Second Edition

Object-Oriented Programming

An Evolutionary Approach

Brad J. Cox, Ph.D.
Andrew J. Novobilski, MSCSE
The Stepstone Corporation

▲▼▼ ADDISON-WESLEY PUBLISHING COMPANY
Reading, Massachusetts • Menlo Park, California • New York
Don Mills, Ontario • Wokingham, England • Amsterdam
Bonn • Sydney • Singapore • Tokyo • Madrid
San Juan • Milan • Paris

Library of Congress Cataloging-in-Publication Data

Cox, Brad J., 1944–
   Object-oriented programming : an evolutionary approach / by Brad
J. Cox and Andrew Novobilski.—2nd ed.
      p.   cm.
   Includes index.
   ISBN 0–201–54834–8
   1. Object-oriented programming (Computer science)   I. Novobilski,
Andrew.   II. Title.
QA76.64.C68   1991
005.1—dc20   90–24501
                                                                                        CIP

Objective-C, ICpak, and Software-IC are registered trademarks of The
Stepstone Corporation. All rights are reserved.

Ada is a trademark of the U.S. Department of Defense.

NextStep is a trademark of NeXT, Inc.

Unix is a trademark of Bell Laboratories.

1 2 3 4 5 6 7 8 9 10 MA 9594939291

Preface

When this book was first published in 1986, object-oriented technologies were unknown except in the research community. The book's goal was to introduce an exciting new technology to a far broader audience, and in this it was emphatically a success. The subsequent explosion of interest in object-oriented technologies is now well known. I find it deeply gratifying that people seek me out to express their appreciation for explaining the new technology so that its value could be understood by all.

Now objects are turning up all over! There are object-oriented databases, object-oriented drawing programs, telephone switching systems, user interfaces, and analysis and design methods. And, oh yes, there are object-oriented programming languages. Lots of them, of every description, from Ada at the conservative right to Smalltalk at the radical left, with C++ and Objective-C somewhere in between. And everyone is asking "What could such different technologies possibly have in common? Do they have anything in common? What does "object-oriented" really mean?

Software Crisis

Twenty years ago, a single IBM 7094 served the entire University of Chicago campus. Today, I have more computing power on my desktop. In 1970, it was newsworthy to link this machine with laboratories across the street. Today, transcontinental electronic mail is routine.

To bring about such an explosion in hardware capabilities, hardware engineers underwent repeated revolutions in their way of working. Early computers were developed by hand, using tubes and later discrete transistors, resistors, and capacitors. Then came board-level integration, integrated circuits, LSI, VLSI. Now we hear talk of wafer scale integration.

Is there a similarly significant change in how software is produced? Although nascent examples can be seen in the recent interest in open standards for operating systems, user interfaces, and communication networks, programming is still primarily a cottage industry based on cut-to-fit craftsmanship rather than a mature discipline based on interchangeable, reusable parts.

I learned to program in assembly language, and then spent the next twenty years doing the same thing in FORTRAN, Pascal, C, and Lisp. While hardware engineers were learning to build with modules whose size and power were increasing exponentially, programmers continued to build programs as always, choosing programming language statements one by one, putting them side by side to make a program.

To demonstrate how far these trajectories have diverged, notice that computer memory can be purchased today for about $50 per megabyte. A typical high-volume software product like Microsoft Word sells for about $250 for three 800K diskettes. This works out to $104 per megabyte, twice as much for software bits that you can't even touch or see!

Hardware engineers discovered how to reuse each other's efforts, to stand on the shoulders of giants instead of their toes. Software engineers have hardly begun to tap such resources, and we can't afford to wait much longer. We are face to face with the software crisis, the awareness that ambitious software systems are generally too expensive, of insufficient quality, hard to schedule reliably, and nearly impossible to manage.

Software Revolution

According to the historian, Thomas Kuhn,[1] science does not progress continuously, by gradually extending an established paradigm. It proceeds as a series of revolutionary upheavals. The discovery of unreconcilable shortcomings in an established paradigm produces a crisis that may lead to a revolution in which the established paradigm is overthrown and replaced.[2]

The software development business is in such a crisis, and the software revolution is such a revolution. The familiar process-centered paradigm of software engineering, where progress is measured by advancement of the software development process, entered its crisis stage a quarter-century ago.[3]

---

[1]Thomas Kuhn, *The Structure of Scientific Revolutions*. Chicago, Ill.: University of Chicago Press, 1962.

[2]See Brad Cox, "Planning the Software Industrial Revolution." *IEEE Software* magazine, November 1990, for a historical comparison between the introduction of interchangeable parts technology during the industrial revolution and the software industrial revolution advocated here. Several paragraphs are used, by permission, from this article.

[3]The term "software crisis," was coined at the NATO Software Engineering conference of 1967.

The paradigm that will move the Information Age forward is the same as the one that launched the Manufacturing Age two centuries ago. It is a product-centered paradigm where progress is measured primarily by the accretion of standard, interchangeable, reusable components, and only secondarily by advancing the processes used to build them.

As the Manufacturing Age declines and the Information Age proceeds, an irresistible desire for change is building in the community that pays our salaries. I only wish I were confident that the changes will come quickly, and that we, the present software development community, will be the ones who make it happen. Or will we stay busy at our terminals, filing away at software like cottage-industry gunsmiths at iron bars, and leave it to our consumers to find a solution that leaves us sitting there?

Object-oriented Technologies

The software revolution did not begin when object-oriented programming languages were invented, and it is certainly not over now that they are widely available. Programmers have been reusing code for decades. For example, first-generation languages like assembler introduced instruction-level reusability. Subsequent generations supplanted this with expression-level and sub-routine-level reusability. Expression-level reusability is a tightly-coupled modularity/binding technology similar to what silicon chip designers call gate-level integration, the reuse of low-level silicon mask layouts in different circuits. Subroutine-level reusability is a less tightly-coupled modularity/binding technology similar to what silicon chip designers call block-level integration, the reuse of large functional blocks of gates in diverse products. The recent generation of tightly-coupled, so-called object-oriented, languages have continued improving along this same trajectory, for example by providing explicit support for encapsulation and inheritance in order to formalize how the best programmers have been hiding complexity for decades.

The languages featured in this book are about something different. They introduce a new software architectural level based on an entirely new modularity/binding technology one notch higher than subroutine libraries. Software-ICs are chip-level modules. These are unlike the tightly-coupled gate- and block-level technologies that silicon experts use to build chips from silicon wafers. They are similar to the pluggable chips that a much larger group uses to build higher levels of electronic functionality. This distinction, one of loose versus tight coupling, or binding; is what distinguishes the assembly-intensive, loosely-coupled modularity/binding technologies featured in this book from the fabrication-intensive, tightly-coupled technologies of languages like C, Cobol, Pascal, Ada, and C + +.

Expressions, subroutines, and Software-ICs play the role in software that gates, blocks, and chips play in hardware. They are all means for hiding complexity. They differ only in how thoroughly they accomplish this and in how tightly the modules are coupled to their environment, but this is a big difference indeed. Building a large system with only gate- and block-level modules is the same as wafer-scale integration, something that the hardware community can barely manage to this day. The strongly-coupled, gate- and block-level object-oriented programming languages that are becoming so popular today, especially those, like Ada, that support only tight coupling and strict type-checking, cannot support a software revolution by themselves, just as the hardware community could never have attained its phenomenal achievements without loosely-coupled modularity/binding technologies like silicon chips and cards.

In this book, "object-oriented" will mean loosely-coupled chip-level objects, or Software-ICs, and this meaning will be defined in detail. When discussing other levels of integration, I will indicate which level of integration is being discussed by using the integration-level qualifiers from hardware engineering. I will speak of gate-level objects and block-level objects when referring to the expression- and subroutine-level objects featured by tightly-coupled languages like Ada and when describing recently-added tightly-coupled features of Objective-C. And I will speak of chip-level objects, or Software-ICs, when discussing the loosely-coupled features of environments like Smalltalk or CLOS, and the Software-IC constructs for which Objective-C is particularly noted.

This terminology will also be used to indicate higher levels of integration that are only beginning to be recognized by the object-oriented community today. In this book I will speak of card-level objects when referring to iconic, nontextual languages like Fabrik[4] and Metaphor[5] whose objects operate as coroutines of one another, not subroutines. And I will even speak of rack-level objects when discussing the software architectural level at which command languages like the Unix shell reside. These highly unconventional uses of the term "object-oriented" reflect our conviction that, on the scale of any significant system, gate-, block-, and even chip-level objects are extremely small units of granularity—grains of sand where bricks are needed. Furthermore, since even chip-level objects are no less procedural than conventional expressions and subroutines, they are just as alien to nonprogrammers. Until invoked by passing them a thread of control from outside, they are as inert as conventional data, quite unlike the objects of everyday experience.

Fabrik pioneered a path that we hope the object-oriented world will soon notice and follow. Since Fabrik was written in Smalltalk, it consists internally of chip-level objects. But externally, it projects a higher-level kind of object, a "card-level object," to the user. These higher-level objects communicate, not synchronously through procedural invocation, but asynchronously by

[4]Fabrik is a research system described in Dan Ingalls, et al., "Fabrik; A Visual Programming Environment." OOPSLA T88 Proceedings.
[5]Metaphor is a commercial office automation product of Metaphor Computer Systems, Mountain View, California.

sending chip-level objects through communication channel objects such as Streams. They amount to a new kind of "object" that encapsulates a copy of the machine's thread of control on a software "card," along with the chip-level objects used to build that card. Software cards are objects of the sort that programmers call lightweight processes; objects that operate as co-routines of one another, not subroutines.

Since these higher-level objects can operate concurrently, they admit a tangible user interface that is uniquely intuitive for nonprogrammers and, for this reason alone, more fundamentally object-oriented than the procedural, single-threaded languages of today. Like the tangible objects of everyday experience, card-level objects provide their own thread of control internally, they don't communicate by procedural invocation, they don't support inheritance, and their user interface is iconic not textual. By adding these and probably more architectural levels, each level can cater to the needs, skills, and interests of a particular constituency of the software components market. The programmer shortage can be solved as the telephone-operator shortage was solved, by making every computer user a programmer.

But what exactly does "object-oriented" mean? This book does not provide a comprehensive answer for two reasons. The first is that the question does not have a comprehensive answer that is true for all levels of software integration. Just as "small" means entirely different things in nuclear physics, gardening, and geology, object-oriented has no absolute meaning that is true at all levels of integration. This issue separates hybrid object-oriented languages like CLOS and Objective-C from "pure" object-oriented languages such as Ada and Smalltalk. Although hybrid language advocates do admire the simplicity that is possible in either a purely tightly-coupled environment like Ada or a purely loosely-coupled one like Smalltalk, it is hard to see how purist solutions can span problems as broad and as deep as software developers face today.

The second reason this book can't comprehensively define "object-oriented" is that the same word is being used by advocates of two different viewpoints to mean very different things. The first viewpoint, the intangibility imperative, is most common in computer science circles. Its advocates view software as a solitary, mental, abstract activity akin to mathematics. The opposing viewpoint, the tangibility imperative, is more common in software engineering circles. Its advocates counter that although software is like mathematics or novel writing in many ways, the intangibility imperative works best for problems that do not exceed the abilities or the longevity of an individual. Intangibles are notoriously hard to produce by committee. Whereas the first group sees objects as empowering software producers via techniques like inheritance that foster abstraction, the second group values techniques like encapsulation that make software more concrete, less abstract, and more approachable by software consumers. Both factions have embraced object-oriented technologies, but for opposite reasons—tangibility advocates for encapsulation and dynamic binding; intangibility advocates for inheritance and static binding. This apparent convergence but actual divergence is responsible for much of the confusion as to what object-oriented means.

Of course, neither of these imperatives eliminates the need for the other. Software really is an abstract/concrete swamp, a hybrid for which dual perspectives can be useful as first-order approximations to a complex reality. Rather, this book proposes a paradigm shift to a new frame of reference in which both imperatives coexist, each predominating at different times and places. It usually emphasizes the tangibility imperative because of the need to begin building and using commercially robust repositories of trusted, stable components whose properties can be understood and tabulated in standard catalogs like the handbooks of mature engineering domains. But it recognizes that the intangibility imperative will always retain its role as the premier tool of solitary, mental creativity. And it anticipates that this imperative will acquire even greater utility for predicting how trusted, quantifiable components, the raw materials of a mature software engineering discipline, will behave when assembled and placed under load.

Evolution, not Revolution

Although the destination is a software revolution, this book emphasizes getting there through evolutionary extensions to present-day programming languages rather than by relinquishing compatibility with the past. It shows how Stepstone built a thoroughly state-of-the-art object-oriented programming language, Objective-C, by simply grafting a small number of new syntactic features alongside the existing capabilities of C. The new language retains the efficiency and compatibility of C for those engaged in gate- and block-level programming, but adds the reusability and productivity of a loosely coupled chip-level object-oriented programming language in order that the rest of the community can build upon the smaller group's efforts. The hybrid supports all three styles of working as modularity/binding tools that can be picked up or laid aside according to the problem at hand.

As with any language that has been described in a publicly accessible form such as this book, Objective-C is nonproprietary. Compilers are available, from multiple sources, on almost every imaginable mainframe, workstation, or personal computer platform including Unix, MS/DOS, Mach, Windows, and OS/2. And successful ports for MVS, Cray, Macintosh, and others may be commercially available soon.

Objective-C is the enabling technology for at least two well-known families of Software-IC libraries, one by Stepstone and the other by NeXT. Although these libraries are written in the same language, they share no code in common. NeXT's library and programming environment are bundled as a single product, NextStep, which is based on Display Postscript is available on NeXT's Cube and on IBM's RS/6000 platforms. Stepstone supports, in a platform-independent manner, two separate libraries, and has several others underway. The first, ICpak, 101, is automatically bundled with our compiler to support foundation functionality and commonly-used data structure Software-ICs, several of which are described in this book. The second, ICpak 201, is sold separately. This is a graphical user interface library that is portable to almost any hardware and software platform, but is most commonly based on X-Windows. Stepstone also provides an Objective-C Browser, which is based on ICpak 201 and is described in Chapter Six.

However, this book is not specific to Objective-C. It shows how similar hybrids can be developed for any base language, including Ada, Cobol, Pascal, PL/I, and C + +. Paradoxically, the oldest and most intractable program-building tools are often used to build the largest and most complex systems. New systems must somehow be compatible with mountains of old code accumulated over the decades. Such system-buildings need the machine efficiency and compatibility with existing code that traditional languages provide. But they also need help and need it now, to cope with the complexity of the systems being built in well-proven antiques like Cobol and Fortran. We enthusiastically support the Codasyl subcommittee that is considering such extensions to Cobol, and hope that our advocacy of similar extensions for Fortran, Ada, PL/I, and C + + will quickly come to fruition.

About This Edition

Many changes have happened since this book was first published in 1986.

I would like to thank Andy Novobilski for taking on the challenge of bringing this book up to date with respect to changes in the Objective-C language, its compiler and libraries, and its support tools. He accomplished this without sacrificing his many other duties in order that I might concentrate my own free moments on writing a new one.

The first group of changes are with respect to the Objective-C language itself. Objective-C was originally envisioned as a hybrid object-oriented programming language to support the chip-level objects of Smalltalk as a strictly upwards compatible extension to the gate- and block-level capabilities of C—beauty marks, warts, and all. However, during the seven years since Objective-C was first developed and the four years since this book was published, Objective-C has been enhanced to also provide strong type-checking and early binding facilities to strengthen C's existing capabilities at gate- and block-level programming. Making these lower-level extensions more widely known was a key motivation for publishing this new edition.

The second group of changes are with respect to the classes discussed throughout this book and detailed in the specification sheets in Appendix A. In previous editions, these classes were specific to this book and not the same as the classes in ICpak 101. One sign of this change is the replacement of the old ByteArray class with the newer String class throughout this book.

The third group of changes are localized in Chapter Seven, Iconic User Interfaces. Given the interest that platform-independent iconic user interfaces are receiving today with the advent of graphic standards like X-Windows, Motif, and Open Look, it is easy to forget that none of these existed when this chapter was written. During the last four years, the classes in this chapter evolved to become a platform-independent graphics library product, called ICpak 201, which Stepstone supports today on almost every software/ hardware platform with the requisite graphics and memory capabilities. On many of these platforms, ICpak 201 is based on X-Windows, but its platform-independence also allows it to be supported almost anywhere including bare graphics hardware. Chapter Seven was rewritten to demonstrate how these libraries are used in building end-user applications, and to reduce the earlier focus on how these libraries work internally.

The last category of changes are my own contribution to this edition. These are the result of retrospection as to the successes, and the failures, of the ideas advocated in this book after seven years of living with them as a day-to-day reality within Stepstone. These changes are described in this preface and in a new section in Chapter Five titled "Specification and Testing." These reflect my conviction, based on seven years in a company whose primary business is selling small-granularity reusable software components for its living, that the software community's adoption of object-oriented programming languages is only the barest beginning of what is needed to escape the software crisis, and nowhere close to the end. Some indication of the distance we have yet to cover can be seen from the following observations:

First, although "object-oriented" languages are now enthusiastically accepted by the software development community, there is still little real agreement as to what the term means. Object-oriented is still a fashion statement, a way of indicating disapproval of the old-fashioned ways of C, Cobol, Fortran, and Pascal, rather than as an exciting new concept to be integrated with the well-proven concepts of the past. This appreciation for the value of diverse modularity/binding technologies is reflected in the gate-, block-, chip-, card-, and rack-level terminology, which appears in this preface as a new feature of this edition.

Second, the importance of commercially robust libraries of small-granularity software components has only begun to be accepted by the software community at large. For example, in spite of this book's emphasis on Software-IC libraries and environment support for using them, and in spite of the far greater investment Stepstone has made in libraries and environments in comparison to the compiler, Objective-C continues to be thought of as yet another programming language to be compared with Ada and C++. Our cottage industry's process-centered paradigm is remarkably ingrained. I would never have predicted that a community that views itself as leading edge would be so slow in moving to a product-centered paradigm based on libraries of trusted components.

Third, our attention is still riveted by object-oriented programming as a new approach to implementing code, whether from libraries or frist principles. We have not noticed the lack of tools for specifying what the code

should do and then testing whether it complies to specification within tolerance. This is one of the main insights Stepstone learned by actually building
small-granularity components for a living. Questions of "what does this library do?" Arise in every sales call, and compatibility of every new version
with those already in the field becomes dominant in every bug repair, improvement, or port. The newly added section on "Specification and Testing"
outlines the approach we are presently using to address these questions in
our commercial products. Although this approach is very low-tech and manual, it establishes the starting point for a new research direction that may
ultimately lead to object-oriented specification/testing languages. These are
a new class of tools to be deployed in parallel with the object-oriented implementation languages of today, just as mechanics use calipers and lathes, independently yet interdependently, together, but ever apart.

This book retains its original focus on technical matters. Although these
are really what revolutions are about, it only touches on cultural issues, matters of value systems, laws, economics, and policies. As the Manufacturing
Age declines, the entire world is looking to the Information Age as the prom-
ising new frontier. The software crisis is the primary barrier to entry, but
this barrier will not stand forever. Since the United States presently produces
nearly 70 percent of the world's software, some believe that this gives it a
commanding lead in winning the software revolution and thereby dominating
this new frontier.

The United States' success over England during the industrial revolution
should prove otherwise. Technical innovations as described in this book are
almost always subordinate to, and far easier to acquire by newcomers than,
cultural innovations such as changes to long-established value systems, laws,
policies, economics, and power balances. These nontechnical issues will be
the subject of a new book, *Planning the Software Industrial Revolution*, to
be published by Addison-Wesley in the future.

Acknowledgments

I want to express my appreciation to the Smalltalk-80, Simula, and Lisp
communities for pioneering object-oriented programming, and the Unix/C
community for developing the substrate that made this book and Objective-
C possible.

I thank Adele Goldberg and Glenn Krasner of Xerox Parc, Dennis McLeod
of the University of Southern California, Tom Plum of Plum-Hall Associates,
Alan Shaw of the University of Washington, Creon Levitt of NASA Ames
Research Center, and Tom Love, Kurt Schmucker, and Bryan Lockwood of
The Stepstone Corp. (formerly PPI), for their thoughtful reviews and criti-
cism.

I thank the stockholders of The Stepstone Corp. (formerly PPI), for the
time and resources used in producing this book, and its employees and cus-

tomers for their patience, support, and encouragement throughout the often trying development process.

I owe a special debt to Gerald Weinberg. Without his steadfast encouragement I would not have undertaken this project in the first place, nor finished it once started.

And most of all I thank Etta, my wife. Precious, we did it!

Sandy Hook, Connecticut   B.J.C.

Over the past several years, I have been fortunate to work with some very talented people at Stepstone, including Brad Cox. I wish to thank Brad for his help and guidance, not only in writing the second edition, but for all the time and patience spent in helping me learn this new technology. I would also like to thank my teammates at Stepstone for their willingness to help as I finished this project. Finally, I wish to thank my wife, Mary Ellen, for accepting this crazy vocation of mine with patience and understanding. Her encouragement and support throughout this project helped me keep it all in perspective.

Sandy Hook, Connecticut   A.J.N.

Contents

| One

System Building

Two hundred years ago, Connecticut was famous for its firearms and textiles industries. Many of the firearms companies are still here today, but the textile industry has long ago moved elsewhere and the old mill buildings have been renovated to house a diversity of modern enterprises such as my own software company, The Stepstone Corporation (formerly PPI). In 1798, very near the mill in which this book was written, Eli Whitney introduced an innovation that revolutionized manufacturing forever. Today a similar innovation is under way that promises to do much the same thing for software.

Before the industrial revolution, the firearms industry was hardly an industry at all but a loose coalition of individual craftsmen. Each firearm was crafted by an individual gunsmith who built each part from raw materials. Firearms produced in this way were expensive and each was the distinctive product of a gunsmith's personal inspiration.

The revolution was sparked when Eli Whitney (the inventor of the cotton gin) received a large manufacturing contract to build muskets for the government. Whitney's innovation was to divide the work so that each part was produced by a specialist to meet a specified standard. Each gunsmith focused on a single part, using sophisticated tools to optimize that task. This produced economies of scale that drove down manufacturing costs, and best of all, Whitney's customer, the government, quickly realized that the standards would allow parts to be interchanged, greatly simplifying their firearm repair problems.

The importance of object-oriented programming is comparable to that of Whitney's interchangeable part innovation, and for many of the same reasons.

1

Both redefine the unit of modularity so that workers produce subcomponents instead of complete solutions. The subcomponents are controlled by standards and can be interchanged across different products. Programmers no longer build entire programs from raw materials, the bare statements and expressions of a programming language. Instead they produce reusable software components by assembling components of other programmers. These components are called Software-ICs to emphasize their similarity with the integrated silicon chip, a similar innovation that has revolutionized the computer hardware industry over the past twenty years or so.

Of course, the industrial revolution was not a true revolution at all, except for those who paid no notice until Whitney had cornered the firearms market. For the winners, it was not a revolution, but the culmination of a gradual process of evolutionary change. This book shows how the same evolutionary process can produce a similar revolution in the software industry.

What Is System Building?

Harvey is the systems architect for Objective Solutions International (OSI), a well-funded startup software company that hopes to win its fortune by making the electronic office a reality for large, paper-intensive customers like insurance companies, banks, and government offices. He is responsible for OSI's new office automation product, a state-of-the-art system that will apply distributed workstation and high-resolution raster graphics technology to handling arbitrary office forms such as WhileYouWereOutNotice, OfficeMemo, PriceList, InsuranceClaimForm, LoanRequestForm, DriversLicenseApplication, TravelExpenseVoucher, and so forth, ad infinitum, because the set of data types that offices handle are ever changing.

OSI's customers are willing to pay handsomely for workable solutions to their paper-handling problems. But because of low computer skill level and rapid turnover, they insist that any computer-based solution emulate their existing (paper) system as closely as possible, improving on it in speed and reliability. Computer-based forms must look and behave like existing paper forms, with preprinted text and rulings that cannot be erased. For example, conventional electronic mail systems are unacceptable because it would be too difficult to train workers to manage important forms with standard text editors. Besides, some customers are looking forward to enhancements to support integrated text, voice, and even video annotations.

OSI plans to build a prototype system capable of demonstrating the concept for a few common office forms, and to demonstrate this prototype to their customers. They would then contract to extend the prototype to support forms required by each individual customer, and to keep the system up to date with the changing needs of their customers. The initial prototype would support a few forms chosen by OSI. Most of the development effort would be downstream as additional forms are added over time.

Harvey is responsible for selecting, verifying, and recommending a software architecture that would allow this ambitious system to be built and then extended, without crippling losses to ripple effects as this complex system evolves over time.

A terrific plan, isn't it? It has something for everyone. Customers will like it because it directly addresses paper-handling costs and the difficulty of acquiring trained personnel. They could use this system to automate not only the forms but the office procedures by which the forms are managed. It could be extremely lucrative for OSI and its stockholders. The prototype would attract new customers, and they can certainly expect a long-term repeat business extending older installations as well. Change is eternal, and OSI is positioned for a long-term, highly profitable market.

And it is certainly an exciting opportunity for Harvey. Harvey has the lead responsibility right at the cutting edge of technology. This system has it all! It is highly distributed, uses high-resolution raster graphics workstations, and provides an iconic user interface, each exciting in its own right. The forms will probably be produced using special-purpose forms-generation languages, and the automatic handling of office procedures will probably involve rule-based (artificial intelligence) technology too. The development methodology will probably encourage rapid prototyping, probably mixed judiciously with a more formal structured methodology. This system is a programmer's dream!

Software Crisis

That of course is possible. But unfortunately, it is not probable. As Figure 1.1 shows, the programming industry has a remarkably bad record delivering systems less ambitious even than this one. The probable outcome is that OSI's project will be canceled before delivering a single line of code, bringing disappointment to the customers, financial ruin to OSI, and personal disgrace to Harvey. The fatal symptoms are uncomfortably familiar: over budget, behind schedule, out of control, low quality, leading eventually to cancellation and disgrace.

What makes OSI's system so ambitious? Hardware is certainly not the problem, because today's hardware is capable of supporting systems of this sort, and more. Distributed systems are nothing new; nor are forms-oriented user interfaces, friendly or not. Nor are electronic mail systems, archival systems, and workstations. Granted, these technologies have usually been exploited in isolation, not in combination, and combining them can certainly cause trouble.

The real problem is that this system involves an attitude toward change that is not provided for by our programming tools, methodologies, and

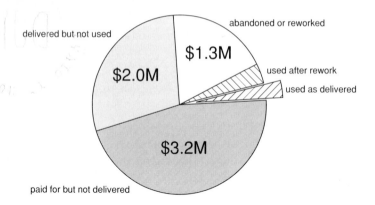

Figure 1.1. Software costs versus results. The U.S. Government Accounting Office 1979 report (FGMSD-80-4) describes this breakdown of results from $6.8 million in nine federal software projects: 47% ($3.2M) were paid for but never delivered, 29% ($2.0M) were delivered but never used, 19% ($1.3M) were abandoned or reworked, 3% ($0.2M) were used after change, and only < 2% ($0.1M) were used as delivered.[1]

concepts. OSI's system is beyond the state of the art because the software industry has not discovered how to produce systems that can survive the kinds of design changes that OSI must expect.

Change: The Enemy

Harvey, as system architect, is responsible for defining the architecture of OSI's new system. But what does this mean? What should Harvey concern himself with, and what should be left to other team members? Certainly, architecture does not include coding. But does it include design? Many architects would argue that Harvey should begin by selecting the hardware and software components of the system and deciding how they interrelate. They would have Harvey refine the hardware makeup of the system (workstations here, minicomputers there, mainframe over yonder), define which software components go where (forms editing here, departmental files there, archival and backup services yonder), and choose a networking strategy for tying these pieces together. Refining this architecture into a detailed design would be done by others, with Harvey's advice and assistance.

But is this architecture, or is this merely an early phase of design? Harvey is probably the first to look at this project with an eye to its technical feasibility and his first responsibility should be to avoid the statistically likely danger. Of course, he cannot shirk the traditional concerns of the architect, because the project could certainly die from a slipshod, poorly documented

[1]ACM Sigsoft Software Engineering Notes, vol 10 no 5, Oct 1985.

architectural specification. But a brilliant decomposition into hardware, software, and network components will do little toward improving the prognosis for this project. On a safari, it is usually appropriate to kill mosquitoes since malaria is a valid and important concern. But it is inappropriate when stopping a charging elephant. Harvey is facing an attack by change, the largest and meanest antagonist any large software project can face, and his first efforts should be to defend this project from destruction by change.

There was a time when the virtue of software over physical media like paper and pencil was in its very responsiveness. Software was exciting because it was so malleable. The computer was a medium for creative inspiration; infinitely moldable to the programmer's desire. Nearly anything could be done with this wonderful stuff.

Although this may be to some extent true for small projects (program building), it is not (and has never been) true for ambitious undertakings (system building). In fact, software systems are usually the least responsive element in many organizations today. The organization as a whole is able to adapt more fluidly than the software upon which it has grown dependent. The primary difference between programs and systems is in their ability to adapt to change. Programs are generally small, lightweight targets, and they can be relatively nimble and adapt as fast as conditions change. But large software systems are anything but responsive. They are large, complex, and brittle, easily disrupted by the slightest impact from outside. There are several schools of thought about what to do about this: the first, firmly entrenched as the current dogma of software design; the others, clamoring for attention from the sidelines.

Maginot Line Defense

The conventional strategy for dealing with change is to build elaborate defensive structures to prevent change altogether. Every software manager knows this one chapter and verse. Software, especially large software systems, should be developed by first determining and documenting the system's requirements. The requirements are turned into specifications, and these are discussed with and ultimately approved and signed by the customer before further work is done. Once the requirements have been frozen, a succession of designs are developed, reviewed, and exhaustively documented as formal design specifications. Ultimately the designs are transformed into code, a step that should be routine assuming a sufficiently rigorous design process has been followed. Finally, the code is tested (in case a bug has crept in somehow) and ultimately delivered to the customer.

Work must of course be scheduled carefully. Assuming this, the customer has to be happy with the result, since the delivered system will be precisely the system he signed off on originally. "Change the requirements? Preposterous! Look at these documents, with your signature at the bottom! The design will have to be redone! You'll disrupt the schedule! It will cost you extra!"

The defenders lay down a withering fire from behind the barricades, and the forces of change crumple and fall. Heigh ho!

The glory is on the front lines. What remains is maintenance, a grubby activity that goes on out of sight in the back room, well outside the mainstream of exciting new development where the really talented programmers gravitate.

Software is not at all like wood or steel. Its paint does not chip and it does not rust or rot. Software does not need dusting, waxing, or cleaning. It often does have faults that do need attention, but this is not maintenance, but repair. Repair is fixing something that has been broken by tinkering with it, or something that has been broken all along. Conversely, as the environment around software changes, energy must be expended to keep it current. This is not maintenance; holding steady to prevent decline. Evolution is changing to move ahead.

Harvey should probably ignore maintenance as a murky nonissue, but he cannot ignore repair and certainly not evolution. His competitive edge depends on being able to evolve that product to meet the changing needs of his customers. But precisely what should he do? He could make sure that code has lots of comments. He could make sure that the programming language is readable (whatever that is). He could outlaw goto's (for whatever good that is supposed to do). He could write lots of internals documentation, and try to keep that up to date with code that is changing all the while. But would doing these things really affect the technical feasibility of this system?

Probably not, because these nostrums do not address the root problem; that the real world actually does change and the Maginot Line defense tries to deny it. The Maginot Line attitude permeates nearly all of the programming industry's tools, methodologies, and concepts. Programming languages make the programmer responsible for building source files that reflect the intended situation, while the compiler is responsible only for turning source files into hard code. The generated code can be extremely efficient because it is not responsible for anything more than the situation described by the programmer. But this code is brittle and unmalleable, efficient but unable to withstand impact from outside. The Maginot Line attitude makes malleability the responsibility of the programmer, not of his tools.

The Maginot Line mentality manages change by trying to prevent it. When that fails (and it nearly always does fail eventually), the task of repairing the damage is passed off to the back room, to the maintenance team. The rest of the team moves on to the next project while everyone tries to ignore the clamor as the maintenance team struggles to keep a ravening horde of changes from devouring these brittle and nearly unchangeable software systems.

Swiss Defense

OSI's business plan amounts to an explicit rejection of the Maginot Line defense. They plan to build a prototype product and to use that to attract customers who will pay them to change the prototype to suit needs. OSI cannot outlaw change, or shove it off on a maintenance group. Their plan requires a radically different view about the software development process; one that addresses change as a vital and integral part of the overall software development process.

OSI might plan to use something like Switzerland's defense strategy of about the same time as the Maginot Line. Rather than invest in expensive (and given their neighbors, unreliable) border defenses, Switzerland declared itself an open country and welcomed visitors from any country, race, or religion. This policy allowed them to weather the world-shaking consequences of World War II while collecting a tidy profit from all sides, simply by adapting to events responsively.

Can this defense work with software? Probably yes, because it has already been applied in several specialized, exceedingly complicated systems. Smalltalk-80 (described in Chapter 3) is one of the purest examples of this strategy, although examples abound in other domains in which the Maginot Line defense is not tenable, such as knowledge engineering. Smalltalk-80's designers produced a system that is capable of being bent in nearly any direction. The entire system, down to the hardware level, is compartmentalized into armor-plated objects that communicate by sending messages. There is no protected (and therefore unchangeable) operating system. The source for the whole system is immediately available online to any programmer, and that programmer's entire programming environment can be immediately changed in almost any manner just by changing a few lines of code.

This book emphasizes how several Smalltalk-80 tactics, particularly object-oriented programming, provide new leverage for building malleable systems. But it does *not* advocate the Swiss Defense as a way of building large systems. Although the concepts of objects, messages, classes, and inheritance provide great potential for building large yet malleable systems of the size that OSI is considering, there are several reasons why other parts of the Smalltalk-80 philosophy are almost certainly inappropriate for projects of this scale.

Machine efficiency is one rather obvious reason. Smalltalk is hard on machine resources, spending computational power lavishly to provide productivity features like automatic garbage collection, a highly graphic user interface, and a uniform environment based on objects. Hardware cost is not the compelling objection it once was because costs are dropping so quickly. Nonetheless OSI's customers can probably find other ways to use almost any amount of hardware power, and are predictably reluctant to spend much of it on a comprehensive environment for the programmers.

Control is a more fundamental reason. OSI's system will involve large numbers of programmers, who must work together as a coordinated organization if a system of this complexity is ever to be delivered. The ability for any programmer to change anything he likes is not a benefit for this kind of work, although the potential liability could be managed via Smalltalk's powerful set of change management tools.

Compatibility is the most fundamental, and nearly unfixable, reason. Nearly all modern organizations have at least some prior investment in software developed in older languages, and OSI's customers will insist that the older software continue to be viable. Short of providing separate hardware for these applications (possibly using Smalltalk-80 as a front-end), there seems to be no way around the fact that Smalltalk-80 needs a complete, stand-alone environment unto itself.

Hybrid Defense

The hybrid defense is like the one preferred by a competent combat commander using every possible strategy in active combination. Defensive breastworks are used to defend important structures against frontal assaults, dispersed commando units are used to provide reconnaissance, maneuverability is used to avoid attack if possible, and diplomacy and other peacetime tactics are used to avoid shooting in the first place.

The conventional software engineering dogma is to build efficient but brittle software systems, surrounded by static defensive structures that protect them from change. The value of this is undisputed, since uncontrolled change ("hacking") is no way to build complex software systems. But even more can be done:

1. Systems can be made malleable by retaining some elasticity into run-time. This involves relaxing the usual demand that everything be accomplished at compile-time. Dynamic binding, described later, is a move in this direction.

2. Systems can be made more changeable by making them smaller and lighter in weight, thus transforming systemlike functionality into programlike size. The encapsulation and inheritance techniques described later do this by integrating reusability into the mainstream of the software development process.

3. Systems can be more tightly encapsulated as objects that behave as armor-plated black boxes to limit the ripple effect when a penetration of the static defenses does happen. A change to one part of the system need not affect the rest of the system, but can be dealt with inside the part directly affected.

Object-oriented Programming

This book has no panacea that will magically eliminate problems of this magnitude. But it does propose several new tools and concepts that can help to produce software that is far more tolerant of change:

Encapsulation is the foundation of the whole approach. Its contribution is restricting the effects of change by placing a wall of code around each piece of data. All access to the data is handled by procedures that were put there to mediate access to the data. By contrast, conventional programming makes the consumer of each operand (defined by one of possibly many suppliers) responsible for choosing operators (again, defined by one of many suppliers) that are type-compatible with the operand on hand. Object-oriented programming moves this responsibility from the consumer and onto the operand and its supplier. These encapsulated operands are called objects. Whereas consumers once specified *how* each operation should be performed by naming a specific piece of code, they now specify only *what* should be done, leaving it to the object to choose code that is appropriate to its type or class.

Inheritance is the more innovative part of the approach because it is not provided by conventional languages. It is a tool for automatically broadcasting code to classes developed by different members of a team. Programmers no longer start each module with a blank page, but instead write a single statement that references some class that is already in the library. Each subsequent statement describes how the new class differs from the one in the library.

To see how these techniques apply to Harvey's problem, take a closer look at the capabilities of the prototype system and how they must change over time. The initial system will support a number of generic office objects like desktops, filefolders, mailboxes, envelopes, memos, and whileYouWereOut-Notices.[2] The prototype must demonstrate that Harvey's design meets the objectives described at the beginning of the chapter. For example, it must demonstrate that these electronic objects can emulate the way familiar office objects behave, and that the system can be extended with new office objects over time. For example:

Container objects must hold arbitrary kinds of things, just as a physical office desktop does. For example, if I decide to mail a filefolder instead of the usual memos, the system should not forbid it on the grounds that the mailbox designer intended mailboxes to hold only memos.

Container objects must be able to contain arbitrary numbers of items, subject only to physical limitations of the machine. For example, workers who work best with cluttered desktops, even with hundreds of open items, should not be prevented from doing so.

---

[2]This spelling convention will be used to create symbols from short descriptive phrases. Many programmers use underscores the same way; i.e., WHILE_YOU_WERE_OUT_NOTICE.

Desktops, envelopes, mailboxes, and filefolders are loosely coupled collections, where coupling refers to the degree to which the design of the collection depends on the design of its contents. Obviously, an electronic desktop cannot be redesigned and recompiled whenever a new kind of electronic object is added to it since the user makes this decision at run-time. Furthermore, the repertoire of items that the desktop must hold will change over time as the system is extended with new kinds of office forms. However, some amount of coupling must occur since an electronic desktop does need to interact with its contents.

For example, suppose that the mailbox has an option that displays a menu of current contents that help the user choose the next item for detailed reading. To implement this option there must be a way to obtain summary information about any item that might appear in the mailbox, and this amounts to an operation that the mailbox must apply to its contents.

This class of problem is not easy to solve with conventional programming languages because conventional programming makes the consumer of an operand responsible for choosing the correct operator for the kind of operand on hand. In this case the mailbox developer is the consumer for the items to be mailed. To get summary information from these items correctly, he must choose operators (functions) that extract the needed information from the various items somehow. The usual solution is to store the type inside each item in a standard place, like this:

```
struct item { int typeCode; ... }
```

and to test the type in a switch statement. Based on the type of item, the mailbox can call the correct function for that type:

```
displaySummaryOf(nextItem)
    struct item *nextItem;
{
    switch (nextItem->typeCode) {
    case MEMO: displayMemoSummary(nextItem); break;
    case FILEFOLDER: displayFolderSummary(nextItem); break;
    case WHILEYOUWEREOUTNOITCE: displayOutNoticeSummary(nextItem); break;
    case ENVELOPE: displayEnvelopeSummary(nextItem); break;
    }
    ...
}
```

Notice what happens if Harvey actually tries to build a system like this. The mailbox code is now explicitly dependent on the kinds of items that were known when the mailbox was written; the case labels explicitly state that this mailbox will not work for contents other than MEMO, FILEFOLDER, WHILEYOUWEREOUTNOTICE, and ENVELOPE. Something has crossed the boundary that should have separated what the mailbox developer is doing and what his suppliers are doing. Every time a new kind of datum is added to this system, the mailbox code must be changed and recompiled.

Furthermore, these switch statements are not localized in any way. They reflect the consumer's responsibility for choosing operators that are compatible with operand types, so they appear throughout the system. Every time a new data type is added, every single switch statement must be changed to add a case for the new type. The ripple effect of even simple changes cannot be bounded, but spreads throughout the system.

Notice what happens when the responsibility for choosing how to implement each command is moved to the objects' supplier instead of their consumer:

```
displaySummaryOf(nextItem)
{
    [nextItem displaySummary];
    ...
}
```

How does one differential between the named object & its function call?

This commands the object named nextItem to perform the command named displaySummary. The consumer doesn't know or care how nextItem performs displaySummary because that is the job of nextItem's supplier. Although different kinds of objects like filefolders, memos, and envelopes may displaySummary in very different ways, the consumer's code needn't care. When the system is extended with a new kind of item, the change does not spread beyond the code written by the supplier of that item. This encapsulation makes systems more malleable by restricting the amount of damage a change can cause.

Inheritance, by contrast, serves to broadcast effects throughout a system. Desktops, filefolders, envelopes, and mailboxes are, on the face of it, different kinds of objects. Nonetheless, they do have many things in common since they are just different kinds of containers. Inheritance allows their similarities to be described in one central place (a Container class) and broadcast to all the classes that behave like containers. The desktop developer need not build these common properties. Instead he describes how desktops are different from plain vanilla containers. Envelopes, filefolders, and mailboxes are described in the same way. Since generic functionality can be developed once and used many times, inheritance provides a powerful boost to productivity. It quickly becomes unthinkable to develop code from scratch because it is nearly always easier to inherit powerful, well tested capabilities from a library of earlier work.

Summary

Eli Whitney is not remembered as the inventor of a better gunsmithing tool, but for inventing a new way for gunsmiths to work together. The result was a revolution in firearms manufacturing that eventually spread to all of manufacturing.

Object-oriented programming is revolutionary in exactly the same way. Its primary new features are summarized in two key words, encapsulation and inheritance. Encapsulation means that the consumer no longer applies operators to operands while taking care that the two are type-compatible. Instead the consumer tells the object what needs to be done, and the object chooses the correct operator from a table of things that the object knows how to do. The result is that the effect of adding a new kind of object does not spread beyond the place where the new type is defined.

By contrast, inheritance is a way of defining some useful contruct in a central place and then automatically broadcasting that construct to all the places where it could help. New functionality is no longer developed by coding each line from scratch, but by inheriting some useful class and describing only how the new one differs. The effect is to put reusability squarely in the mainstream of the software development process.

| Two

Why Object-oriented Programming?

O bject-oriented programming is not so much a coding technique as it is a code packaging technique, a way for code suppliers to encapsulate functionality for delivery to consumers. It is this increased emphasis on the relationship between consumers and suppliers of code that separates object-oriented and conventional programming (Figure 2.1).

Binding is the process of integrating functionality from different suppliers into a consumer's code (Figure 2.2). Binding is more than what most programmers call linking; determining which binary modules must be combined to produce an executable image, assigning a memory address to each one, and patching external references with the correct memory addresses. Binding is the process whereby operators and operands of potentially many different types are published by suppliers and used by consumers.

There are several schools of thought about when and how binding should be done, each with distinct strengths and weaknesses. The early binding approach is the most widely known because it is the only approach provided in most conventional languages. With early binding, binding occurs while the consumer's code is being compiled so that the consumer and his tools (the compiler) bear responsibility for binding. Delayed binding (also known as late binding or dynamic binding) means that binding is done later than compile-time, generally while the program is running. Delayed binding moves responsibility for binding away from the consumer and onto the operands, effectively onto the supplier who defined this type of operand.

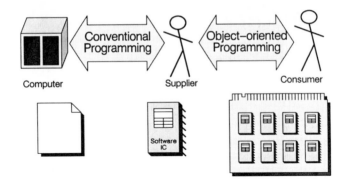

Figure 2.1. Program-building versus system-building. Conventional programming tools emphasize the relationship between a programmer and his code, while object-oriented programming emphasizes the relationship between suppliers and consumers of code.

Open vs. Closed Universe

The early and late binding approaches discussed above are hardly equivalent. Early binding works in a closed universe in which all potential interactions between the parts of that environment can be declared when these parts are created by the compiler (Figure 2.3). Late binding becomes essential in an open universe, when the parts that might interact are not known until the program is running.

For example, suppose you are building a Point class where X and Y coordinates are both 16 bit integers. The Point class is a closed universe, because you have decided (and intend to enforce) that only 16 bit integers can appear there. If someone wants to reuse the Point class in a continuous domain where coordinates must be floating point numbers, they will have to discard your work and build anew, or edit your class and recompile.

The mailbox example is entirely different. The mailbox is an open universe, not a closed one. In an open universe where you cannot outlaw change, a change-tolerant mailbox is an attractive candidate for reuse. Since the mailbox must hold any object that responds to a published protocol, it can be used off the shelf without having to be modified each time a new kind of object is to be mailed. Possibly, the next client of mailbox won't use it to mail memos at all, but to deliver tractor parts to Russia!

This chapter shows the effects of choosing to work in an open or closed universe by contrasting several binding approaches in a small example—a program for counting the number of unique words in a file.

Software Productivity

Most would agree that software productivity is low; lower than we'd like certainly, and probably lower than it needs to be. It is harder to agree what productivity is, at least in a quantifiable sense that would allow controlled

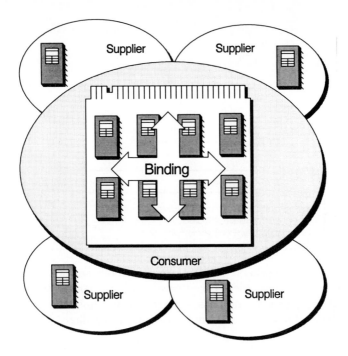

Figure 2.2. Binding. Binding is the process of assembling components from different suppliers into a larger component belonging to the consumer.

experiments to be defined and measured scientifically. What is software productivity? Or much the same thing, How do you measure it? In measuring something, one hopes to understand the factors that influence it, and from these to discover ways to control it to advantage. This is the goal of Software Metrics, the study of factors influencing productivity by measuring real or artificial software development projects.

Bulk Is Bad

Although many of the hypotheses in this field are unproved and controversial, there is little disagreement with the most basic one: *Bulk is bad.* Study after study has confirmed that development costs increase and productivity decreases more than linearly with the size of the overall project. Who has not accomplished phenomenal productivity as a solitary individual, designing and then building some small project as a solitary task? And who has not been frustrated by slower progress in a larger project that required coordinated teamwork? As project size increases, the number of individuals increases, and this increases the amount of effort wasted in coordination overhead.

A common measurement of code bulk is to count the number of lines of code, and a common measure for software productivity is to count the number of lines of code produced per unit time. These numbers are relatively easy

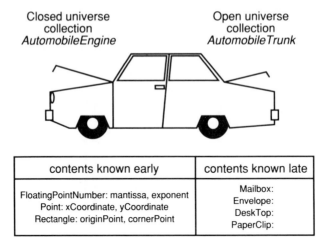

Closed universe collection *AutomobileEngine*	Open universe collection *AutomobileTrunk*

contents known early	contents known late
FloatingPointNumber: mantissa, exponent Point: xCoordinate, yCoordinate Rectangle: originPoint, cornerPoint	Mailbox: Envelope: DeskTop: PaperClip:

Figure 2.3. Open versus closed universe. An automobile engine is a closed universe collection. This means that the types of its components can be stringently specified long before the engine is put into use. An automobile trunk is an open universe collection. The kind of contents it will hold cannot be predicted in advance.

to collect, and have actually demonstrated remarkable success in getting a quick reading of where things stand. But of course the code bulk metric pleases almost no one. Surely more than code bulk is involved in software productivity. If productivity can really be measured as the rate at which lines of code are produced, why not just use a tight loop to spew code as fast as possible, and send the programmers home?

Surface Area Is Bad

When the Aswan Dam in Egypt was being constructed, a different activity was under way upstream. The dam's reservoir would eventually flood a number of ancient temples and monuments of collosal historical value. To save these treasures, some could be protected by coffer dams, but others would simply be moved. And moved they were. Entire temples were carefully sawed into manageable pieces, shipped to a new, safe location, and there reassembled into their original form, an immense jigsaw puzzle. The cost was tremendous and must have been scrutinized as carefully as we study software development costs today. There must have been time to measure productivity while the first temples were being moved, and experts to study these figures with an eye toward optimizing temple-moving productivity.

Clearly, temple-moving costs depend on the number and size of temples moved, or temple bulk. But so does the cost of shipping rock and gravel. Bulk is a factor in the cost of almost anything. But bulk was hardly the only factor, even the predominant one, in the cost of moving these temples. Since they were to end up with temples, not rock and gravel, the cost depended also on the number and complexity of the temple parts that would have to be reassembled. The cost of shipping rock and gravel depends primarily on bulk; the cost of shipping temples depends as well on surface area.

Software productivity depends not only on sheer bulk but also on surface area, the number of things that must be understood and properly dealt with for one programmer's code to function correctly in combination with another's. Some things that influence software surface area are:

1. Information hiding: Surface area increases with the number of names that are visible at the interface between a supplier and consumer. This includes data element names (structure member names), data type names (structure names), and function names. Software packaging schemes that reduce the number of names that a consumer must learn and use correctly decrease surface area.

2. Abstract data types: Each type dependency between these names increases the surface area of the interfaces. For example, a requirement that a function take two arguments, the first of type complex and the second of type float, increases the number of things that the consumer must get right to use this function successfully.

3. Time sequence of operations: Each requirement that the consumer perform operations in a particular order increases surface area. For example, requiring the consumer to know that an object must be allocated, then initialized, then accessed increases the number of things a consumer must get right, and thus the surface area of the consumer-supplier interface.

4. Garbage collection: If the consumer is responsible for releasing objects when they are no longer needed, he must be aware of the entire system to ensure that each object is freed once and only once during the lifetime of the program, and never accessed afterward. This increases surface area tremendously, since it forces every consumer to understand the entirety of the application, not just the interface to his suppliers.

5. Protection domains: Large systems involve processes running inside a protection domain such as a personal computer address space or a process in a timesharing system. The protected processes communicate via files, pipes, packets, transactions, or messages. Each communication between protection domains increases surface area by exposing a new influence, different from those that operate in the main body of code.

6. Concurrency: Concurrent problems have higher surface area than sequential ones because interactions can now occur across time as well as space.

UniqueWords

Object-oriented programming is a packaging technology. It allows suppliers to crate up units of generic functionality such that consumers can apply them in their specific application. It packages functionality so that it can be reused. Object-oriented programming is only one of many ways for packaging code. This section contrasts three common packaging techniques by putting them to work in a simple exercise, which is to build a program, UniqueWords, that counts the number of unique words in a document. Document sizes are such that the words can be held in main memory.

Packaging Technology 1: UNIX Pipes/Filters

One of the most programmer-efficient technologies for packaging code for reuse was introduced in UNIX and has now spread to other programming environments as well. The pipes and filters technology packages reusable code into small, stand-alone programs, in which each program is a tool (a filter) that does a single job well. The filters can be connected by pipes, a communication channel through which the output of one filter can be received as the input of the next.

This technology is at its best on problems like this one. The job can be done in a single line of code by connecting three filters with two pipes like this:

```
tr -cs 'A-Za-z0-9' '\012' | sort -u | wc -l
```

The | symbols denote pipes; the others denote tool invocations. The first tool is the tr program which translates characters. With the options used here (-cs), it translates each nonalphanumeric character ('A-Za-z0-9') into a newline character (' \012') to produce a byte-stream with each word on a separate line. This stream is piped into the sort program which sorts the words. Sort is used here with an option (-u) that makes it discard duplicate words, producing a new stream that contains only unique words. These are piped into the wc (word count) program which counts the unique words in the document.

This is one of the most potent reusability technologies known today. The small tools are neatly encapsulated, easily documented, and require no recompilation (e.g., their source does not have to be available) to reassemble them to solve problems in an open universe that their builder never imagined. Nonetheless, this technology is not a panacea for packaging reusable code. For one thing, passing bytes along a pipe is orders of magnitude more costly than passing arguments between two subroutines. More importantly, pipes only carry streams of bytes, not the highly structured data that abounds in system building. You cannot pass a pointer or a linked list across a pipe without great difficulty.

Packaging Technology 2: Subroutine Libraries

Certainly the most successful packaging technique, judging from the frequency with which it is used today, is the tried-and-true library of subroutines and macros. Nearly every programming language provides some way to store compiled modules in a library, and to link that code into applications. It is the reusability workhorse of the programming industry.

Applied to the UniqueWords example, this technology would deliver packaged functionality (from the UNIX I/O library) for opening and closing files, reading characters, and printing results. It would supply a library of string-handling functions to deal with words, stored as character strings. And from the point of view of the application builder, the operating system itself is a package of function calls for reading and writing files, etc. But this technology provides no way to keep track of the unique words read thus far, so these would have to be developed from scratch.

This points to the major weakness of subroutine libraries as a reusability technology. Why wouldn't a programming environment as rich as UNIX offer a subroutine for solving problems as simple, and as ubiquitous, as searching? The needed algorithm exists in there already. The C compiler contains algorithms for searching for symbols, the text formatter contains algorithms for managing macro definitions, the file search utility contains algorithms for searching for strings in text buffers, etcetera and ad nauseum. Yet to proceed with this exercise requires building yet another search algorithm from first principles.

The reason is hardly subtle and is central to everything this book has to offer. The subroutine library technology is limited by the fact that it requires each piece of code to be tightly bound to the environment for which that piece of code was developed (i.e. to exist in a closed universe). The algorithm that the C compiler uses to search for defined identifiers cannot be lifted out and reused, because it is tightly bound to its environment (the C compiler application) and the specific kind of datum that it is prepared to search over (the data structure used for identifiers in the C compiler).

Of course, this limitation is offset by a corresponding benefit: superb machine efficiency. A qualitative estimate for these trade-offs can even be derived. Appendix B contains a C program that manages a hashed table of symbols. A perfect reusability technology would have allowed this algorithm to be used here, but the packaging technology required that it be bound to manage Nodes, and here we need one that manages Words. That algorithm was written in 103 lines of moderately complex C code, a figure that serves to estimate the amount of code that would have to be written from scratch to solve the UniqueWords exercise. These 103 lines implement the hash table itself, a function for computing hash codes from Nodes, logic for managing collisions, and so forth.

While the pipes/filters technology solved the problem in one line, the subroutine library technology required over a hundred—a difference of over two orders of magnitude! But of course machine efficiency can be expected to differ as well.

Packaging Technology 3: Software-ICs

The prior two solutions provide fixed points of reference with which to compare the packaging technology emphasized in this book. The Software-IC technology is similar to pipes and filters in that much of the work is done at run-time, but different in that machine efficiency is much higher, although somewhat less than the subroutine library technique. But it is like the subroutine library technology in that complicated data structures can be managed easily.

This solution also uses the UNIX libraries of functions for managing files, reading characters, and comparing strings. But it introduces an additional library, called an IC pak, that contains a pair of Software-ICs named Set and String. Software-ICs are binary files just like those in a conventional subroutine library. The String IC implements a class of object that holds character arrays, and these will be used to represent the words in the document. The Set IC implements a class of objects that hold sets of other objects. Since sets do not allow duplicate members, these objects use a hash table to rapidly check that each newly added object is not a duplicate of some existing member.

These components can be used as follows. First create an empty set. For each word in the file, create a String instance containing the word's characters and add this instance to the set (rely on the set to reject duplicate members). When the file is empty, report the size of the set as the number of unique words in the file.

This description can be translated line for line into a programming language and compiled to produce an executable program. For example, the following is coded in Objective-C, the hybrid programming language to be described in this book (see Chapter 4).

```
uniqueWords = [Set new];          /* uniqueWords is an empty set */
while(getWord(buf) !=EOF) {        /* read a word into buf */
    currentWord = [String str:buf];  /* currentWord is a byteArray */
    [uniqueWords add:currentWord];   /* add currentWord to the set */
}
printf("The number of unique words is %d\n",[uniqueWords size]);
```

In most respects, this fragment is a perfectly ordinary C program. The assignment expressions, the while loop, and the getWord and printf functions work exactly as in ordinary C. It differs from C in that it contains three message expressions, enclosed in square brackets (e.g., [Set new]). These extensions are added to C by Objective-C.

The first message expression commands the object named Set to perform the operation named new and stores the result in the local variable uniqueWords. Objects whose names begin with an upper-case letter, such as Set, are called factory objects. Every Software-IC contains its own factory object, and these are used to produce instances of the class of objects that the Software-IC supports. This line causes the Set factory to produce a new set (in other words, a new instance of class Set) and gives that instance the name uniqueWords.

The second line uses an ordinary C function, getWord(), to read the next word from the file, storing it in an ordinary C character array, buf. The third line is another message expression, this time telling the object named String to perform the operation named str:. The colon in the operation name signifies that the operation takes an argument, buf. This statement commands String, the factory object of the String Software-IC, to produce a new instance holding the characters that getWord has obtained from the file. The identifier of this new object is stored in the local variable, currentWord. The next statement commands the set, uniqueWords, to perform the operation, add:, on the argument, currentWord.[1] Finally, once the file is empty, the C printf function is used to print the number of unique words in the document. This number is computed by commanding the set to report how many members it contains by sending it the message size.

This solution involves about ten lines of code (the six lines shown above plus about four lines of declarations). This is an order of magnitude fewer lines than the subroutine library approach (100 lines), but an order of magnitude more lines than the pipes and filters approach (1 line). Conversely, the subroutine library version will run the fastest, the Software-IC version somewhat slower, and the piped version slowest of all.

Discussion

These three solutions represent three points on a continuum for when, and how tightly, one programmer's work should be coupled to another's. The subroutine library solution represents one end of the spectrum, the closed universe. Binding is done by the consumer when he writes each line of code. This produces highly machine-efficient solutions, but the cost in programmer efficiency can be high. The pipes and filters technology represents the opposite end of the spectrum, the open universe, and delivers the opposite trade-off in man-machine efficiency.

The Software-IC approach lies somewhere in between. Like the pipes/filters solution, no recompilation is needed to reuse code. The Set and String ICs were compiled in binary and archived long before the UniqueWords application was conceived. Binding did not occur until an application compiled, linked, and finally executed. At some point in the computation the set instance needed to determine whether its argument was a duplicate of any other member in the set. It did this by sending its argument, an instance of class String, a message that requested it to determine whether it is equal to some other object, its potential duplicate.

Binding occurs only at this point. Until now, the Set IC was not coupled to the String IC in any way. A compiler could use sets to manage symbol tables, an accounting application could use sets to manage customer accounts, and an office automation application could use sets to manage filefolders, all without changing or even recompiling the code that implements the

---

[1]To simplify this introduction, the algorithm uses memory inefficiently. Each time the set fails to add a member because a duplicate member is already in the set, the new entry is not deallocated. A practical implementation would use the filter: message instead of add:. This causes the set to deallocate potential entries that fail because a duplicate member exists.

Set class in any way. The same Set code can support sets of different kinds of contents within the same application. It is even possible to have sets of mixed kinds of contents, such as a set of information about customers where the customer information is held in different kinds of office forms. The application contains only a single copy of set, and this single copy supports sets of anything that might get tossed in at run-time.

Binding Time and Coupling Strength

Early binding and late binding are fundamentally different tools for different jobs, but this distinction is routinely misunderstood. For example, consider the recent enthusiasm for strongly typed languages with operator overloading, such as Ada.

> One of the design concepts behind Ada is that the semantics of a given program should be static to the largest degree practical. Reliability is therefore enhanced because much of the analysis of a program can be done at compilation time. Thus, in Ada, we see that the basic type of any object is designed to be static and that the number, scope, and visibility of entities are known prior to execution. When we abstract objects in the problem space, however, we find that the world is not so nicely static.[2]

Ada's answer for open universe situations is the access type or pointer variable, which allows the programmer to implement loosely coupled collections by doing dynamic binding himself with conditional statements.

The world contains both kinds of collections. For example, consider an automobile engine and an automobile trunk. The engine is a closed universe tightly coupled collection. Early in the automobile's lifecycle (as early as design time), it is possible and desirable to know that the engine will be composed of an engine block, pistons, rings, and a crankshaft. On the other hand, the automobile's trunk is an open universe, a loosely coupled collection. It is not possible or desirable to specify what that trunk will hold any earlier than when the car is put to use.

Static Binding and Tightly Coupled Collections

In programming, a floating point number is an example of a tightly coupled collection. As early as design time it is known that each number will consist of precisely one mantissa and precisely one exponent. This knowledge can be hard-wired into a programming tool like a C compiler, and the programmer can forget about mantissas and exponents and think only in terms of higher level concepts—real numbers and the operations they support. The compiler translates high-level notations like "a = b + 2.3" into operations on mantissas and exponents based on its knowledge that a, b, and 2.3 are of type floatingPointNumber. This knowledge is used early, at compile-time,

---

[2]Grady Booch, *Software Engineering with Ada,* Benjamin/Cummings, 1983.

which is why this way of translating symbols into code is called early or static binding.

C language also provides ways for the programmer to define new data types as well. For example, a graphics programmer might decide to define a new data type, vector, as a tightly coupled collection of two integers describing the end points of a geometric vector:

```
typedef struct { int x, y; } vector;
```

Ideally, the language would allow as much flexibility for writing operations on vectors that C provides for writing operations on floating point numbers. For example, given the origin of a rectangle (its top-left corner) and its extent (its diagonal dimension),

```
vector origin, extent;
```

a programmer might like to compute the vector to its bottom right corner by writing

```
vector bottomRight = origin + extent;
```

This is not possible in C, nor in other conventional languages like Pascal, FORTRAN, and COBOL.[3] These languages do not allow the programmer to change the meaning of built-in operators like +, so that these operators cannot be applied to newly added data types like vector. These languages require the programmer to decompose each operation to primitive types manually and write:

```
bottomRight.x = origin.x + extent.x;
bottomRight.y = origin.y + extent.y;
```

The supplier of a new data type like vector cannot hide the implementation of this new type from consumers. They must know the implementation to use the type, because they must do all binding between vector and operations on vectors manually when they write their code.

The recent trend is toward languages that do provide this flexibility, as long as all types are known at compile-time. For example, languages like Ada allow vectors to be defined as a new data type with +, a legal operation on that type. When compiling the expression

```
bottomRight = origin + extent;
```

the compiler notices that both origin and extent are vectors, and determines that a special meaning for the + operator is to be used—the one defined by the supplier of the vector type. These languages provide early binding in a more powerful way than C because the meaning of predefined operators like + can be changed for newly defined data types.

---

[3]But it is possible in C++. See Chapter 3.

This approach can address some of the difficulties encountered when applying subroutine libraries to the UniqueWords problem. The problem was to build a new data type, Set, without prematurely committing to the kind of elements to be stored in the Set. Ada's solution to this class of problem is called a generic package, which is a package of code with a compile-time parameter that specifies which type is to be managed by the set. The Unique-Words application would be solved by writing a statement in the consumer's code that directs the compiler to compile a Set that expects to manage Strings.

Dynamic Binding and Loosely Coupled Collections

The statically bound languages are perfect for building tightly coupled collections like vectors and rectangles. They can even be pushed to handle some harder cases like the UniqueWords example. Of course recompiling a supplier's code every time a consumer provides a new data type can be a problem, and not only because of the time to compile these custom sets and the memory to store them in. A more fundamental concern is that the supplier must trust the compiler to protect any proprietary interest he might hold in those sources. It is hard to see how a commercial marketplace in generic packages could develop as long as suppliers must trust the compiler to protect their proprietary interests in source code.

It is less widely recognized that statically bound languages are extremely poor for building loosely coupled collections—open universe problems are more like the automobile's trunk than its engine. Loosely coupled collections abound in applications like office automation, in information-oriented ensembles like DeskTop, Envelope, FileFolder, PaperClip, Mailbox, and FileCabinet. A desktop or a mailbox is a loosely coupled collection because it is neither possible nor desirable to state, at any point earlier than when the desktop is in use, what kind of items it contains.

When every data type is known when the code is compiled, the closed universe approach of static binding works. Otherwise binding must be done dynamically, period. There is no choice between static and dynamic binding, since dynamic binding is intrinsic to the very essense of a loosely coupled collection. However, there is a choice between one method of implementing dynamic binding and another, since dynamic binding can be done either manually, by conditional statements written by the programmer, or automatically, by the programming language and the run-time environment.

The choice is shown in Figure 2.4. This figure shows the kinds of objects in an office automation project as seven folders, each representing the work of a different programmer. The mailbox folder is open to show the mailbox developer's two choices for how to implement dynamic binding.

The left fragment shows the manual approach. A switch statement determines which kind of object is on hand, passing control dynamically to the operation (a C function) that properly manipulates that kind of object. The

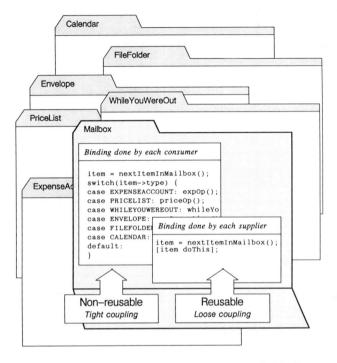

Figure 2.4. Binding in a loosely coupled collection. Dynamic binding can be implemented either by the consumer or by the supplier. The former leads to nonreusable code, because the consumer's code enumerates the set of data types that were known when the consumer's code was written. The latter can produce reusable code, because data types are mentioned in only one place—in the files that define each data type.

kind of object is represented in a field inside each object, represented as a C structure:

```
struct OfficeMemo { int type; ... } ;
struct WhileYouWereOutNotice { int type; ... } ;
struct FileFolder { int type; ... } ;
```

The fragment on the right shows the other approach in which dynamic binding is provided automatically by the programming language. The mailbox developer, as consumer of the other six data types in this system, specifies what each item is to do by writing the message expression [item doThis], and it is up to the object to decide how the command, doThis, should be accomplished for that kind of object.

The difference between these two approaches is crucial to the separation of responsibility between supplier and consumer. The mailbox developer is the consumer of functionality provided elsewhere in his project. The first approach requires that he, the consumer, bear the responsibility for determining which supplier's data is at hand in the mailbox and for selecting which one of the supplier's subroutines is proper for that kind of data. This is called consumer-side binding. By contrast, the other approach puts that responsibility right where it belongs, on the supplier's side.

The problem with consumer-side binding can be seen in the case labels in the switch statement. These labels explicitly enumerate the data types this mailbox is prepared to handle, so each time a new type is added anywhere in this system, the mailbox code must be changed. Something foul has leaked across the boundary that should have isolated suppliers from consumers. This mailbox is useless in any other application, because the case labels explicitly state that it will only work correctly for those six types.

One effect of consumer-side binding is lack of reusability. It forces the mailbox to be written in a way that prevents it from ever being reused in other applications. Consumer-side binding also leads to lack of malleability. Each time a new data type is added to the system, the source for the mailbox must be modified. It cannot withstand the kind of evolutionary changes discussed in Chapter 1. Supplier-side binding, by contrast, increases the chance that the mailbox can be reused in other applications because it no longer mentions types that might change in some new application. And the system becomes malleable because new data types can be added over time without impacting working code.

This benefit is called encapsulation. It is the first and foremost contribution of the dynamically bound style of object-oriented programming. A second benefit, called inheritance, becomes possible once encapsulation is available. Inheritance is a technique for defining new data types by describing how each new type differs from some preexisting type.

Software-IC Implications

The appeal of all this is the possibility that the software industry might obtain some of the benefits that the silicon chip brought to the hardware industry; the ability of a supplier to deliver a tightly encapsulated unit of functionality that is specialized for its intended function, yet independent of any particular application. The silicon chip is the unit of hardware reusability that has most conspicuously contributed to the hardware productivity boom. Might the Software-IC concept do the same for software?

Gordon Moore, the chairman of Intel Corporation, once predicted that the number of components on a silicon integrated chip would continue to double yearly. The prediction, now known as Moore's law, has held up remarkably well during the twenty years I've been in this business. One of its many implications is that during the same period that my productivity has been growing arithmetically with each improvement in programming language technology, the productivity of my friends in the hardware industry has been growing geometrically as the capability of the building blocks that they work with doubled each year for twenty years. My productivity certainly improved in moving from assembly language to FORTRAN to C to Lisp. But it certainly did not improve by a millionfold, as is implied by Moore's law:

$2^{20} = 1,048,576$

Objects are tightly encapsulated and thus relatively independent of their environment. They can be designed, developed, tested, and documented as stand-alone units without knowledge of any particular application, and then stockpiled for distribution and reuse in many different circumstances. A reusable module acquires value unto itself, while the value of application-dependent code has no value beyond that of the application as a whole. It can be tested and documented to much higher standards than has been done in the past. What might this do for software reliability, or for quelling the usual objection, "I can develop it quicker than I can understand somebody else's code."

Board designers routinely reuse the work of circuit designers, who reuse the efforts of workers at even lower levels—wafer manufacturers, mask fabricators, printing shops. Communication channels (trade magazines) allow suppliers to communicate with potential consumers, and consumers have catalogs, filing systems, performance tests, price comparisons for selecting among multiple suppliers. The impressive vitality of the marketplace in reusable hardware components is legendary.

Might a similar marketplace be possible for software? What might a marketplace for reusable software components be like? How might a SymbolTable supplier describe this product to a community of potential consumers? How will a consumer community choose between SymbolTables supplied by a community of suppliers? Might an office automation systems builder go comparison shopping for a DeskTop object as the cornerstone of his office automation system? Might he choose between a fully optioned model with DeskDrawer and FilingDrawer objects already built-in, versus a bare-bones model that he can integrate with drawer objects from competing vendors? Might he then shop for RolodexFile objects, AppointmentBook, DeskCalendar, and DeskCalculator objects with which to stock his office automation product? Or choose instead to build inhouse, perhaps shopping elsewhere for lower level components like OrderedCollection, SortedCollection, Text, TextView, Window, and the like?

How might full software reusability affect the software industry as a whole, given the slipped schedules, overstretched budgets and canceled project that typify ambitious projects today? Wouldn't this go far toward reducing the software backlog that is tormenting us right now? Or free us from the slipped schedules and canceled orders that so often produce that chasm between our dreams and what we can reasonably expect to produce?

Summary

This chapter has described a number of technologies for packaging a supplier's code for reuse by a consumer. These technologies are tools, not panaceas. Each of them has its place, and none replace the others. I'd no more relinquish Smalltalk-style late binding for C-style early binding than I'd relinquish subroutine libraries for pipes and filters. They are each different solutions for different jobs, and they all deserve their place on a programmer's workbench. They each have a specialized purpose for which they are the best tool for the job. Whether early binding or late binding is better or worse cannot be discussed in the abstract, but only in relation to how well it serves a specific task.

Early binding is best when building tightly coupled collections in a closed universe environment where the types of all members can be specified early. By making this information available to the compiler, it can prevent a certain class of programming error by verifying that all members are as the designer specified them, a language feature known as strong type checking.

Static binding is of little use when the problem involves the open universe environment of a loosely coupled collection. But it is possible to use a statically bound programming language for such problems, by having each consumer provide statements that accomplish the dynamic part of the problem. This solution is highly undesirable, because it makes the consumer's code highly dependent on the supplier's. Such code is not reusable in other applications, and the application itself is unmalleable because of extremely high coupling.

Chapter 4 will show how support for supplier-side dynamic binding can be grafted onto almost any statically bound programming language. This produces a hybrid language that offers the best of both worlds. These hybrids are a lot like a skilled cabinetmaker's workbench. To a novice it seems cluttered with random tools of many descriptions, but to the craftsman's eye each tool is there for a reason, and each leaps to hand in a twinkling. Beauty may be found in how each tool makes its unique contribution to the job as a whole.

Supplier-side binding makes the Software-IC approach feasible. It allows suppliers to collect large bodies of tested code into libraries, where it can be drawn upon by consumers. Software-ICs are binary representations that protect any proprietary interests the suppliers have in their code. This satisfies an important commercial prerequisite for any marketplace in reusable software components.

However, tools alone are not enough to affect the powerful forces that could easily prevent dreams like the Software-IC marketplace from becoming reality:

A serious, and very possibly fatal, objection is that software can be copied (i.e., pirated) so easily that it removes any incentive to invest in building software for reuse.

The effort of documenting a module such that others can really use it is substantial, and could even exceed the effort required to build the module from scratch.

Reusing code means trusting that code to work properly. Although encapsulation and inheritance do help with this, they don't eliminate the possibility of applications failing when software they depend on changes.

Underlying these concerns, and others as well, is the inescapable fact that programming is really different from other manufacturing of physical objects. Eli Whitney's interchangeable parts notion can only be approximated in the computer, where the opportunity for unforeseen interaction is so much greater than in physical media like iron or brass.

| Three

What Is Object-oriented Programming?

Object-oriented is well on its way to becoming the buzzword of the 1990s. Suddenly everybody is using it, but with such a range of radically different meanings that no one seems to know exactly what the other is saying. It is hard to imagine two languages more different than Smalltalk-80 and Ada, yet both are sometimes called object-oriented languages. Others think of objects as primarily a way of expressing concurrency, and yet others as a way of organizing complex facts into hierarchies. How can the same term refer to things as different as programming languages, user interfaces, schemes for representing expert knowledge, distributed operating systems, telephony switching systems, and many others? What *does* object-oriented mean?

Outside the computer domain, the word object means anything with a crisply defined boundary. Pencils, hummingbirds, molecules, and galaxies are objects, but oceans, fog, and measles are not. Although the von Neumann concept of the computer's address space defines no such thing as a crisply defined boundary, programmers have none the less chosen to adopt this word. Without first defining key terms like boundary, no understanding about the meaning of words like object can be expected.

This chapter surveys several meanings for this term by describing how the word is used in several modern programming languages. The goal is not to provide a comprehensive survey of all that has been done or said under the name object-oriented programming, but to describe a few key points that have been explored in the spectrum of possibilities. Although this provides a perspective that some may find helpful, it is also tangential to the chapters that follow and might well be skipped on first reading.

Smalltalk-80

Smalltalk-80 is an integrated programming language and programming environment. It is the result of over a decade of research by the Software Concepts Group at Xerox PARC. Smalltalk is a remarkably influential system. It has affected not only other Xerox commercial products like the Star office automation system and Interlisp-D knowledge engineering systems, but has also influenced many other academic and commercial systems as well. Its influence on Apple's Lisa and Macintosh systems is widely acknowledged, not to mention its effect on a variety of lesser known systems in office automation, inhouse publishing, and computer-aided design. Much of today's enthusiasm for high-resolution graphics workstations, iconic user interfaces, and personal computing can be traced directly to its demonstration of the value and feasibility of these ideas.

Until recently, Smalltalk's value has been in proving concepts that are subsequently exploited in other systems, not as a commercially important system in its own right. This is changing as cost-effective commercial implementations become available, and as the marketplace begins to discover how Smalltalk fits within the traditional range of programming solutions.

From the beginning Smalltalk's designers have steadfastly emphasized a number of innovative and controversial ideas about what computing could be like:

1. *Personal computing:* Computers are cheap and people are expensive. Computers should not be shared. Giving each person his own private machine would multiply the available computing horsepower and allow machine efficiency to diminish as a design issue.

2. *Interaction:* The computing environment should go to any lengths to provide immediate feedback for all user actions.

3. *Graphics:* People are most adept at visual thinking. Text should be replaced by graphic images as far as possible.

4. *Object-oriented programming:* People work with problem-domain concepts, while hardware works with different (operator/operand) concepts. Some of the conceptual burden in translating from problem-domain to computer-domain should be carried by the machine, by making the machine work in terms of concepts closer to the user's everyday world.

Smalltalk-80 is the name of several layers of abstraction which together implement these assertions. From the beginning, Smalltalk-80's designers were inspired by Alan Kay's vision of the future, the Dynabook. This is a powerful personal computer, as capable as the most powerful graphics workstations available today, but the size of a small notebook. Smalltalk-80 was designed to be the system programming language for computers of this power.

Virtual Machine

In Smalltalk-80, an object is some private data and a collection of procedures that can access that data. The data is private to the object, and cannot be accessed without help from one of that object's procedures. The procedures are public to all consumers, who access the object by writing message expressions. A message expression tells an object what it should do. The object responds to a message by selecting and then performing a procedure whereby all objects of its class perform this message. This procedure is called a method, and the command carried by the message is called a selector.

Smalltalk adheres to this principle exhaustively. Literally everything is an object—not only large infrequently used high-level entities like windows, directories, and projects, but heavily used low-level entities like integers and stack frames. (Of course, heavy optimization is applied in these and other cases.)

The advantage is consistency, which shows up throughout the system. The whole integrated system is organized by a single principle, so a user need understand only this principle to explore any part of Smalltalk-80. Once he has learned to use the debugger (the inspector) to examine an object, he knows everything he needs to inspect and understand stack frames, integers, floating point numbers—literally anything in the system (Figure 3.1).

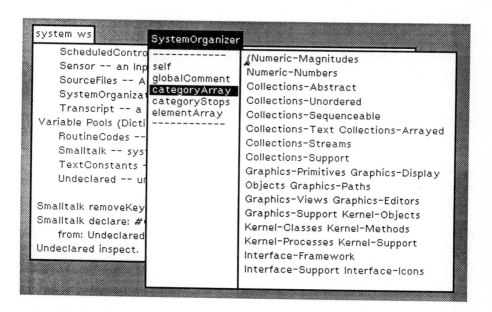

Figure 3.1. The Smalltalk-80 inspection facility can be used to examine and change the state of any part of the system.

This book adopts the Smalltalk-80 definition of all object-oriented concepts, including object, message, class, method, and inheritance. Full definitions are provided in Chapter 4. The primary exception is how object lifetimes are determined. Smalltalk-80 provides automatic garbage collection, which means that the lifetime of all objects is determined, not by the programmer, but by the system. When an object is no longer referenced, its memory is automatically reclaimed for reuse.

To accomplish this efficiently, and to allow free space to be compacted easily when memory becomes fragmented, Smalltalk uses a meaning for the term object identifier that is more powerful than that used in the rest of this book. Here, objects are identified directly, by their memory address. But in Smalltalk they are identified by offset into a table of object descriptors, the object table, one of whose entries is the memory address of the object. This hides memory management from the programmer, making address handling the business of the system and allowing it to move things around as needed.

Everything is an object, even low-level entities like small integers. A typical implementation represents object identifiers as 16 bit integers, using 15 of the bits to identify small integers directly (i.e., small integers occupy no slots in the object table). The other bit is used to signal that the id is not that of a small integer, but an offset into the object table.

The benefit of automatic garbage collection is not small, because it eliminates a whole class of truly nasty bugs. It eliminates the dangling pointer problem, in which invalid object identifiers (produced by freeing the object they point to) can lie dormant for arbitrarily long periods and then cause hard-to-diagnose problems (crashes) when they are finally accessed. And it prevents the equally dangerous problem in which a long-running application strangles from lack of memory because unneeded objects have not been freed.

But it is also a liability. In combination with Smalltalk's extensive use of dynamically bound messaging, it can cause monumental costs in machine resources, effectively prohibiting the use of Smalltalk-80 for some performance-critical applications. These resources are hardly wasted, but they were spent deliberately to move work that is normally borne by increasingly expensive programmers onto increasingly cheap machines.

Programming Language

The simplicity of the Smalltalk-80 virtual machine allows the programming language to be unusually small as well. The complex syntax most languages provide for declaring data types is completely unnecessary because everything is of only one type, an object. No control structures are needed either, since these are all achieved by messaging. In fact, the Smalltalk-80 language only defines syntax for

1. declaring object names and assigning them values,
2. sending messages, and
3. defining new classes and methods.

The last two really need no special syntax at all, since they are accomplished through mouse commands to the browser; a tool in the Smalltalk-80 environment that is used for reading, changing, and compiling methods.

Messages

The simplest kind of message is the unary message expression. A unary message is a message with no arguments, so it consists of only two parts:[1]

1. The name of an object to receive the message, followed by
2. The name of the message.

```
theta sin
quantity sqrt
nameString size
```

A second kind of message is a keyword message expression. These can have arguments; as many as there are parts in the keyword. The selector of a keyword message is composed of one or more keywords, one preceding each argument. A keyword part is a simple identifier and a trailing colon:

```
index max:limit
householdFinances spendAmount:548.00 forReason:'rent'
```

Both examples send a single keyword message, even though the keyword selector in the second example is written in two parts separated by the argument, 548.00. The first statement sends the message, max:, to the object index, and the second statement sends the message, spendAmount:forReason:, to the object, householdFinances. In both cases the colons are an inseparable part of the message selector, and are even retained in spoken conversation. For example, the message in the second line is spoken spend-amount-colon-for-reason-colon. The colons describe places where arguments are to be provided. Both the receiver and the arguments can be variable names, constants, or other expressions.

Binary messages behave just like keyword messages of a single argument. The selector of a binary message is always one or two characters from a designated set of special characters. Examples of binary message expressions are

```
3 + 4
total - 1
total <= max
```

Finally, the assignment operator is used to store values into variables

```
sum ← 3 + 4
x ← theta sin
```

---

[1]Some phrases and examples are used verbatim from Goldberg and Robson, *Smalltalk-80: The Language and its Implementation*, Addison-Wesley, 1983.

Since message expressions can be (and often are!) deeply nested, one inside the other, precedence rules are provided to sort things out, and parentheses can be used to override the precedence rules when necessary.

Blocks

Smalltalk is an interactive environment, so expressions are normally evaluated immediately. Expressions can be stored for subsequent execution by enclosing them in brackets. This creates a remarkable construct called a block. A block is an object (an instance of class Block) that represents a sequence of instructions whose execution is to be deferred until the block is sent the message, value. Most of Smalltalk's control structures are implemented as messages to objects that take blocks as arguments. For example,

```
index <= limit
    ifTrue:[total ← total + (list at:index)]
```

The index < = limit expression is a binary message to the object, index, an instance of some class of Number (precisely which kind of number cannot be determined from this fragment). The number creates a new instance of class Boolean, and the next line sends this boolean the message ifTrue: with an instance of class Block as the argument. The boolean evaluates the block by sending it the message value if the boolean's state is TRUE.

Blocks are deceptively simple. Surprisingly powerful facilities are hidden within that terse phrase, a sequence of instructions whose execution is to be deferred. For example, even though a block looks like, and is often used like, a C compound statement or a Pascal BEGIN ... END pair, it shares few of the limitations these languages place on how long execution might be deferred. In most languages, execution can be deferred no longer than the lifetime of the enclosing scope, a restriction derived from the hidden assumption that the execution state of any block of code is held on a simple hardware stack which always grows and shrinks from one end.

Smalltalk-80 blocks have no such restriction because stack frames are objects and are allocated and deallocated with all the generality provided for any other kind of object. In particular, blocks are allocated from the heap and are disposed of by the garbage collector, not when the scope which created them terminates. Any block, as well as the environment in which it was originally created (its context), can be held indefinitely and executed long after the message that created it returned. For example, the following provides the object aSet instructions about what to do if removal of anElement fails; e.g., because the set includes no such element:

```
aSet remove:anElement ifFail:[ ... ]
```

This block will be executed by aSet, not by the caller, but nonetheless it will have full access to the context of the calling method, including its local variables and arguments. The block is given a reference to the caller's context when the block is created, and this context persists as long as a reference to it exists anywhere in the system. For example, it is permissible to hold references to blocks in long-lived objects, like menus, that outlive the procedure that created them.

This extraordinary facility derives directly from the decision to make no exceptions to the rule that everything will benefit from the full power the system provides for any object, even low-level entities that most languages handle specially, like stack frames. The benefit is large, because this single concept, the block, moves a number of difficult topics outside the language and puts them at the disposal of its users. The price is also large because even heavily used operations like messaging cannot benefit from fast special-purpose sequential stacks, but incur the full garbage collection treatment.[2]

Programming Environment

No discussion of Smalltalk-80 is complete without mentioning its extraordinary integrated programming environment (Figure 3.2). The programming language, supporting tools (text editors, linkers, debuggers), and the operating system itself are an integrated, tightly coupled whole which co-reside within the same virtual (and in some implementations, physical) address space.

This environment emphasizes personal creativity. This is nowhere as obvious as in its philosophy of making the entire system accessible, even things that most programmers would not dream of changing, like the operating system or the representation for floating point numbers. Neither of these things are protected, and the full source for both is available online and easily changed by any programmer. Anything can be changed as easily as any other, even changes that are inconsistent with the rest of the system and cause it to crash, or changes that could make subsequent work incompatible with work being done on neighboring systems.

The turmoil that unconstrained hacking can cause was obvious to Smalltalk's designers, and it forced them to think creatively about tools for managing change. The result was a beautifully designed environment for dealing with change in a convenient, disciplined way. A Smalltalk-80 user works at a high-resolution screen, using a tool called the browser to explore and possibly modify any part of the system. The browser is like a text editor, in that it can display source code for reading or for editing. It is also the primary way of running the compiler, thus modifying the system in place.

The browser also provides a way for team members to communicate about their software. Each programmer's personal environment is constructed by periodically integrating the work of the entire team. A tool similar to the browser is used by the person responsible for integrating the team's work. It checks each change for consistency and flags suspicious items for detailed

---

[2]Of course, the faster Smalltalk-80 implementations go to considerable lengths to determine when it is safe to create and dispose of blocks in traditional, faster ways.

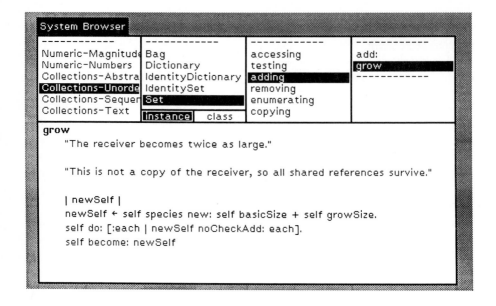

Figure 3.2. The Smalltalk-80 browser is used to examine, change, and compile classes and methods.

attention. This produces a new release of the base system to be distributed to all team members.

Each new release includes the full source for the system, including comments, so the integration/release cycle periodically publicizes the work of each individual to the rest of the group. Group members use the browser to learn what others have contributed, and to study how this can be reused in their own efforts, and the browser supports this search with cross-referencing aids. This amounts to an electronic means for publishing and studying the kind of information that most programmers handle less efficiently on paper.

Smalltalk Is Clearly the Solution. But What's the Problem?

From the beginning, the goal of Smalltalk's developers was research. The utility of any by-products, such as Smalltalk-80 itself, was purely secondary. In this, they were successful, for the fruits of their work have spread widely. But what of Smalltalk-80 itself? Does it have a place outside the research environment, alongside conventional programming languages like C or even robust dinosaurs like COBOL and FORTRAN?

The obvious application is for building prototype systems that will be re-coded in conventional languages, and this seems to account for most of its use today. But even more creative uses are imaginable that exploit the potential symbiosis that could exist between Smalltalk-80's world of personal computing and the COBOL/IMS world of organizational computing.

These behemoth databases exist because executives need timely, accurate information on which to base decisions. But they complain of delays and inconveniences of getting to the data, separated from it as they are by a multi-layered data processing staff. Smalltalk-80 might well have a role even in this gray pin stripe world. A Smalltalk-80 programmer might develop classes that encapsulate the knowledge required to draw data from the mainframe environment, and these classes used to allow less experienced programmers to serve the executive directly. The personal computer environment could serve as an impedance matcher between the executive's needs and the constraints of organizational computing.

Similar niches exist in scientific computing as well, plagued as it is by a bewildering diversity of data collection machines, computational/data storage machines, and number-crunching machines. One of a kind experiments are common, and the results must usually be interpreted with throw-away analysis programs. Today, these programs are written in FORTRAN. Smalltalk could well provide a better alternative, especially given its facility with graphics.

My own interest in hybrid object-oriented languages developed from the dream that organizational computing and personal computing could meet each other halfway, via a bridge over which arbitrary data could flow with minimum programmer intervention. The bridge is created by providing the organizational computer with its own object-oriented programming language so that data can be put into object form. Object passivation machinery (discussed on page 144) can automatically convert this data into a form that Smalltalk can read and vice versa, so that much of the information transfer could be done automatically. This, and C's ability to access databases maintained in older languages like FORTRAN, creates a bridge between data locked in the mainframe and the user by relying on the ability of Smalltalk-80 to build user interfaces rapidly.

Ada

So great is the publicity surrounding this language that it needs little introduction here. Commissioned by the U.S. Department of Defense (DOD), Ada was designed as a state-of-the-art replacement for the diverse collection of languages now used to build embedded computer systems. Throughout, there was an explicit intention that Ada would be mandatory for embedded systems work in which the computer is an integral and relatively small component within a much larger system involving aircraft control surfaces, weapons systems, navigational aids, communications systems, and the like. Just how embedded systems differ from ordinary ones where the computer is embedded in a maze of magnetic media drives, printers, typesetters, communications networks, and industrial control hardware, has always been unclear. This ambiguity is probably intentional, because the goal from the beginning has been to reduce the number of language dialects that DOD must contend with.

Ada has always been shrouded in controversy. Its designers are accused of the kitchen-sink syndrome, because Ada is a large, feature-laden, and extremely complicated language. Complex and possibly ill-understood features like multitasking and exception handling are defined as part of the language when these features should have probably been left out of the language itself and provided in detachable appendages like subroutine libraries or Ada packages. The arguments on both sides are understandable, given DOD's emphasis on preventing a proliferation of possibly incompatible dialects. Nonetheless, the size and complexity of the language has certainly increased the delay in getting satisfactory Ada compilers, as well as the antipathy toward this complex language that few will ever comprehend fully.

Object-oriented Features of Ada

Be that as it may, my purpose is not discussing Ada, the language, but the sense in which Ada, and languages like Ada, are said to support object-oriented programming. It should be clear by now that Ada's objectives are not to extend the realm of things that computers can do, but to provide a single way to do the things that are now done in numerous incompatible but similar languages.

The complexity of Ada's features often obscures the fact that Ada is basically a conventional language. Ada contains nothing that would surprise any C, Pascal, or FORTRAN user who is used to multitasking and exception handling as tacked onto the base language with subroutine libraries. Ada is a strongly typed language that performs all binding at compile-time. The types of all data are declared explicitly, and all decisions are made by the compiler at compile-time, not by the objects at run-time.

By Smalltalk-80 definitions, an object is some private data plus the group of procedures that can access that data. This encapsulation of data and procedure is accomplished by making the message expression the sole way of accessing any object. Since binding is deferred until the message has been sent, there is no difficulty working with loosely coupled collections that hold objects of different types.

In Ada, the encapsulation mechanism is provided entirely by the compiler and has vanished before run-time. This is Ada's strength and its weakness. It is a strength for the purpose for which Ada was designed; eliminating the need for multiple conventional languages for building conventional applications. It is better for building tightly coupled collections in which the type of each component can be known and specified in advance, because the compiler can check that each component is of the type specified. It is a weakness in problems in which change cannot be managed by editing the source and recompiling. The key distinguishing factor is the degree to which change can be dealt with early in the design process, before the program reaches the compiler.

Packages

In Ada, the supplier of a new capability does so by defining a package. The package contains parts that are to be private to the supplier, and others that are to be published to the consumer's code. Typically, the code and the precise layout of the fields in the object are held private, but this is by no means necessary. The supplier decides what to publish and what not to.

For example, the supplier of a graphics package might define a new data type, vector, to manage two-dimensional coordinates.

```
package TwoDimensionalGeometryPackage is
   type vector is record
      x : integer;
      y : integer;
   end record
   function "+" (a, b : in vector) return vector;
   function "-" (a, b : in vector) return vector;
end TwoDimensionalGeometryPackage;
```

This package defines an interface between the consumer and the supplier, but not the implementation underlying this interface. This is described separately in a package body:

```
package body TwoDimensionalGeometryPackage is
   function "+" (a, b in vector) return vector is
      begin
         -- instructions
      end
   function "-" (a, b in vector) return vector is
      begin
         -- instructions
      end
   begin
   -- instructions for initializing
end TwoDimensionalGeometryPackage
```

The consumer signals the compiler to use a package in a "with" statement, causing the public parts of the package to become known to the consumer's code. The consumer can use the services of the package in any way that the supplier made provision for. For example:

```
with TwoDimensionalGeometryPackage;
origin, extent, corner : vector;
corner = origin + extent;
```

Notice that Ada allows operator overloading, so that conventional operator names like + can be given meanings for user-defined data types. The compiler can tell that

```
corner = origin + extent;
```

should be handled differently from

```
sum = 2 + 2;
```

because the compiler knows that origin and extent are of type vector, and that a package has overridden the conventional meaning of the + symbol for this type. While the advantages of operator overloading are obvious for conventional mathematical symbols like +, it applies as well to conventional function names like sqrt, computeGyroCorrection, or accelerateToMaximum-Thrust.

Discussion

Ada's approach to object-oriented programming has its strengths and weaknesses, and it is inappropriate to state, categorically and self-righteously, "This is a strength" or "That is a weakness," without making clear "With respect to what alternative?" or "In the context of what problem?"

One of Ada's key decisions is that the semantics of a given program should be statically determined. Ada carries static binding further than older languages like C. But for programs that cannot be statically specified, Ada provides only access types. Access types are simply pointers; loopholes that allow the programmer to implement loosely coupled collections in the same way it would be done in C, implementing dynamic binding manually with consumer-side binding.

A real disappointment is Ada's limitations on defining new types by reusing some existing type. Although Ada does provide subtypes and derived types, these are only ways of restricting a general type, like integer, to some specific range or purpose, like dayOfTheWeek. Neither makes it possible to extend a preexisting type by adding additional fields and operations. This is a serious shortcoming because it removes the possibility of even limited kinds of type inheritance and forces the developer of each new type to duplicate code held in more general types.

The package concept is a genuine improvement over conventional languages like C. But its magnitude is hard to quantify. I think of it as comparable to the improvement of moving from an unstructured language like FORTRAN to a structured language like C, but less than the improvement of moving from assembly language to FORTRAN. Other parts of the Ada philosophy, primarily the insistence on a single language for all software development, have more likelihood of delivering truly significant improvements.

Static binding gains its efficiency by coupling decisions made by the supplier with those of the consumer at compile-time, just as in the conventional languages that DOD has been using for decades. Ada provides few features for decreasing this coupling, but it does provide outstanding support for managing tight coupling in a convenient manner. And perhaps that is just as well, because Ada is already bigger and more complicated than may be good for it. Why bemoan the fact that it supports only static binding, when dynamic binding can be added when needed through the techniques described in this book?

C++

C++ is an evolutionary enhancement to C language developed at Bell Laboratories. C++ is particularly interesting given this book's emphasis on Objective-C because it contrasts what can be accomplished by redefining the programming language itself as opposed to adding object-oriented capabilities to an immutable base language.

Objective-C adds dynamically bound objects, classes, and inheritance to plain vanilla C language. This adds just enough capability to support encapsulation and inheritance, sufficient that Software-IC technology can be applied to system-building problems, not on improving the programming language itself.

Bell Laboratories

However, these restrictions don't apply at Bell Laboratories. C, and now C++, were invented there. C is the standard programming language for AT&T and is its primary language for building telephone systems; systems that must be repaired and evolved throughout a traditionally long (40+ years) lifetime. This software is highly complex in its own right, and the job is doubly complicated by stringent reliability constraints. This enormous body of complex, touchy, and rarely compiled code is an important factor that governs all change to C language.

In this day of rapid turnover, Bell has retained nearly every individual who has been influential in defining and evolving C language. This includes Ken Thompson (best known as the original impetus behind UNIX and the inventor of Belle, the world champion chess computer, but also the inventor of B, an ancestor of C), Dennis Ritchie (the inventor of C itself), Steve Johnson (the creator of the subsequent, so-called portable C compiler, upon which most modern C compilers are based), Brian Kernighan (co-author with Ritchie of the book that was for years the sole reference book for C language[3]), and many others, including Bjarne Stroustrup, the primary force behind C++.

This pool of talent makes Bell Labs uniquely able, and highly motivated, to ensure that C language remains a vital, modern language, while the rest of the corporation acts to dampen change for change's sake. C++ evolved in this crucible to meet the following goals:[4]

1. Retain the extremely high machine efficiency and portability that C is famous for.

---

[3]Kernighan and Ritchie: *The C Programming Language*, Prentice-Hall Software Series.
[4]Ellis and Stroustrup, *The Annotated C++ Reference Manual*, Addison-Wesley, 1990.

2. Retain compatibility between C++ and C.

3. Repair long-standing flaws, particularly C's lax treatment of types. C has long been criticized for its weak type checking even inside a given function, and no type checking across functions even inside the same file.

4. Upgrade C in line with modern data-hiding principles.

C++ is very nearly a proper superset of C language, with a few modest incompatibilities. Its enhancements include the ability to define new data types (classes), operations on those types (operators and functions), and a comprehensive set of ways to control operations on these types, including operator overloading, constructors, and destructors.

Classes

New data types are defined through the class statement; a generalization of the old struct statement which it largely replaces but which is retained for backward compatibility (struct is treated as a special case of class in which all members are public). For example, the following is equivalent to a struct declaration

```
class ostream {
public:
    FILE *file;
    int nextchar;
    char buf[128];
};
```

This declares a new class ostream with three members, file, nextchar, and buf. The keyword, public:, makes these names public and accessible to any program that incorporates this declaration. The only difference between a class and a struct is that struct members are public by default, whereas class members are private unless explicitly designated otherwise. While structs could have only data members, classes may also have procedural members, or functions. These functions may be of two kinds, *friend* functions and *member* functions.

Friend Functions

Friend functions are conventional C functions. They have no particular connection with the class, except in being allowed to reference any data members that have been declared private (by appearing in advance of the public: marker)

```
class date {
    int day, month, year;
public:
    friend void setDate(date*, int, int, int);
    friend void nextDate(date*);
    friend void nextToday();
    friend void printDate(date*);
};
```

This makes the implementation for dates private, accessible only by the four friend functions. Notice the argument types accepted by these functions are also declared; these types are not only checked by the compiler, but are also used to guide binding decisions as well. This class might then be used as follows:

```
date myBirthday, today;
setDate(&myBirthday, 30, 12, 1950);
setDate(&today, 23, 6, 1983);
printDate(&today);
nextDate(&today);
```

Member Functions

Whereas friends are conventional functions, member functions are actually linked to the class in the same sense that data members are. Member functions provide the object-oriented flavor of C++. They implement operations on an instance of some class, whereas friends are just standard C functions that have been allowed to reference private members by name. Member functions are declared by mentioning their declaration inside the class declaration, alongside the declarations of member variables:

```
class date {
    int day, month, year;    /* the implementation for dates */
public:
    void set(int, int, int);   /* the interface to dates */
    void next();
    void print();
};
```

Member functions are called by syntax that reflects their role as operations performed by a specific object, and parallels the way structure members are accessed.

```
myBirthday.print();
today.next();
```

To define a member function, the name of its class must also be provided

```
void date.next() {
    day = day + 1;
    if (month == FEB && day > 28)
        ...
}
```

Such functions always receive an implicit argument, this, which identifies the object performing the function. In this example, the day field can be referenced as either day or this>day.

Derived Classes

C++ also provides the ability to define subclasses with inheritance, by describing how a new (derived) subclass differs from some older (inherited) superclass. The technique is different from Objective-C's in detail, and it trades generality and memory space to gain greater compile-time type checking and a measure of machine efficiency. For example, a class of shapes could be defined as follows:

```
class shape {
    vector center;
    int color;
    shape *next;
public:
    void move(vector);    /* reposition a shape */
    vector where();       /* reply location of a shape */
    virtual void rotate(int); /* rotate a shape */
    virtual void draw();    /* display a shape */
};
```

Virtual functions are functions that could not be implemented without knowing the specific shape, and that must therefore be overridden in each subclass, like this:

```
class circle : public shape {
    float radius;
public:
    void rotate(int) { ; } /* how to rotate a circle */
    void draw();          /* how to draw a circle */
    ...
};
```

The virtual keyword signals that these functions must be dynamically bound, and triggers the compiler to add an invisible member to each instance that explicitly indicates its class at run-time. It is now possible to define subclasses that obey a common protocol, so that any instance can be drawn by:

```
anyInstance.draw();
```

C++ allows you to derive a new class from multiple superclasses (multiple inheritance). Conflicts that arise due to the new class inheriting members with the same name from more than one base class are handled according to a set of language rules. For example, to derive a dish class from pre-existing circle and container classes, you would create the following declaration:

```
class dish : public circle, container {/* ... */};
```

In addition to showing that dish is to be implemented by copying the variables and methods of circle and container, this statement also indicates the kinds of access a user of dish will have to the members of the circle and container base classes. The public keyword in front of circle indicates that users of dish share the same access privileges to the protected and public members of circle as dish does itself. On the other hand, the absence of a keyword in front of container marks it as private. Access to the public and protected members of circle is restricted to dish only; users of dish can not access members of container at all. This mechanism allows the class designer to selectively restrict access among its superclasses.

The issue of multiple inheritance and how it affects software development is discussed in Chapter five.

Protected Data

When a new class is derived from an old class, the question arises as to what the derived class should have access to. In C++, the derived class's access to the members of the base class is handled by the implementer of the base class. The implementer can specify members of a class as public, private, or protected access. Suppose we change the definition of the shape class to read:

```
class shape {
private:
    shape *next;
protected:
    vector center;
    int color;
public:
    .....
};
```

Member and friend functions from classes derived from the shape class would be able to access the "center" and "color" data members from the shape class, since they were designated as protected. However, they could not access the "next" data member, since it was marked as private.

Operator Overloading

The facilities described for functions apply to other operators as well. By prefixing an operator token with the keyword *operator*, a new implementation for that operator can be provided. For example, the last pair of declarations below define how '+' should work for the class of vectors:

```
class vector {
    int x, y;
public:
    vector(int xc, int yc) { x = xc; y = yc; }     /* constructor */
    vector(int xc) { x = xc; y = 0; }              /* constructor */
    vector(vector p) { x = p.x; y = p.y; }         /* constructor */
    friend vector operator+(vector, vector);  /* add two vectors */
    friend vector operator+(vector, int);     /* add vector and integer */
    ...
};
```

This defines vectors on a two-dimensional integer coordinate plane. The three functions named vector are called constructors. Constructors define how new vectors are constructed when they appear in initialization statements and also when new vectors are constructed on the stack in calling a function. Since the declaration also includes the implementation for these operators, the implementation will be expanded inline, and no function call overhead will be incurred to initialize vectors. The inline expansion feature applies to any kind of operator that may be declared in a class, not just constructors.

The remaining three operators define how the + operator works when both sides are vectors, or when the right side is an integer. The declaration could be extended to build a complete vector class, with scalar products, dot products, cross products, tensor products, etc.

```
vector east = (1), north = (0, 1);
vector northEast = north + east;
```

Memory Management

In C++ new objects can be allocated dynamically on the heap and then referred to by address. Objects can also be allocated statically and referred to by name, as for the three vectors shown in the previous example. At run-time, space for objects known by name must be initialized whenever their name enters scope. For example:

1. Objects passed as arguments to functions, and objects declared as local (auto) variables, must be initialized when that function is called.

2. Objects returned from functions must be initialized as that function returns.

3. Objects in the function's call stack (arguments and local variables) must be destroyed when the function returns and the stack collapses.

C++ provides a way for the class developer to specify what should happen in these cases. The vector example shows how constructor operators are specified. The inverse is a destructor operation, whose name is the name of the class prefixed with a ~ token. For example, a string class might be

```
class string {
    int length;
    char *bytes;
    string(char*);              /* string constructor */
    ~string() { delete bytes }  /* string destructor */
public:
    int length() { return length }
    char *text() { return bytes }
};
string.string(char *s) {
    length = strlen(s);
    bytes = new char[length+1];
    strcpy(bytes, s);
}
```

This guarantees that each string instance created when strings are passed to and returned from functions is a unique copy. But it does not handle multiple references created when one string is explicitly assigned to another in an assignment statement. This can be arranged by overriding the assignment operator.

Notice that although this does not replace automatic garbage collection, it can sometimes reduce the need for it. Automatic garbage collection is still desirable when objects are multiply referenced via pointers. By copying objects each time they're needed, multiple references do not occur, so objects can be disposed of whenever they go out of scope. Of course, this is feasible only for very small objects. For example, the string implementation shown here involves allocating and initializing a new copy every time the string is passed to a function, and the overhead could easily become intolerable. C++ does not provide automatic garbage collection.

Separate Compilation

Each compilation is performed in isolation. C++ retains no memory of past compilations, so all declarations about external classes must be manually incorporated into each source file. C++ provides no assistance for doing this other than the usual #include statement. It imposes no restriction on how this is accomplished nor any checks to ensure that information is consistent across compilations.

In practice two files are prepared for each class. The first is a file of declarations that must be included in every file that uses the class. The second is a file of definitions, which is compiled, archived, and combined into the executable image by the linker. The entire contents of the first file is therefore public information, while only the second is truly private when compiled into binary. This makes the private/public distinctions provided by a class declaration something of a misnomer. The file can be read from outside the language; even copied and modified to make private information accessible to a consumer's code.

What Does "Object-Oriented" Mean?[5]

We started this chapter by asking the question "What does object-oriented mean?" But even after studying several different languages that are object-oriented, there is still considerable uncertainty over what this adjective means. No one is confused when adjectives like "small" or "fast" mean entirely different things in nuclear physics, gardening, and geology. But in the abstract murk of the software domain it is all too easy to lose one's bearing, to misunderstand the context, to confuse the very small with

[5]Brad Cox, "Planning the Software Industrial Revolution," *IEEE Software*, November 1990. Copyright © IEEE 1990, used by permission.

the extremely large. So, to understand the meaning of any adjective, especially "object-oriented" we must take special care to specify the context in which it is applied.

Let's return to the question "What is object-oriented?" by introducing a vocabulary for specifying software "context" as it relates to level in a software producer-consumer hierarchy. We can then use this vocabulary to summarize the attributes of the languages we have just explored.

The new vocabulary is simply the level names of hardware engineering: gate-level, block-level, chip-level, card-level, rack-level, and so on, to higher and lower levels, applied to an analogous multilevel software architecture. Figure 3.3 defines a software meaning for each of these names by demonstrating the extent to which various programming languages provide modularity/binding technologies at each level.

The lowest level of integration provides gate-level objects—components at the expression and statement level of a programming language. The next highest level provides block-level objects—components at the subroutine and function level of a programming language. Some of the languages discussed in this chapter, such as Ada, support these levels with compile-intensive technologies with strong type checking. Others, such as C++, even provide inheritance. These gate- and block-level languages, especially Ada and to a

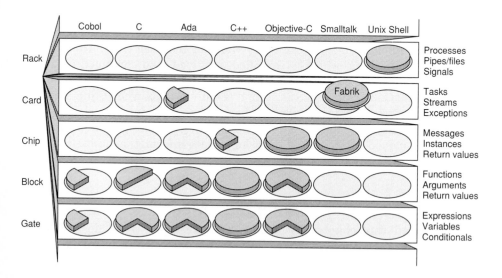

Figure 3.3. Object-oriented means different things at different levels of integration; that is, in different contexts or levels of the producer-consumer hierarchy. Pie slices represent the extent to which several popular languages support work at each level. (Brad Cox, "Planning the Software Industrial Revolution," *IEEE Software,* November 1990. Copyright © IEEE 1990, used by permission.)

great extent C+ +, are for dealing with closed universe computing problems. But when an open universe problem arises, you are no better off with Ada than any conventional language. At least C+ + does provide an approximation of what is needed in its virtual function mechanism.

Time will show that the objects of all the languages in this book are only a beginning, not an end. The transition from how the machine forces programmers to think to how everyone expects tangible objects to behave is not a single step but many.

At the gate and block levels of Figure 3.3, object-oriented means encapsulation (Ada) and in some languages (C+ +), inheritance, but the dynamism of everyday objects has been intentionally relinquished in favor of machine-oriented virtues like computational efficiency and static binding.

The intermediate (chip) level introduces the open-universe model of everyday experience. For the chip-level objects of Objective-C and Smalltalk, all possible interactions between parts and the whole do not have to be known and declared in advance, when the universe is created by the compiler.

But on the scale of any significant system, gate-, block-, and even chip-level objects are extremely small units of granularity—grains of sand where bricks are needed. Furthermore, since chip-level objects are no less procedural than conventional expressions and subroutines, they are just as alien to non-programmers. Until invoked by passing them a thread of control from outside, they are as inert as conventional data, quite unlike the objects of everyday experience.

Fabrik[6] pioneered a path that I expect the object-oriented world to soon notice and follow. Since Fabrik was written in Smalltalk, it consists internally of chip-level objects. But externally, it projects a higher-level kind of object, a "card-level object," to the user. These higher-level objects communicate, not synchronously through procedural invocation, but asynchronously by sending chip-level objects through communication channel objects such as Streams. They amount to a new kind of "object" that encapsulates a copy of the machine's thread of control on a software "card," along with the chip-level objects used to build that card. Software cards are objects of the sort that programmers call lightweight processes; objects that operate as coroutines of one another, not subroutines.

Since software cards can operate concurrently, they admit a tangible user interface (as Figure 3.3 shows) that is uniquely intuitive for non-programmers and for this reason alone, more fundamentally object-oriented than the procedural, single-threaded languages of today. Like the tangible objects of everyday experience, card-level objects provide their own thread of control internally, they don't communicate by procedural invocation, they don't support inheritance, and their user interface is iconic, not textual.

<hr>

[6]Dan Ingalls, et al.: "Fabrik; A Visual Programming Environment," OOPSLA 1988 Proceedings.

By adding these, and probably more, architectural levels, each level can cater to the needs, skills, and interests of a particular constituency of the software components market. The programmer shortage can be solved as the telephone-operator shortage was solved, by making every computer user a programmer.

Summary

These languages are not a comprehensive sample of all object-oriented languages. Important object-oriented languages like Flavors and Loops, which emphasize class hierarchies to organize facts about a problem domain are not represented. Although Smalltalk and Ada do emphasize concurrency to varying degrees, some languages, like Carl Hewitts Actor languages and Yanezawa's ABCL, carry this theme much further. And I've excluded other important languages like Object-Pascal, Neon,[7] Modula-2, Mesa, Cedar, and others.

Table 3.1
Characteristics of Programming Languages

	Smalltalk-80	Ada	C++	Objective-C
Binding time	late	early	either	either
Operator overloading	yes	yes	yes	no
Garbage collection	yes	no	no	possible
Inheritance	yes	no	yes	yes
Activation/passivation	yes	no	no	yes
Multiple inheritance	yes	no	yes	possible
Commerical availability	yes	yes	yes	yes
Software-IC libraries	yes	no	no	yes

The languages that were discussed do have points in common, but their differences are dramatic (Table 3.1). Binding is done entirely at run-time in Smalltalk, entirely at compile-time in Ada, and can be done either way in Objective-C and C++. Inheritance is central to many of these languages, but is missing altogether in Ada. Although derived types, subtypes and generic packages are certainly useful features of the language, they are no substitute for inheritance.

---

[7]For an excellent survey of these languages and their uses, see Kurt Schmucker's book, *Object-oriented Languages on the Macintosh*, Apple Press, 1986.

| Four

Objects, Messages, and Encapsulation

This chapter marks the beginning of a shift in emphasis away from concepts of object-oriented programming to how these concepts are implemented in a hybrid programming language, Objective-C. Objective-C implements the dynamically bound style of object-oriented programming used in Smalltalk-80 as a set of extensions to a conventional base language, C. Few of the techniques used in doing this are specific to C, so Objective-C serves to demonstrate how this style of programming can be grafted onto other conventional languages as well.

This chapter and the next will define the basic concepts implemented by this language and enough of its syntax to work examples and to get a feel for how they are applied in practice. The subject matter divides naturally into two parts: the programming concepts used by a consumer of object-oriented functionality and those used by the supplier of that functionality. This chapter introduces the concepts used by a consumer. Those used by a supplier will be described in the next chapter.

| Objects, Messages, and Encapsulation

Objective-C is a hybrid programming language sold by The Stepstone Corporation (formerly Productivity Products International). It was formed by grafting the Smalltalk-80 style of object-oriented programming onto a C language rootstock. Objective-C adds precisely one new data type, the object, to those C provides already, and precisely one new operation, the message expression. This small piece of language-level surgery, coupled with a run-time (dynamic) binding mechanism, supports an open universe computing model in which the relationship between the individual parts and the whole need not be known and declared at compile time. This open universe computing model, like the one found in Smalltalk-80, places the emphasis on human efficiency (the next chapter describes several additional features that are specific to Objective-C) by enabling software component reuse. The approach shown here for Objective-C can, and should, be supported for nearly any other language apart from C.

An object is some private data and a set of operations that can access that data. An object is requested to perform one of its operations by sending it a message telling the object what to do. The receiver responds to the message by first choosing the operation that implements the message name, executing this operation, and then returning control to the caller.

Newcomers accustomed to applying functions to data find this terminology unsettling. How can ordinary bits and bytes be requested to do something? Are Objective-C programmers just being cute with all this talk about intelligent actors that know how to do things?

This manner of speaking reflects the fact that objects really are different from conventional operators and operands. A conventional operand just lies around passively waiting to be stepped on by some operation. But an object is active data because each one has a set of operations inextricably bound within it. It is not proper or even possible to treat an object the way programmers treat data by doing something to it directly. We can "apply a function to some data" but not to an object. An object's data is private to it, and the only way to access that data is to request the object to do it by running one of its procedures at our request.

To request means to execute a programming language statement called a message expression. A message expression is analogous to an ordinary function call with one extra step; a selection mechanism that provides dynamic binding. Both functions and messages carry arguments, and either can return values. In both, the context of the calling function is saved on a stack and restored when the computation finishes. In both, the caller is blocked until the callee finishes.

However, using the word message for anything as simple as this does complicate matters, because the word bears such strong connotations of concurrency. Every programmer knows that calling a function blocks the caller until the called function finishes. But message sounds like something more is going on. Newcomers struggle, searching for the implied promise of a concurrency mechanism and miss the real contribution. Messages are not a concurrency mechanism, but a modularity mechanism. Messaging creates the encapsulation of data and procedure that is called an object.

Objective-C messages have nothing to do with concurrency, either pro or con. They neither encourage nor discourage building and using concurrency mechanisms on your own. You can even package these mechanisms inside objects and trigger these objects with messages. But these messages are precisely as good as, no better and certainly no worse than, function calls in this respect.

Functions and messages differ in several ways. For one thing, functions can have zero or more arguments, while messages always have at least one that identifies the object that is to receive the message. The part of a message that tells the object what to do is called the message selector. It corresponds to the function name determining what will happen, but with one crucial difference. A function name always identifies a single piece of executable code, but a message selector does not, because the code that will be selected also depends on which object was sent the message.

For example, consider the square root function, sqrt. This name uniquely identifies the piece of code that computes square roots of floating point numbers. If the result bears any similarity to the mathematical concept of a square root, we conclude two things (1) sqrt worked correctly and (2) its user supplied the correct kind of argument, a floating point number. By contrast, message selectors identify the logical operation directly, and the precise piece of code is chosen by the receiver of the message. If a sqrt message is sent to some arbitrary kind of number, the result depends entirely on whether the code works correctly. One of the user's responsibilities has been given to the machine. While function names specify how to do it, message selectors specify only what should be done, leaving how to be determined automatically while the message expression is being executed.

The anthropomorphic way of speaking is solely because of this selection mechanism; a dimwit intelligence to be sure, remarkable only because of its absence in conventional programming. Telling an object, deskTop, for example, to do something like print means only that the machine shall execute a message expression whose receiver is deskTop and whose selector is print. This triggers the selection mechanism to decide how print should be implemented for the deskTop object. It looks up print in a table of things that deskTop knows how to do and branches to the piece of code stored there. Saying "deskTop objects know how to print" is no more mysterious than the search that a menu system performs to find a piece of code for a function key. Saying that an object knows how to do something means only that when a message is executed with that object as receiver, the selection mechanism's search succeeds and triggers one of the object's operations.

Except for the selection mechanism, each aspect of this terminology has its exact counterpart in conventional operator/operand programming:

object	a block of data
object id	pointer to block of data
send message to object	apply function to data

One last time: the only substantive difference between conventional programming and object-oriented programming is the selection mechanism.

This is not to minimize its importance, but to demystify what is basically a very simple notion. Its significance is that it moves a single responsibility across the boundary between the consumer of a service and the supplier of that service. In conventional programming, the consumer is responsible for choosing functions that operate properly on the data managed by that service. The selection mechanism moves that single responsibility off the consumer and onto the supplier. In this small change lies all the power of the technique.

This is in no sense a panacea. It is a simple, yet reasonably effective, system-building tool. It allows suppliers to present cleanly specified interfaces around the services they provide. A consumer has full visibility to the procedures offered by an object, and no visibility to its data. From a consumer's point of view, an object is a seamless capsule that offers a number of services, with no visibility as to how these services are implemented (see Figure 4.1).

The technical term for this is encapsulation. How an object implements its actions, and how its internal data is arranged, is encapsulated inside a procedural shell that mediates all access to the object. This chapter will focus

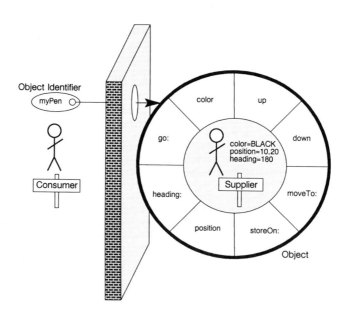

Figure 4.1. Consumer/supplier viewpoints. Encapsulation means that a consumer sees only the services that are available from an object, but not how those services are implemented. Only the supplier has visibility into the object's procedures and its data.

on techniques for using these encapsulated units of functionality. The next chapter will show how objects are built, introducing classes and inheritance.

Objective-C

Objective-C is a tool for writing programs that involve objects and messages. Equally, it is a tool for expressing the kind of programs that C programmers have been writing for years. It is a hybrid language that contains all of C language plus major parts of Smalltalk-80.

Objective-C works just like a C compiler (Figure 4.2). The programmer develops source files with a text editor, compiles them to binary with the Objective-C compiler, stores them in libraries with a standard librarian, links

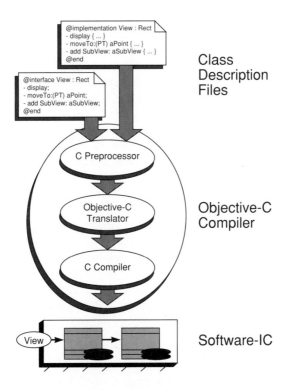

Figure 4.2. The Objective-C compiler. UNIX-based C compilers are implemented as multiple passes. The C preprocessor, cpp, transforms statements like #import and #define into C source, which is compiled into assembler source by the C compiler. The C compiler (often implemented as several passes) produces assembly language code which is compiled to binary by an assembler. For such implementations, the Objective-C front end runs after the C preprocessor.

them with a standard linker, and debugs and tests them just as any C programmer would. Objective-C is a superset of C. It is permissible, even typical, for files to contain only ordinary C statements. C statements pass through Objective-C unchanged to be compiled into binary exactly as if Objective-C were not present. Other files make heavy use of object-oriented constructs; sometimes to the point that they look more like Smalltalk-80 than C language. These statements are transformed to produce source acceptable to the C compiler. For brevity, the entire ensemble is called the Objective-C compiler, even though Objective-C seems to simply pass C constructs through to the C compiler unchanged. C is a low-level language that is best thought of as a portable, structured assembly language. This makes it an ideal base language for the purposes of this book, because it imposes few strong-minded notions that would have to be overcome by the front end and distract from the main objective.

One of Objective-C's key features is that it is always possible to bypass the object-oriented machinery to access an object's private information directly. This is one of a hybrid language's greatest theoretical weaknesses and one of its greatest pragmatic strengths. Low-level code is often best developed in a conventional manner, exploiting static binding to obtain high machine efficiency and strong type checking. Conversely, user-level code is often best written as objects. It is important that these levels interface smoothly and efficiently. In a hybrid language, this is done by adopting the appropriate programming convention at the various levels. It is relatively common in these areas of transition to use C constructs to access object memory directly.

This chapter describes the object-oriented capabilities of Objective-C to the point that it can be used to work exercises. A secondary goal is to define a particular implementation of object-oriented programming constructed around a particular point in design space. This will help the exploration in Chapter 10 of how these design decisions might be modified to accomplish different design goals such as automatic garbage collection, concurrency, virtual object memories where objects live primarily on disk, or distributed object systems where objects live on more than one machine.

Object Identifiers

Objects are identified by a new Objective-C data type called an id, or object identifier. An object identifier provides a handle by which that object can be manipulated in a message expression, the sole legal operation on an object's id. An object identifier provides an unconditional capability to access an object, without any form of access right restrictions.

Object identifiers must uniquely identify as many objects as may ever coexist in the system at any one time. They are stored in local variables, passed as arguments in message expressions and in function calls, held in instance variables (fields inside objects), and in other kinds of memory structures. In other words, they can be used as fluidly as the built-in types of the base language.

How an object identifier actually identifies the object is an implementation detail for which many choices are plausible. A reasonable choice, certainly one of the simplest, and the one that is used in Objective-C, is to use the physical address of the object in memory as its identifier. Objective-C makes this decision known to C by generating a typedef statement into each file. This defines a new type, id, in terms of another type that C understands already, namely pointers to structures.[1] Thereafter ids are treated as legitimate new types that can be used as freely as the standard C built-in data types (char, int, float, etc.).

```
int maximumCapacity;  // declare an integer
id thisObject;        // declare an object identifier
```

This declares two C variables of type int and id, respectively. The variable named maximumCapacity can be used to hold any integer value, and the one named thisObject can be used to hold an identifier for any kind of object.

An id consumes a fixed amount of space, wide enough to identify as many objects as may exist at any one time. This space is not the same as the space occupied by the private data in the object itself. Object identifiers are fixed-size numbers, whereas the space occupied by an object differs for each kind of object. The consumer of an object sees only object identifiers, not the objects themselves. The objects are allocated by suppliers, not by consumers. The consumer controls only the identifier, and may assign values to it, copy it, and hold it in permanent data structures, exactly as might be done for any C data type like char, int or float.

Message Expressions

Once a user has an object's identifier he may access its services by writing a message expression. A message expression is a command for an object to do something, during which the sender waits until the receiver has done it and returned a reply. Sending a message is exactly the same as calling a procedure, the only difference being that messages involve dynamic binding.

In an object-oriented system, operations are done by objects, not to them. Operations are requested by writing a message expression that specifies some object and tells it what to do by specifying the name of an action to be performed. This name is called the message selector. The object receiving the message looks up the selector in a table of things it knows how to do to decide how to implement this command.

---

[1]The specific declaration that is generated is typedef struct_PRIVATE *id. This defines the new type id as pointer to a struct_PRIVATE. The fields inside struct_PRIVATE vary with the kind of object and are described in the next chapter.

As a matter of implementation convenience, all objects translate selectors to implementations in a uniform manner, and the selection mechanism is centralized in a single function called the messager.[2] All message expressions compile into calls on the messager function; their arguments specify the id of the receiver and the message selector. The object contributes a dispatch table that the messaging routine searches to determine how this kind of object implements this selector. This table is built when the object is defined, and is not usually changed dynamically. It identifies the selector of every message that this object knows how to perform, and a pointer to a procedure whereby this object implements that message. This procedure, called the implementation or the method, is a compiled C function body.

Messages are sent by writing message expressions, which are translated directly into calls on the messager. In fact, were it not for needing a bit of compile-time assistance in defining new classes, the special syntax might well be dispensed with altogether and calls written directly on the messaging routine, like this:

```
reply = _msg(aReceiver, "aMessage", argument1, ...);
```

This would not require any special syntax and no new tools to handle the modified syntax. And it models the intended semantics perfectly. In fact, the only reason for not adopting this path here is efficiency. A compile-time tool is needed to convert message selectors into some representation that can be compared efficiently to avoid string comparison overhead in the messager.

Unary Message Expressions

Objective-C's messaging syntax is an adaptation of Smalltalk-80 syntax modified for compatibility with C language. Message expressions are written as a pair of balanced square braces surrounding the receiver, selector, and arguments. The simplest kind of message expression is like the Smalltalk-80 unary expression which takes no arguments.

```
aSet = [Set new];
```

This message expression sends the unary message new to the object identified by the C variable Set. The reply from this message is stored in another variable, aSet.

Message expressions are allowed anywhere function calls are allowed in C. C is relatively generous in this regard, being an expression-oriented language that allows function calls, and therefore message expressions, wherever a computational expression is allowed. For example, message expressions can appear as arguments to function calls

```
printf("The size of this set is %d\n", [aSet size]);
```

[2]The C name of this function is __msg().

They can appear inside conditional expressions and looping constructs

```
if ([container isEmpty]) ...
```

or

```
while (member = [sequence next]) ...
```

They can even appear inside other message expressions:

```
[aSet size];                        // receiver = a variable
[someFunction(someArgument) size]   // receiver = a function call
[[Set new] size];                   // receiver = a message expression
```

Most C programmers would never dream of writing deeply nested function calls like this:

```
printf("(%d,%d)\n", xCoord(originOf(aRectangle)), yCoord(cornerOf(aRectangle)));
```

But oddly, they quickly become accustomed to doing the same thing with message expressions

```
printf("(%d,%d)\n", [[aRectangle origin] x], [[aRectangle corner] y]);
```

Keyword Message Expressions

Messages that take arguments are called keyword expressions. These are written in the rather unique fashion described earlier for Smalltalk-80.

message	selector	arguments
[anObject doThis]	doThis	none
[anObject doThis:arg1]	doThis:	arg1
[anObject do:arg1 with:arg2]	do:with:	arg1, arg2

The first message has the unary selector doThis. Unary selectors are just selectors that have no arguments. The second and third messages have keyword selectors doThis: and do:with:. Keyword selectors take arguments, as many as there are colons in the selector, and the arguments are written inside the keyword, immediately after each of the colons. There is no deep significance to this rather odd convention. The only difference between a unary and keyword selector is in number of arguments. Every character of both kinds of selector is significant, including the colons and the various keyword fragments strung out among the arguments. In spoken conversation the third message expression is pronounced "send anObject the message do-colon-with-colon with arguments arg1 and arg2."

This convention seems strange to those accustomed to conventional function call syntax, and frankly, I find it a mixed blessing. It does provide tight syntactic control over the number and meaning of method arguments, and it does lead to surprisingly readable code, once you've become accustomed to the new conventions. But it is hard to explain, and the keyword notion is superficial in that the keyword fragments are immediately joined in the compiler and dealt with thereafter as a single concatenated string. It has the definite disadvantage of making it more difficult to locate messages in source code by searching for a simple string, because arguments inside the keyword get in the way of string search tools.

Message Expression Types

Message expressions can return values, so they have types in exactly the same way that functions do. For example, the new message always returns a value of type id, while the size message always returns a value of type int.

```
id aSet = [Set new];
int n = [aSet size];
```

The type of any given message is determined when the first method with that name is defined and is automatically made known to all sending sites.

Factory Objects

To back away from the trees and look at the forest, imagine a large object-oriented application just after it has been loaded into memory but before it has begun to execute. Eventually, it will contain many objects of many types (instances of many classes) but initially, none have been created yet. But objects are created by sending the message, new, to other objects. How can this be before any objects have yet been created?

Put simply, the programmer conceives the initial object, the compiler builds it, the linker delivers it, and the loader gives it life by installing it in memory, along with all the other paraphernalia that constitutes the application as a whole. This is true for each class in the system. These primal objects are called factory objects. The compiler guarantees that the binary file produced by compiling each class contributes one factory object to each application that uses that class. The factory objects are unique only in that they are built at compile-time and are assembled into memory by the loader. In all other respects, they are objects like any other, and like other objects, their behavior is controlled by the programmer who defined them. Their purpose is in providing a way to create initialized instances of their class, in ways that are special to each class. This is why they are called factory objects.

Producing instances is only one of the functions of factory objects, just as manufacturing new products is only one of many functions of real-life factories. They also consume resources, produce payrolls, pay taxes, and produce garbage. Factory objects are objects like all others in that what they actually do is determined by the programmer that defined them. Producing new instances of their class is only typical of what factory objects can do. It is by no means exclusive.

A complete system will contain many kinds of factory objects and many objects produced by these factories. The following conventions are used to keep them straight.

1. Factory object names always begin with an upper-case character.
2. Factory object names describe the class of the objects they produce.
3. Instance names always begin with a lower case letter.

For example, the name of a factory object that produces Strings would not be factoryThatProducesStrings, but String. This is shorter and there is little chance of misunderstanding String to mean any specific array, because String instances will be named with a lower case letter; e.g., currentWord, capitalOfTexas, firstArgument, or even aString.

Factory objects are built by the compiler and the linker, so they are automatically available for messaging at run-time. Every factory's name is published in a global variable, which can be accessed by making that name visible to C's scoping machinery through an extern statement, like this:

```
extern id ByteArray;
```

Examples

I've described enough syntax to begin working with some sample classes.

In what follows, the focus will be exclusively on the consumer's code, because I have not yet introduced syntax that a supplier uses to define new classes and methods. The text will make clear the behavior to be expected of the various messages.

Pen Example

Consider an object named Pen. From the naming convention you can conclude that (1) Pen names a factory object that (2) produces new writing instruments, each of class Pen. As subsequent material is presented, it will turn out that we also know, or can easily determine, even more about what pens can accomplish. Until then, I'll introduce each new fact piecemeal, and concentrate on the big picture.

All factory objects understand the message new to mean "Create a new instance of your class and reply its id." The semantics of this message is always the same, system-wide. All factory objects know new to mean only one thing: the consumer wants a new instance. They may (and often do) execute different code to implement this request, but each factory duly allocates a new instance, initializes its variables to some known state, and returns the resulting id to the caller.

So much for what the supplier does. Let's focus now on how the consumer sets this up and uses the results:

```
#import "Pen.h"³
id myPen;
myPen = [Pen new];
```

³The "#import" statement works just like the "#include" C Preprocessor except that it will only include the contents of a named file once per compile.

The first line of this fragment is a C preprocessor command that includes the interface file for the Pen class. This provides the compiler with explicit information about the methods used to create and access instances of the Pen class. The second statement defines a symbol, myPen of type id that will be created in the caller's local namespace. The last statement initializes my Pen with the value returned by the Pen factory in response to the message expression [Pen new].

This new entity is a fully functional object in its own right, but it is different from the object that produced it. It contains different information, and it responds to different messages. The objects Pen and myPen are as different as a ballpoint pen is from the plastic factory that manufactured it. For example, if you sent the message new to myPen, you'd get an error diagnostic: "Pens do not know how to new."

Sending new to a factory object is just like telling an automobile factory that you want a new car. Unless you're more explicit, you can only expect to receive a car of some kind, because you've left it to the factory to choose all the details. If you need a red pen, you must tell the factory which color you need explicitly:

```
id redPen, bluePen, blackPen;
redPen = [Pen red];
bluePen = [Pen blue];
blackPen = [Pen black];
```

The messages red, blue, and black are just like the message new in that they create a new pen and reply its id. The only difference is that the factory initializes the pen differently, perhaps setting a variable in the new pen to describe its color.

The new pens are objects too, so they can respond to messages. For example, a pen's color can be determined by requesting the pen to report its color, like this:

```
penColor = [myPen color];
```

PencilCup Example

Pens are capable objects that could be explored in arbitrary detail. For example, they implement the store of abilities that Seymour Papert described in his book, *Mindstorms*.[4] Instead of pursuing pens further at this point, consider how pens might be integrated into a larger system.

Say you have before you a pencil cup that contains pens of various colors, several pencils, a letter opener, and a pair of scissors. A computer-domain model of this situation could be constructed by using the same techniques used above:

[4]Papert, Seymour: *Mindstorms: Children, Computers, and Powerful Ideas,* Basic Books, 1982.

```
#import "Container.h"
#import "Pen.h"
#import "Pencil.h"
#import "LetterOpener.h"
#import "Scissors.h"

id pencilCup = [Container new];
[pencilCup add:[Pen blue]];
[pencilCup add:[Pen red]];
[pencilCup add:[Pen green]];
[pencilCup add:[Pencil new]];
[pencilCup add:[LetterOpener new]];
[pencilCup add:[Scissors new]];
```

The first message expression commands the factory object for the Container class to produce an empty container named pencilCup, and pencilCup is told to add: some objects. Each of the objects is produced on the fly by sending additional messages to various other factories.

One of the things containers can do is compute their weight by adding their own weight to that of their contents. The weight could be printed by putting the message expression directly into the function call that prints the result like this:

```
printf("The weight of my pencil cup is %f\n", [pencilCup weight]);
```

The supplier of class Container is responsible for making containers compute weights correctly, but examining how he does this will help to establish one of the things that is so different about object-oriented programming; shifting responsibility for managing operator-operand type interdependencies from the consumer of a data type to the supplier.

```
float total = tareWeight;        // start with weight of empty container
int i, n = [self size];          // n = number of members
for (i = 0; i < n; i++) {        // loop over each member
    id member = [self at:i];     // get next member
    total = total+[member weight]; // accumulate weight of contents
}
return total;                    // return total weight to caller
```

Notice the looseness of the collaboration between the supplier of this container and the suppliers of any object that might ever be added to the container. The items in the container were chosen dynamically. No one warned the container supplier that the container would someday need to compute weights of pens, scissors, and letter openers. The container code was not changed, and nothing was recompiled. This would be impossible in any event because the decision of what to add was made at run-time. But a number of different kinds of object were placed into that container without concern as to how the container should go about determining the weight of each one. No agreements were made that might allow the container to determine weights from some convention like "the third field in every element contains its weight."

Instead, a much weaker and easier standard was applied, one that was established and documented by the container supplier. "I warrant that my container will hold any kind of object, so long as it knows how to report its own weight." The container supplier, acting as consumer of the data types provided to it as arguments, freed his code of assumptions like how to compute weights by pushing this responsibility off on his suppliers. His container can work for any kind of contents, so long as the contents provide a method for computing weights.

The container code becomes reusable and independent of the kind of contents its developer had in mind when he developed it. This container works for any kind of object, whether now or in the future. It even works if an item in this container is another container![5]

The distinction is subtle and easy to miss, yet absolutely crucial. The point is not that objects and messages make it possible for electronic containers to magically compute the weight of whatever is tossed into them. If weights are to be computed, somebody still has to write code that computes weights. The difference is in where the decision is made about how to compute the weight of some arbitrary kind of object. With object-oriented programming, the objects make this decision. With conventional programming, the consumer does, and must therefore write code like:

```
float total = tareWeight;          // start with weight of empty container
for (i = 0; i < numberOfItems;  i++)  {// loop over each item
    item = contents[i];            // the current item
    switch (item->type) {          // determine its type
    case PEN:
    case PENCIL:
    case LETTEROPENER:
        total += item->weight;     // grope his private data
        break;
    case CONTAINER:
        total += weightOfContainer(item);
        break;
    ...
    default: fatalError("bad contents");
    }
    ...                            // use the total weight
}
```

While the earlier implementation works for any data type that understands a weigh message, this one is useless for anything but those types listed in the case labels.

Admittedly, computing weights of electronic objects is a contrived and rather trivial example. But it is tiny by design, to illustrate one of the things

---

[5]However, consider the consequences of [pencilCup add:pencilCup]. This leads to a situation like that of the dragon who ate his own tail and turned himself inside out.

that makes system building hard. The pencilCup is a system-building project in microcosm. It involves multiple different programmers, one for each of the different data types. Three of these will probably leave the project within six months, two of them are changing things for one reason or another, and one of them has lost the requirements page that mentioned the need to keep track of weight. Several more are hard at work building additional data types, in anticipation of the long-awaited release of the Phase 2 Enhanced Automated DeskTop that also supports calligraphy pens, cuneiform writing implements, and lost car keys.

The two implementations differ in that the object-oriented version makes the supplier of each data type responsible for implementing all operations that are required on that data type. The conventional version makes the supplier responsible for supplying the necessary operators, and the consumer responsible for choosing the correct ones. This amounts to a leakage of information into the consumer's domain, with the consequences seen in the second container implementation. Every time a new data type is added to the system, the container code must be changed.

Furthermore, notice that this example is not improved in any fundamental way by any statically bound language. The pencilCup example is by its very nature dynamic, and in at least two ways resulting from at least three agents of change operating over different time spans.

1. The container user, not its developer, controls what goes into it. The container code has to adapt dynamically to whatever data type the user might decide to drop in next, out of all the data types implemented within the present system.
2. The system as a whole is changing as new data types get implemented and put at the user's disposal.
3. Reusing the container code introduces that code into a new environment, full of new potential contents.

The problem is a dynamic problem, and therefore not solvable with any static tool.

Summary

This chapter has described the outer shell of concepts to be used in this book. An object is a pool of private data and the procedures that can access this data. A message requests an object to perform one of its procedures. These concepts provide encapsulation, which means that an object's data is hidden within, and protected by, a shell of procedures. I have shown how this pair of concepts can be added to a conventional programming language, using Objective-C as an example. Objects are identified with the new data type, id, and requests to objects are written as message expressions.

Finally, I have shown how the concepts are used and have contrasted the new programming style with the conventional style. The primary difference is that a single responsibility has been moved from the consumer of a service to the supplier of that service: the responsibility for choosing the operator (procedure) that is type compatible with the kind of operand (data) to be operated upon.

| Five

Classes and Inheritance

The previous chapter defined the terms object, object identifier, and message and described how they are expressed in Objective-C. Together these constructs provide encapsulation, by defining what objects are and how they can be accessed. But they do not define how specific kinds of objects are defined. Encapsulation is for the consumer of object-oriented functionality. This chapter defines the constructs used by a supplier.

It introduces the distinction between instances and classes, and exposes how objects are implemented on conventional hardware. The supplier uses Objective-C syntax to describe classes and methods, using both encapsulation and inheritance to reduce programming effort by reusing existing work to an unusual degree. The programming process involves turning class description files into a binary representation, the Software-IC, which is ultimately linked into an application by the linker.

Finally this chapter will present some compiler-related matters that have relatively little to do with object-oriented programming, but are essential when building or using compilers that provide inheritance and other features that make each compilation depend on prior compilations.

Classes

The concepts of class and instance will already be familiar. "Betsy is a cow" is just a short way of saying "Betsy is an instance of class cow." In programming the same concept is often called type. For example

```
int leftEdge, rightEdge;
```

just says "allocate two instances of class int named leftEdge and right-Edge". The languages that support a fixed list of built-in classes tend to use the word type, while those that allow the programmer to define his own types favor the word class.

Instances

Betsy is a cow, but Betsy is also Betsy, the individual. She is like other cows in most ways; yet different in the ways that set her apart from the herd. The instance, Betsy, is a tangible, flesh and blood creature, but a class is an abstraction. Betsy, the instance, can moo, but cow, the class, cannot.

Classes are arranged in hierarchies with specific classes like holstein at the leaves, intermediate classes like cow or mammal at the trunk, and generic classes like vertebrate or animal near the root. Betsy is a holstein, so she is equally a cow, a ruminant, a mammal, a vertebrate, and an animal. Such hierarchies allow a wealth of information to be derived about any given instance. By knowing that Lassie is a dog, one can immediately conclude that Lassie does not eat grass and chew a cud (dogs are not ruminants) but that she is nonetheless warm-blooded, feeds her young on milk, and shares many other features with Betsy. (Both dogs and ruminants are mammals.)

The class hierarchy is a simple technique for organizing facts about the universe, but it is not the only one. It is not even a sufficient one considering all the interests that an organized collection of facts might serve. For example, the class hierarchy helps to determine which animals might chew cuds, but is of little help in determining which animals might be found in a zoo.

This chapter will describe how class hierarchies can be used to organize and reason about software entities; how programming languages apply instances, classes, and hierarchical inheritance to designing, building, storing, understanding, and using software objects.

Parts of an Object

It usually makes sense to describe, not how individual objects should work, but how classes of objects should work. It would be silly to develop a program that models an individual pen, and have it all to do over again when another pen is needed. It makes more sense to describe how all pens should behave, yet leave some room for pens to be individuals as well. Therefore, at some cost in generality, Smalltalk and Objective-C assume that each instance will have its own private place to store data values, but will share the following things with other instances of its class:

1. Data declarations: All pens will share the same memory layout. Differences between pens will be represented by storing different values into the same field names and types.
2. Method definitions: All pens will use the same methods (code) in responding to messages.

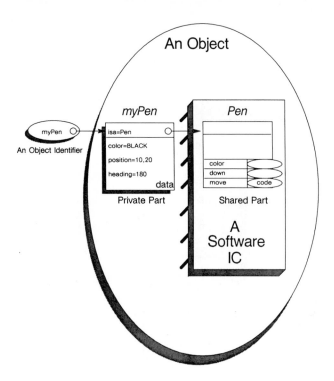

Figure 5.1. Private and shared parts of an object. The shared part describes what is similar about the instances of a class. The private part describes what is different.

In other words, the instances of a class will share the same code and the same field names and field types within their private block of memory. Individual differences between instances are described in the field's values. Figure 5.1 shows how this is accomplished in practice. Each object is made up of two parts: a private part and a shared part. The private part holds the instance's private data fields, and the shared part holds information, such as code, that this instance shares with the other instances of its class. The two parts are linked in a standard way understood by the messager which uses the link to find tables describing the things the receiver (and all other objects of the receiver's class) knows how to do.

Instantiation

Most objects are created at run-time by factory objects in response to statements like:

```
myPen = [Pen new];
```

The result is shown in Figure 5.2. A new instance named myPen has been constructed by the factory object's new method, which has allocated memory

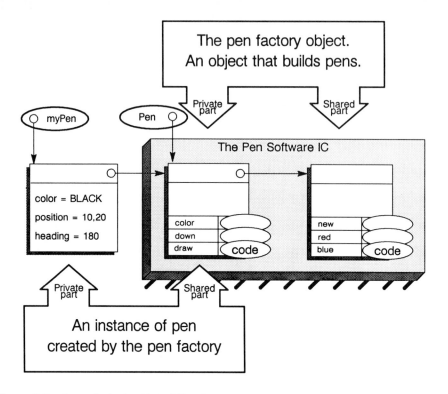

Figure 5.2. A newly instantiated Pen instance.

for the new object's private part, and initialized the link between its private
and shared parts. The rest of the fields in the private part have been initialized to some standard initial state. From here on, the new pen controls its
own destiny, since the encapsulation principle guarantees that its state can
only be modified by one of its own procedures.

Before this object could have been created, two preconditions must have
been met somehow:

1. The factory object identified as Pen must have existed.
2. The shared part of myPen must have existed.

In Objective-C, these preconditions are handled by conventional means.
The compiler builds them into a binary file, and the linker/loader makes them
available in memory. For example, the global variable Pen is initialized to
point to a statically allocated object, both of whose parts[1] were in the binary
file.

---

[1]In the case of factory objects, the name, shared part, can be misleading. Only a single instance of each kind of factory object ever exists, so its shared part is shared by only this
single instance.

Sending this object the message, new, triggers one of its methods to manu-
facture a new instance of class Pen. The method does this by allocating memory, initializing it, and returning the id of the resulting object. The caller
stores this id in the variable myPen. Only at this point does a pen exist.
Before this, only the potential to have pens existed; a potential that is held
entirely within the Pen Software-IC.

Notice that the objects identified by Pen and myPen are both perfectly
ordinary objects. Both have a private part to hold their private data, and a
shared part that holds their code. The only surprise is that the shared part
of the instance and the private part of the factory are the same block of
memory!

Inheritance

It would be possible to stop with the encapsulation concept and build a
language that provides classes and instances, but not inheritance. Some
languages do exactly that (e.g., Ada). Inheritance is not a necessary feature
of an object-oriented language, but it is certainly an extremely desirable one.

Also, the simple linear scheme to be described here is not the only way to
provide inheritance. For example, some languages provide multiple inheritance, which means that classes can have more than one superclass. These
languages provide more generality, solving, for example, problems like expressing what a toy truck is. Is it a kind of toy, or is it a kind of truck? With
multiple inheritance, it can be both.

Inheritance is a tool for organizing, building, and using reusable classes.
Without inheritance, every class would be a free-standing unit, each developed from the ground up. Different classes would bear no relationship with
one another, since the developer of each provides methods in whatever manner he chooses. Any consistency across classes is the result of discipline on
the part of the programmers.

Inheritance makes it possible to define new software in the same way we
introduce any concept to a newcomer, by comparing it with something that
is already familiar; e.g., "A zebra is like a horse, but it has stripes." Inheritance links concepts into a related whole, so that as a higher level concept
changes, the change is automatically applied throughout. When a child learns
that horses like carrots, inheritance implies that zebras might too. Inheritance provides an enormous simplification because it reduces the number of
things that must be specified and remembered. It does this by making them
interdependent. Things that are developed independently often work incon-
sistently, leaving more things to remember and more things to go wrong.
Inheritance has a twofold effect, reducing code bulk by reducing the need
to redevelop common functionality, and reducing surface area by increasing
consistency.

Few programmers realize just how natural it can be to program using inheritance. For example, building a symbol table in C is a noticeable project;

a matter of several hours at least. Inheritance reduces this time to seconds, the time it takes to type a statement that explains symbols to the machine in the same way you'd describe zebras to a child: "A Symbol is like a String, but has an additional field to hold a value."

Software-ICs

The development process centers on producing and consuming Software-ICs. The design phase identifies them, programmers implement them, compilation builds them, linking assembles them to build applications, and loading brings them into memory. A Software-IC carries everything that needs to be known to support a class, packaged as a self-contained unit. A Software-IC is the binary representation of a single class of functionality. It is produced by compiling a source file in which a programmer describes how the class should be implemented. The process starts with a hazy, intangible concept like Pen, ExpenseAccount, or FinancialHistory, and eventually produces a version, the implementation, that runs successfully within some application.

Figure 5.3 represents the stages in the development of the class, from its birth as an unformed concept through its maturity as a tested implementation, a subcomponent within some application. The word class is valid at each stage of this development, and experienced programmers often use class to refer to the artifacts at each stage in the process. For example, Smalltalk-80 programmers do not use terms like class description file, Software-ICs, factory object, or shared part of an object, since the single word class serves for all of them. But there are not so subtle distinctions between these meanings that newcomers must learn, and it helps to have a different name for each stage in the development of the class. These terms are just other names for class, just as egg, larvae, pupae, and adult are other names for butterfly.

Class Implementation File

Given a class (the concept), its programmer describes an implementation in an implementation file, which is the unit of modularity in an object-oriented system. Programmers create classes or implementation files, not programs or modules.

An implementation file begins by providing a name for the new class and the name of another class called the superclass. Inheritance comes into play here. Without inheritance, the rest of the file would describe the new class fully. With it, the file only specifies how the new class differs from its superclass.

Suppose that a class called Symbol is needed in a compiler project to represent the name and memory address of each identifier. This would be done by building Symbol as a subclass of a preexisting class named String. A String is an object that holds an array of bytes, and this can be used to manage the

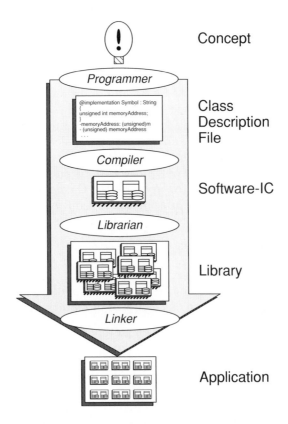

Figure 5.3. Developing a Software-IC. The implementation process from the time a useful class is first identified to the time it is fully implemented inside an application.

symbol's name. But Strings have no way of holding the value assigned to that symbol. To fix this, the file that defines class Symbol (the subclass) will state that Symbol differs from String (the superclass) in having this one additional variable. In Objective-C, this is written as:

```
@implementation Symbol : String { unsigned int memoryAddress; }
```

Symbols are bigger than Strings in having the new variable, memoryAddress, in addition to any variables defined in the String class. Classes always differ from their superclass by having more, never less. There is no way to subtract information in a subclass, because none is needed. Subclasses are always a specialized version of their superclass, and specialization involves adding or modifying information, not subtracting it.

Every class description file contains a declaration for any variables to be added to the instance variable declarations inherited from the superclass, and each of its superclasses in turn. These declarations determine the layout of the private part of that class's instances, by defining a name and a type for each instance variable. Space for these variables will be allocated later when the instance is actually created, at run-time.

Subclasses can also differ by having additional methods or by replacing methods inherited from their superclasses. These methods are described in the new class's implementation file and contribute to defining the shared part of the class's instances. The shared part is physically created at compile time, by allocating space for it and its dispatch table, and assigning values to each slot. For example, Objective-C does this by generating data initialization statements that will be acted upon by the C compiler and the linker.

Furthermore, the above information is required for two different kinds of object:

1. The instances of the class
2. The factory for this class

In other words, an implementation file provides two distinct sets of variable declarations, and two distinct sets of factory methods:

1. Instance variables and instance methods
2. Factory variables[2] and factory methods

Compiling a class implementation like the one shown above for class Symbol produces a Software-IC. The Software-IC can be linked into an application, where it defines a single global symbol named Symbol. This symbol identifies a factory object, which behaves precisely like the factory object named String, except that the instances it produces are longer by the amount of space required to hold an unsigned integer, and it is an instance of class Symbol instead of String. Except for this, Symbols and Strings are indistinguishable. Notice that until some methods have been provided for accessing this extra variable, it will serve no useful purpose.

Inheritance

Before discussing how methods are declared, consider what this single line accomplishes when it has been compiled, linked, and loaded, and the following message expression is executed:

```
mySymbol = [Symbol str:"Bang"];
```

There is no way to decipher what this statement actually does from first principles, just as the statement "A zebra is just like a ⟨BLEEP⟩, but it has stripes" is useless in learning about zebras. Inheritance helps only by making

---

[2]The current version of Objective-C provides no special syntax for defining factory variables. Factory variables are simulated by using ordinary C global variables.

it possible to define new classes in terms of old ones. If the older class is unknown, as String is right now, you are helpless until you learn about String. The indirection can even proceed for several levels, because it so happens that String is a subclass of Array, and Array is a subclass of Object,[3] where at last the indirection terminates on a class that is not defined in terms of some other class. All inheritance chains terminate with the class named Object, which is the only class that has no superclass. Object is a superclass of every other class. Although Objective-C does not require a class to have a superclass, most classes do. Object is a superclass of almost every other class, and is sometimes referred to as the root of the inheritance hierarchy. It contains most of the generic behavior for creating, using, saving, and freeing instances of a class.

Inheritance of Instance Variables

Notice the Symbol instance shown at the bottom of Figure 5.4. This block of memory is allocated and initialized by the factory object, Symbol, and is now pointed at by the variable mySymbol. The declaration for class Symbol is shown alongside, and it shows that Symbol is a subclass of String. Subclasses inherit everything declared in its superclasses, so the variables in the private part of a Symbol duplicate exactly the variables in the private part of a String. The same holds with respect to each class in the diagram. The variables declared by each subclass are simply concatenated onto the end of the variables declared in its superclass.

The concatenation starts with the topmost class, Object, which contributes three instance variables: isa; attr; and objID. The isa instance variable, shown in Figure 5.4, is the all-important variable that links every object to its shared part. Not shown are the attr and objID instance variables. These variables help optimize certain runtime performance aspects, and will be discussed in Chapter Seven.

Inheritance of Instance Methods

Even though no methods have been defined yet in the class interface or implementation files for class Symbol, these symbol instances are by no means without behavior. Inheritance guarantees that every instance of the Symbol class automatically inherits the methods in the String class, plus those of Array and Object as well. Figure 5.5 shows the various parts of this symbol. Its shared part is not a monolith of local and inherited information, but instead, the inherited information is attached by linking the shared parts together. Every shared part holds a dispatch table whose slots define a name and implementation for each method.

---

[3]The properties of these classes will be described in Chapter Seven, after you've become proficient with the concepts discussed in this chapter. For now you'll have to proceed by learning these classes piecemeal.

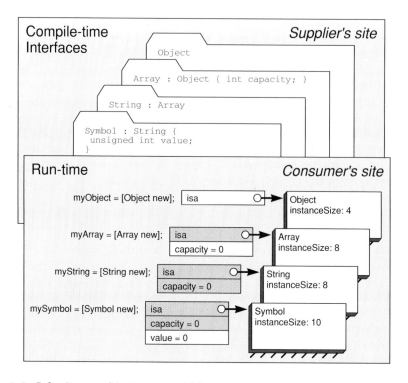

Figure 5.4. Inheritance of instance variables.

The links are visible only to the messager function.[4] This function takes two or more arguments, the first identifying the receiver of the message and the second identifying the message selector. The messager uses the first argument to find the receiver's private data and then follows the receiver's isa link to find the receiver's shared part and its dispatch table of method names and implementations. If the method name column in this table matches the message selector, the implementation column identifies the C function to be called. Otherwise the search is repeated in the dispatch table of every shared part that can be found by following the superclass link. If no superclass link exists (the field contains nil), the search fails and the object reports it does not understand the message.

Inheritance of Factory Methods

The same rules that apply to instances apply to factory objects too. Figure 5.6 shows the various parts of the factory object for class Symbol. It is constructed exactly like the symbol instance. It has its own private and shared parts, and messages and inheritance work exactly the same as they do for

[4]The linear search implied by this discussion is not used in practical systems because it would be too slow. Indexing is far faster and is described in Chapter 7.

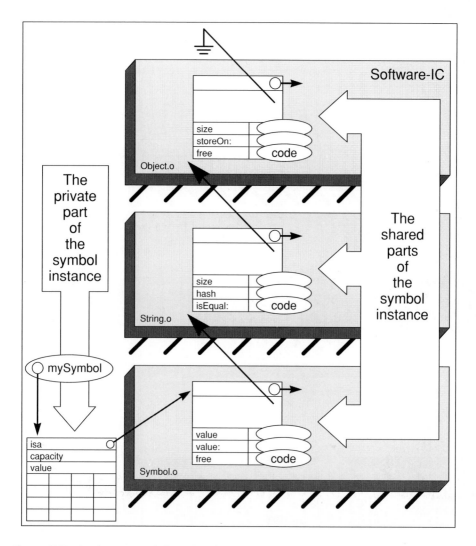

Figure 5.5. An instance of class Symbol. The symbol consists of a private part and a shared part. The shared part is implemented as a linked list of dispatch tables.

instances. Also, notice that the inheritance chain for factories leads to both parts of the Object class, thus ensuring that factory objects inherit the object class's data declarations and method definitions. This guarantees that factory objects are proper objects too.

Figure 5.7 splices the previous two figures together to show the entire inheritance story on a single page. This figure seems complicated until you realize that each of the blocks is an object and that the messager deals with

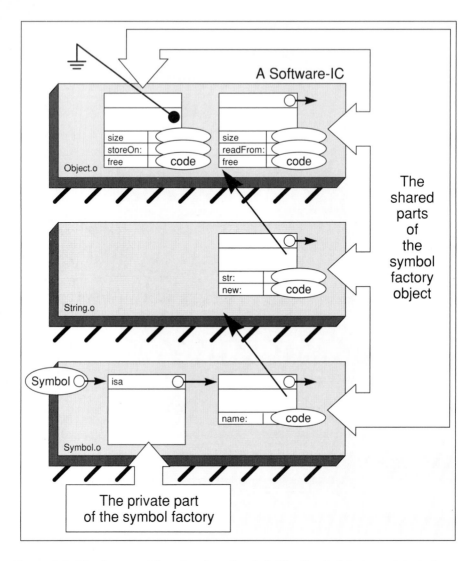

Figure 5.6. The factory object for class Symbol. The Symbol factory object also consists of a private part and a shared part. The shared part is implemented as a linked list of dispatch tables. Notice that the list includes the instance methods of the Object class, because factory objects should behave like objects, too.

objects in only one way. Each one has a private part and a shared part, and each shared part is a chain of inherited subparts. The only surprise is that what is the shared part of one object can be the private part of another. View this figure as the messaging routine sees it, one object at a time, and mentally simulate sending messages to all of the objects in this figure. For

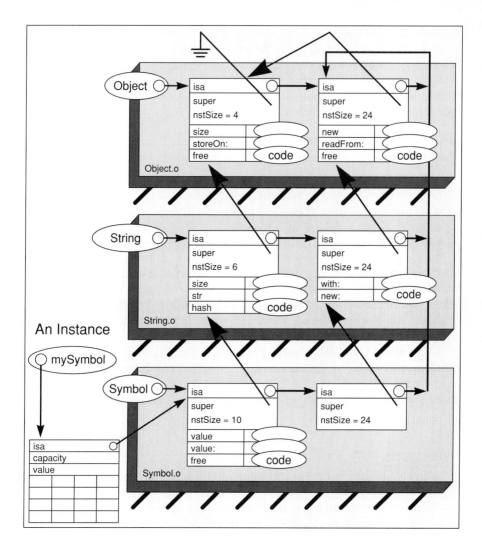

Figure 5.7. The entire inheritance story. Each Software-IC contains a factory object that builds the instances of its class. At link time, the Software-ICs are interconnected as shown here. The messager knows about the interconnections, and (logically) traverses them to implement inheritance of methods. In practical systems, the list traverse is normally optimized away so that messaging usually involves a fast table indexing operation.

example, the shared part of the symbol instance at the lower left corner is also the private part of the factory object, Symbol.

Notice how the name and function of a block changes when the point of view is changed by selecting a different object. What was once the shared part of an instance becomes the private part of a factory object, because the way each block is used depends entirely on which object is being messaged. The leftmost column of boxes are factory objects from one point of view, but from another, they are the shared parts of the instances the factory produces.

I have avoided introducing the terminology used by Smalltalk-80 programmers for these components because the same word, class, is used to mean different things at different times.

1. Class can mean the shared part of an object. For example, "The class holds an object's dispatch table of method names and implementations."
2. Class can mean the factory that produces an object. For example, "To create an object, send a message to its class."
3. Class can mean a unit of programming modularity (e.g., a source file or a Smalltalk browser panel in which both a factory and instances are described). For example, "Joe is developing a Symbol class."

In Smalltalk terminology, the object itself is what we've called the private part, and the class is what we've called the shared part. What we've called the factory, Smalltalk programmers call the class; ergo class methods, class variables, etc. An additional word, the metaclass, occasionally appears as well, and means the shared part of an object's shared part, generally one of the blocks along the right edge of Figure 5.7. Finally, and most confusing of all, notice that block at the upper-right corner of the diagram whose private and shared parts are the same, because its isa variable points to itself. Smalltalk-80 programmers call this one the Class of all classes.

Methods

I've delayed describing how methods are defined to reduce the number of syntactic details required to get this far. It's time to set this right. Recall that each implementation file defines two sets of methods—one for the instances of that class, and another for the factory object for that class. The two sets of methods make up the two dispatch tables that each Software-IC contains, held by the two parts of the factory object in that IC. The factory object's dispatch table (the factory methods) is in the factory object's shared part, and the instance's dispatch table is tucked into the other part of the factory object.

The compiler builds a factory object by generating its two parts in binary form from information provided by the programmer, primarily via method-Definition statements. Each methodDefinition describes:

1. Whether it is an instance method or a factory method. This determines which dispatch table this method will go in.
2. The method's name (the selector), the names and types of any formal parameters, and the type returned by this method.

3. The method's implementation. Implementations are written as an ordinary C function body with enhancements discussed in the previous chapter.

A method definition is like a C function definition in that both have a name, formal arguments, and an implementation enclosed in curly braces. But they have the following differences:

1. Method names need not be, and often are not, unique across different classes.
2. Methods are not called directly by name like functions, but indirectly by messaging.
3. Methods must address an additional address space, the private data inside the object that was sent the message.

In Objective-C, methods are defined much like C functions using syntax that parallels messaging syntax; for example, to pick up the Symbol class where we left it earlier in this chapter,

```
@implementation Symbol : String { unsigned int symbolValue; }
```

This one line of code has gone a long way toward solving the whole problem.

```
symbolTable = [Set new];
currentSymbol = [symbolTable filter:[Symbol str:buffer]];
```

This code fragment parallels the uniqueWords example discussed in Chapter 2, except that now it is Symbol instances that are being collected in the set named symbolTable rather than Strings. The Symbol factory already recognizes the message str: since it inherited this message from String. The Symbol instances are automatically able to support the hashing and string comparison messages required to hold them in a set, because these also were inherited.

A compiler builder could declare this class good enough for now and move on to building other parts of the compiler, trusting that symbols work already. They do work, because no new code has been written. Everything having to do with symbols has been inherited from a library that is already known to work correctly.

Instance Methods

The shortcoming of this class is that it does not provide quite enough functionality, because it provides no way to assign values to the instance variable, symbolValue. Having this variable and methods to access it is the way Symbols differ from Strings. So symbol's programmer adds two methods to support the missing functionality:

```
- (unsigned)address { return symbolValue; }
- (void)address:(unsigned)anAddress { symbolValue = anAddress; }
```

The first method defines a method named address which returns the symbol's value as an unsigned integer, and the second sets the symbol's value to the value provided in an argument, anAddress. A return type is assigned for both methods, so that the calling site can know that messages whose selector is address return an unsigned integer, and messages named address: return no value at all, or void.

Methods that return no value are rare because of the following conventions:

If a method has anything useful to return, it should return that.

Otherwise, it should return the id of the receiver.

The prior value held in symbolValue is potentially valuable to the consumer, so the second method could have been better written as:

```
- (unsigned)address:(unsigned)anAddress {
    unsigned tmp = symbolValue;
    symbolValue = anAddress;
    return tmp;
}
```

More commonly, the second rule of the convention is used and such methods would be written as:

```
- address:(unsigned)anAddress { symbolValue = anAddress; return self; }
```

The variable, self, is accessible inside any method and it identifies the object that is performing the method. I'll discuss this variable more thoroughly in the next section. Since no return type was specified here, Objective-C assigns this method the default type of id. Since C does not specify the value returned by a function that does not return control explicitly, the method exits with an explicit return statement, return self. It is poor practice to fail to do this without specifying a method return type of void. For example:

```
- doThis { doSomething(); }            // poor! return value is ill-defined
- doThis { doSomething(); return;}     // poor! return value is still ill-defined
- doThis { doSomething(); return self;} // good
```

The type declared for a method is important because it influences not only what happens at the called site (i.e., the method), but also at every calling site, system-wide. Because of this, the Objective-C compiler will issue a warning if it encounters the same method name elsewhere in the system with a different return type. This is not a theoretical restriction because the selector is a global name for a service that may be offered by different kinds of objects, but it can be a practical nuisance when code is integrated from different suppliers.[5] By defining the selector address above, the implementor is establishing the service of address reporting. An important part of establishing a

---

[5]I will return to how the compiler defines globals at the end of this chapter.

service is in deciding what C data types cross the consumer-supplier interface, namely, the types of formal arguments and the type returned by the method.

Self

Each of these methods refer to an instance variable, symbolValue, by name. But there will generally be many different symbols in the system, so how does the method know which one is meant?

Methods are triggered by sending a message to some receiver. The messaging routine chooses the proper implementation for this message and invokes it (a C function) with a formal parameter, 'self', set to the id of the object that is receiving the message. The fields of the object are described to the methods in the form of a C structure declaration, struct__PRIVATE, in which instance variables are declared as member names. Objective-C helps methods access instance variables by just looking for instance variable names in a method body and turning each one into a structure member reference. For example, the body of the above pair of methods is transformed into:

```
... { return self->symbolValue; }
... { self->symbolValue = anAddress; }
```

Therefore the hidden variable self is implicitly used every time the code references an instance variable. The variable can also be used explicitly as in the return self statement described earlier. It can even be used in C pointer expressions, but in doing so the programmer is assuming something about the implementation strategy, that objects are identified by their address in memory. If that strategy changes, for example, by introducing an object table as discussed in Chapter 10, the method will no longer work correctly.

Officially, self should never be modified in a method, since giving it a new value conveys unrestricted access to the internal data of some other object to the one that is executing the method. However, one of the practical strengths of a hybrid language is that programmers retain the ability to deliberately break such rules. For example, consider the following declaration:

```
@implementation SinglyLinkedListNode : Object { id successor; }
- successor { return successor; }
- successor:aSinglyLinkedListNode {
    id tmp = successor;
    successor = aSinglyLinkedListNode;
    return tmp;
}
- tail { return successor == nil ? self : [successor tail]; }
```

This implements a node in a singly linked list. Each node provides two methods by which its successor node can be determined or changed, and a tail method whereby the last node in the chain can be found.

An experienced programmer who is more concerned with efficiency might rewrite this method to rely on the fact that self is a variable and can be changed.

```
- tail {
    while(successor) self = successor;
    return self;
}
```

The first implementation is safer, but slower. Code written in this manner is more apt to withstand radical changes in the substrate implementation, and is more general in that the successor of a node can be any kind of object that implements a tail message (i.e., the successor need not be an instance of SinglyLinkedListNode. The latter method, by contrast, runs at full machine speeds, but is less likely to withstand radical changes in the substrate, and might crash if the successor: method were used to change the successor of some node to something other than a SinglyLinkedListNode.

Factory Methods

Factory methods are defined exactly like instance methods, but they begin with a + marker, not the − marker that identifies instance methods. The ability to define new factory objects, or to override inherited ones, does not mean that it must be exercised in every class description file. It is fairly common to find no factory methods mentioned in such files, which indicates that the inherited ones will suffice.

For example, the class implementation file for Object defines a factory method named new. This method is inherited by every factory in the system and is the standard way of building vanilla instances of any class. It is described in greater detail in Chapter 7, so I'll only provide an overview here.

```
@implementation Object ...⁶
  + new {
    id newObject = (* _alloc)(self, 0);
    return newObject;
  }
```

The (* _alloc)() function takes two arguments, the first describing the amount of memory to be allocated. The second argument is immaterial for now. This number and the value stored in newObject's isa variable in the following statement are both determined by self and therefore by which object is executing this method. This will always be one of the many different factory objects.

A consumer triggers this method by sending a message to one of the factory objects.

```
aSymbol = [Symbol new];
```

The factory object named Symbol receives this message and runs its new method, which it happened to inherit from the Object factory. Where the method was defined is immaterial, because the outcome is not determined by

---

[6]The @implementation ClassName ... is a typography convention that is used to indicate which class a fragment of code is defined in.

where the method was defined but by the object that is executing it now, and this is determined by the value of self.

When a class is compiled, the compiler initializes a variable in its factory's private part to indicate the space required to hold that class's instance variables. These variables are set by initializing the C structure struct __SHARED, and this number is obtained with the C sizeof operator;

```
struct _SHARED someDataName = {
    ...
    sizeof(struct _PRIVATE), /* initialize clsSizInstance field */
    ...
};
```

This determines the amount of space to be allocated by the alloc function, which also initializes the space with zeroes. The new method stores its self variable into the first word of the new block and returns its address to the caller as the id of the newly created object. A new instance has been allocated, initialized to vanilla Symbol (containing zeroes except for the first word), and sent on its way as a brand new fully functional instance of class Symbol.

Super

Occasionally an ordinary message expression is not sufficient. The problem occurs when an inherited method is overridden with another method by the same name, but the inherited method must still be accessed from within the overriding method. This situation would arise, for example, if you tried to print some message every time a new symbol is created. You might try

```
+ new { printf("aMessage\n"); return [self new]; }
```

but this just creates an infinite loop because self still points to the Symbol factory object and the messaging logic would always reach the implementation shown here. You might try sending the message directly to Symbol's superclass

```
+ new { printf("aMessage\n"); return [String new]; }
```

but this makes the Symbol factory produce Strings, not Symbols. Try as you might, there is no way to accomplish the desired effect without actually copying the code from Object's new, and it would be a shame to be copying code like this when the real goal is to reuse as much as possible.

The problem cannot be solved with the standard messaging logic, and the solution is a totally separate messager that is triggered like this:

```
+ new { printf("aMessage\n"); return [super new]; }
```

Super is not a variable (like self), but a syntactic device. It changes the way messaging is done by causing the compiler to call a different messager named __msgSuper. Whereas the normal messager's first argument is the receiver of the message, msgSuper's first argument is the shared structure in which the selector search should begin. This messager determines the object to receive the message from the value of self in the sending method by probing into the caller's activation record (stack frame).

Inheritance and Encapsulation in Combination

Inheritance is a technique for bringing generic code into play when producing new code. It is by no means the only way, because the encapsulation provided by messaging provides another way of accomplishing roughly the same effect. For example, imagine a specialized new class in an office automation system, like Envelope. One way to build it would be as a subclass of OrderedCollection, emphasizing the containment attributes of an Envelope.

```
@implementation Envelope : OrderedCollection {
    id toAddress, fromAddress;
}
```

No methods need be written for adding and removing elements, because these have been inherited from OrderedCollection. But another programmer might think first of attributes of an Envelope other than containment. He might emphasize that an Envelope is most like a paper form with fields in which to specify addresses. This programmer might build Envelope as a subclass of Form, and now his problem is to add containment abilities to the envelope.

He can solve the problem using encapsulation, by attaching a collection in one of Envelope's instance variables and providing Envelope its own methods for adding and removing elements from the collection, implementing these by sending messages to the attached collection:

```
@implementation Envelope:Form {
    id toAddress, fromAddress;
    id contents;
}
+ new { return [[super new] initialize]; }
- initialize { contents = [OrderedCollection new]; return self; }
- add:anObject { return [contents add:anObject]; }
- remove:anObject { return [contents remove:anObject]; }
- (int)size { return [contents size]; }
@end
```

Compiling and Linking

This section discusses a number of housekeeping details that have been glossed over until now. You may prefer to skip the rest of this chapter because it has relatively little to do with object-oriented programming. Nonetheless, these details are essential to using Objective-C successfully and are vital to building hybrids for other base languages.

Inheritance requires that the compiler have access to a store of persistent information about the classes being referenced during the compilation process. This persistent store of information are the interface files. As they change over time, they reflect the changes that have been made to the class's interface during the development process. For example, the interface file for the Symbol class discussed earlier contains the following information:

```
#import "String.h"
@interface Symbol : String { unsigned int symbolValue; }
- (void)address:(unsigned)anAddress;
- (unsigned) address;
@end
```

There are several conventions that are used when defining the contents of the interface file, as illustrated here for the Symbol class:

1. The interface file for the Symbol class will be named Symbol.h, and the implementation file will be named Symbol.m.

2. Symbol.h will contain a statement that imports the superclass's interface file, String.h.

3. Symbol.m will contain a statement that imports the class's interface file, Symbol.h. It does not import the superclass's interface file, String.h, since this was done by Symbol.h.

4. Symbol.m will import the interface file for any classes it references internally.

The responsibility for managing this information belongs to the programmer. There are two philosophies for how and when the two files for each class should be created. One philosophy argues that all interfaces should be defined during design, with the implementation file developed later, during coding. The second approach (adopted by this book), does not make this strong a distinction between design and coding. Work occurs primarily in the implementation file and the interface file is derived automatically once the implementation file stabilizes. In other words, the interface is complete only once development on the implementation file is complete.

I use a text editor to create interface files from implementation files mechanically. When development is complete, I examine the interface file to determine whether all of the methods declared there should really be published in the interface declaration that I publish to my consumers. For example, if some methods are provided solely for the class and not for its client (private methods), I may decide to hide them, either by removing them altogether or enclosing them in comments.

I find it convenient to provide all superclass and instance variable information in both files, even though Objective-C only requires this information in the interface file. If you adhere to the first philosophy, you may omit the superclass and instance variable information from your implementation file, and will therefore need to read source code across two files. By duplicating the information about instance variables and superclass information, it is available in the same file with the methods. When the information is present in both files, the compiler requires that it match exactly.

Building Software-ICs

Each implementation file imports the interface files for the classes used in that file by means of the #import preprocessor command—these go at the top of the file, before the code that references them. The #import directive is an optimized form of #include that will only include a file once per compile.

The interface file tells the compiler the name of the class being compiled, the superclass name, the instance variable declarations, and the method declarations. By convention, each interface imports the interface file of its superclass. When a class without a superclass is reached, the compiler has imported everything it needs to assemble a declaration for struct _PRIVATE for this new class.

If classes are the bricks in an object-oriented system, selectors are the mortar. The interface declarations help the compiler to establish three key attributes for each selector:

1. The selector's name, as a string of characters like "new" or "spend-Amount:forReason:."

2. A code that will uniquely identify this selector at runtime. These codes are assigned through a process that operates partially at compile time, partially at link time, and finally at startup time, when the selector string has been completely reduced from a String to a number that is unique within this application. This is to let the messaging logic work with numbers when comparing selectors, instead of strings like "new."

3. The type of this selector and its arguments. For example, the type of the selector "new" is id while the type of the selector "size" is int.

This selector-specific information is consulted each time the compiler encounters a selector in a source file. Both the type and the selector code affect how code is generated, and they both affect the binary results in the Software-IC. For example, the selector's return type affects the way message expressions are generated. The default type declaration for the messager is id, so nothing special is done for messages whose selector is of this type. When the selector has some different type, the base language must be informed that this particular invocation of the messager no longer returns an id, but some other C type. For example, consider the following method declaration:

```
- (struct MYSTRUCT)mySelector { ... }
```

This gives the selector, mySelector, the type, struct MYSTRUCT, such that a calling site elsewhere in the system might write:

```
struct MYSTRUCT someVariable;
someVariable = [someObject mySelector];
```

The base language has to generate some rather elaborate code to move an entire block of memory from the method to the local variable, someVariable, and so the base language must have accurate and comprehensive information about the type being returned from each message expression, particularly those whose return values participate in expressions at the calling site. Luckily, C provides exactly what is needed, although the syntax is so obfuscatory that relatively few C programmers (and some C compiler developers) never even learn that it exists:

```
someVariable = (*((struct MYSTRUCT *)(*)()_msg))(someObject, ... );
```

The effect of this bizarre construct is to typecast the meaning of the symbol, __msg (as opposed to the value returned by the function, __msg()), from pointer-to-function-returning-id to pointer-to-function-returning-MYSTRUCT. This is based on the fact that C treats names as legal expressions and therefore a valid subject for a typecast, including even the name part of the function in an expression calling that function.

If an inconsistent declaration is encountered subsequently, the compiler adopts the new definition, but warns that code has probably been generated and compiled into Software-ICs that already assume the old type. This code should be recompiled manually.

The conversion of selector names to selector codes is straightforward. Whenever a selector name is encountered in the source that is not present in any class declaration, it is assigned the next available code. This ensures that all selectors in a given compilation unit are unique, but another step will be needed when an application is being linked to ensure uniqueness across the class declarations in that application. In other words, unique selector codes cannot be generated into the code directly, but must be drawn from a table so that a later step can assign truly unique numbers.

Working with Multiple Libraries

Now consider a number of libraries being used by a multiperson development effort. Sam is developing the graphics primitives classes in a library called GraphicsPrimitives, Jill is developing user interface classes in a library called UserInterface, and Jane is building the application, workbench, in an application-specific library, Workbench.

Libraries are interdependent. Jane's classes inherit classes from libraries developed within her group, and often libraries from outside her organization as well. For example, her classes will certainly inherit classes like Object, which is a member of the generic foundation library, that Stepstone provided with the compiler. The universe of possible libraries is infinite and it contains many libraries of no interest, such as the libraries in groups similar to this one in other companies.

Implementation   Jane's work consists of a number of source files, a number of interface files, and a number of Software-ICs (binary files). By convention, she will store her files together in a directory area, along with a control file that describes how the files are compiled. The control file describes how to run the compiler, objcc, telling objcc about how the network of libraries should be interconnected and in which directories the libraries can be found:

```
objcc -c -O -I/usr/jill/UserInterface -I/usr/sam/GraphicsPrimitives \
   +WorkBench +UserInterface +GraphicsPrimitives +Foundation
```

The -I prefixes describe directories in which other libraries can be located, and the + prefixes describe the library names to be sought in these directories. For example, Jill's user interface library will consist of two files named UserInterface.a (containing Software-ICs) and UserInterface.h (containing their interface declarations), stored by convention in the directory that contains Jill's libraries. UserInterface.h is actually a collection of the interface files for all the classes in the user interface library. This file can contain all of the actual interface declarations, or it might contain import statements that are used to include all of the interface declarations. Either way, such files are not necessarily prudent, since they violate encapsulation by exposing clients to more information than they need. A better way for Jill to export this information would be to use the conventions outlined earlier for importing interface files only as needed, one at a time.

That suffices for the compilation process, turning source files into Software-ICs. Now consider how Software-ICs are linked to produce an intact application. The standard linker is used for this, with only one difference from the way ordinary C programs are linked to account for the fact that the run-time system needs certain information that is not preserved by standard linkers. For example, the run-time system needs a pair of tables, one that identifies the list of classes that has been installed in this application, and another that identifies the selector tables that the linker has installed in this application. This is currently accomplished by running the compiler in a special mode at link time. The compiler scans the symbol table to generate a table of initialization functions (one per class). This table is then compiled and linked into the application to guide the runtime initialization routine in reconciling the selector tables so that unique codes can be chosen for each selector.

Multiple Inheritance

Some object-oriented languages allow classes to have more than one superclass; a feature known as multiple inheritance. Multiple inheritance allows the envelope to be described as an object that behaves both as a container and also as a form. A workable syntax would be:

```
@implementation Envelope:Form,Container {
   id toAddress, fromAddress;
}
```

With hierarchical inheritance, inherited code is never copied but is acquired via the dynamic lookup mechanism in the messer. Inherited instance variables are laid out sequentially in memory, so methods that access them can be compiled and bound to offsets that are known statically when methods are compiled.

With multiple inheritance, this is possible for only the first of the multiple superclasses. The inherited variables for the others must be added at the end of the block at offsets that are not the same as the offsets that were known when the methods were compiled in a superclass. These methods must be copied into the current class and recompiled there to rebind their instance variable accesses to the new offsets. There are also several conceptual restrictions (error conditions) that should be detected and duly reported. If the same method name is inherited from more than one superclass, this should be reported as a design error. A similar restriction applies to instance variable names.

If the programming language does not support multiple inheritance directly, the programmer can simulate the same effect like this:

```
@implementation Envelope:Form {
    id toAddress, returnAddress;
#include "Container.data"
}
#include "Container.methods"
... Additional methods of Form ...
@end
```

In other words, the base language's facilities for incorporating new files inside the files being compiled can incorporate the data declarations of the superclasses inside the subclass's instance variable declarations, and also its methods in the appropriate place. This solution preserves the semantics of multiple inheritance perfectly, duplicating how the compiler would accomplish the same job. But it is syntactically unwieldy and it is inconvenient to store the data declarations and methods in separate files.

More fundamentally, multiple inheritance requires that the compiler have access to the source of each superclass to build a subclass. This is not a problem with single inheritance because superclass methods are never used by a single inheritance compiler.

Other implementations for multiple inheritance are also possible. This one is based on the assumption that methods are bound statically to instance variable offsets computed from the beginning of the object. This assumption could be relaxed by binding methods to offsets from the beginning of the variables declared by its class, instead of the beginning of the object. This introduces more complexity into the messaging logic, but it does represent an interesting approach you might experiment with in your implementation.

Objective-C does not currently support multiple inheritance. Not because it can't, but because I'm not sure it should, for reasons explained in the next section. Although inheritance is very useful for implementing new classes from pre-existing ones, it has grave shortcomings that are too often glossed over in books about object-oriented programming. Although inheritance is an important and useful tool for *implementing* new classes from existing ones, this is often less than is desired because it is little help in *specifying* classes: describing how they fit into their environment, and in particular, for describing dynamic attributes such as what classes *do*. Adding the ability for a class to inherit from multiple superclasses only compounds the problems resulting from the lack of robust specification tools for software.

Specification and Testing[7]

Once Congress mandated interchangeable parts in the early 1800s, technologies for building them followed posthaste. The first phase focused on water-powered tools such as Blanchard's pattern lathe. This lathe represents the mainstream approach of the software community until now, the search for technologies capable of transforming progressively higher-level descriptions of the problem, like the gun-stock pattern that guides this lathe, into concrete implementations that are correct by construction.

Today, this lathe stands in the American History Museum in Washington, D.C., in an exhibit whose point is that the crucial innovation that made interchangeable parts possible was not only the elimination of cut-to-fit craftsmanship by tools like Blanchard's lathe. The crucial discovery was made, not by Blanchard, but by John Hall, who realized that implementation tools would fail unless supplemented by specification tools capable of determining whether parts complied to specification within tolerance. The museum reinforces this point by displaying a box of hardened steel inspection gauges in the same exhibit with Blanchard's lathe.

This discovery has not yet occurred in software. Although it is easy to find articles with specification in their title, they usually mean implementation, as in "automatically generating code from specifications." Although such higher level implementation tools are clearly worthwhile, it is misleading to call them specification languages because this obscures the absence of true specification technologies in software—the rulers, protractors, calipers, micrometers, and gauges of manufacturing. Programmers continue to rely exclusively on implementation technologies, be they ultrahigh-level programming languages—tools of certainty like the Blanchard lathe—or lower level languages—tools of risk like the rasps, files, and spoke shaves that it displaced.

The confusion of implementation and specification is particularly prominent in that most fashionable of object-oriented features: inheritance. As used in object-oriented language circles, inheritance is the Blanchard lathe of software—a powerful and important tool for creating new classes from existing ones, but not nearly as useful for specifying static properties such as how

---

[7]For a complete discussion of this topic, see Brad Cox, "Planning the Software Industrial Revolution," *IEEE Software* magazine, November 1990. Portions used by permission; © 1990 IEEE

they fit into their environment, and useless for describing dynamic properties such as what these classes do.

Rather than laboriously building each new class by hand, inheritance copies functionality from a network of existing classes to create a new class that is, until the programmer begins overriding or adding methods, correct by construction. Such hierarchies show how a class's internals were constructed. They say nothing, or worse, are misleading, about the class's specification—the static and dynamic properties that the class offers to its consumers.

For example, Figure 5.8 shows the implementation hierarchy for a Semaphore class that inherits four existing classes. Contrast this implementation hierarchy with the following facts:

1. Semaphores are a kind of Queue only from the arcane viewpoint of their author. This hierarchy resulted from a speed optimization of no interest to consumers, who should view them as scheduling primitives with only wait and signal methods. How will the producer tell the consumer to avoid some, many, or all of those irrelevant and dangerous methods being inherited from all four superclasses? And if such static issues are handled statically, where will dynamic ones be handled—the vital question of what Semaphore does?

2. This hierarchy says quite explicitly that OrderedCollection is similar to Set and dissimilar to Queue. However exactly the opposite is true. Queue is functionally identical to OrderedCollection. I carefully handcrafted Queue to have each of OrderedCollection's methods, each with precisely the same semantics, to show that encapsulation lets a class's internals be

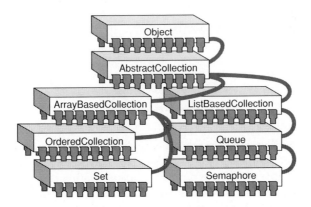

Figure 5.8. This implementation hierarchy shows how new classes are implemented from pre-existing ones. But notice that it provides a misleading picture of what the external consumer is truly interested in, the specification of what these classes actually do.

revised without affecting its externals. But how will the consumer discover that OrderedCollection and Queue provide the same functionality—that they are competing implementations of precisely the same specification? And how will any commercially significant differences, like time/space trade-offs, be expressed independently of these similarities?

Manufacturing handles this issue by providing two separate classes of tools, implementation tools for the producer's side of the interface and specification tools for the consumer's side. Shouldn't we do likewise? Shouldn't conceptual aids like inheritance be used on both sides, but separately, just as Blanchards lathe and Hall's inspection gauges deal with different views of the same object's interface? Shouldn't Semaphore's consumer interface be expressed in an explicit specification hierarchy, as in Figure 5.9, independently of the producer's implementation hierarchy?

Just as a measuring stick is not a "higher level" saw, a specification tool is not a higher level implementation tool. Specification is not the implementation tool's job. Separating the two would eliminate performance as a constraint on the specification tool, allowing knowledge representation shells that already support rich conceptual relationships to be used as a basis for a specification language "compiler." The two tools can be deployed as equal partners, both central to the development process, as shown in Figure 5.10.

The primitives of the specification language are ordinary test procedures—predicates with a single argument that identifies the putative implementation to be tested. A test procedure exercises its argument to determine whether it behaves according to its specification. For example, a putative

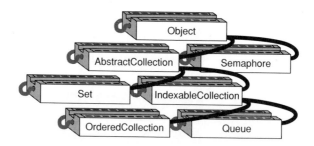

Figure 5.9. A specification hierarchy is entirely different from an implementation hierarchy. The names in this figure are not class names, but the names of test procedures that verify whether a putative implementation complies to a specification within a tolerance embodied in each test. For example, this figure declares that an acceptable Semaphore is any putative Semaphore that passes a Semaphore gauge that consists of the Semaphore and Object test procedures. The test named "Semaphore" might verify that a putative Semaphore provides wait and signal methods (static correctness) and that they behave as they should (dynamic correctness).

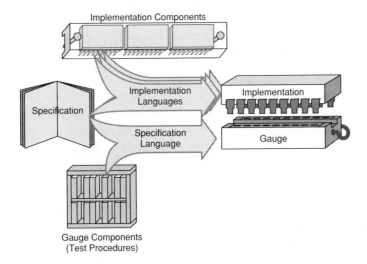

Figure 5.10. A software development process in which specification has as much emphasis as implementation. The specification language "compiler" is a knowledge representation tool. Just as implementation languages preserve code in implementation hierarchies, the specification language preserves specifications by preserving the gauges that determine compliance to specification. Just as implementation language compilers generate implementations from libraries of subcomponents, the specification language "compiler" assembles pre-existing test procedures to form executable gauges that determine whether a putative implementation complies to its specification.

duck is an acceptable duck upon passing the isADuck gauge. The specification compiler builds this gauge by assembling walksLikeADuck and quacksLikeADuck test procedures from the library. The "compiler" is simply an off-the-shelf knowledge representation tool for invoking test procedures stored for this purpose in the test procedure library.

The test procedure libraries play the role in software as elsewhere—defining the shared vocabulary that makes producer-consumer dialogue possible. For example, in "I need a pound of roofing nails," "pound" is defined by a test procedure involving a scale, and "nail" by a test procedure involving shape recognition by the natural senses. Test procedures are particularly crucial in software because of the natural senses' inability to contribute to the specification of otherwise intangible software products like Stack or Set. Making software tangible and observable, rather than intangible and speculative, is the first step to making software engineering and computer science a reality.

Test procedures collect "operational," or indirect, measurements of what we'd really like to know, the product's quality as perceived by the customer.

They monitor the consumer's interface, rather than our traditional focus on the producer's interface (i.e., by counting lines of code, cyclomatic complexity, Halsted metrics, etc.). This knowledge of how product quality varies over time can then be feedback to improve the process through statistical quality control techniques, as described in Deming,[8] that play such a key role today in manufacturing.

The rudiments of this approach are already available today. I recommended that you use the modest tools that do exist today in anticipation of the more ambitious tools of tomorrow. The basis of the whole approach is a simple macro, assert(), that is available in every Objective-C environment in an include file, which can be found on most Unix systems in /usr/include/assert.h. This macro accepts a single C expression as its argument. If the expression evaluates to true (non-zero), the macro takes no action and the computation proceeds as if the macro was not present. Otherwise, the macro prints a fatal error message indicating that an assertion violation has occurred.

For example, if line 12 of file Foo.m contains the statement

```
assert(2+2 == 4);
```

execution continues normally because this assertion is true. But had the line read instead

```
assert(2+2 == 5);
```

a fatal error would result with the error message

```
assertion failer in file Foo.m line 12
```

This behavior can be modified by compiling the program with NDEBUG set. This eliminates the assertion testing altogether, so that the assert() macros can be retained permanently in the code as a form of documentation, imposing no overhead whatsoever.

The most common way of using this macro is for white-box testing, which means that the assertions appear right alongside the code being tested. Although this can be done in a casual unstructured manner, the recommended technique is to cluster the assertions into two groups, preconditions and postconditions.

1. Preconditions: verify that conditions that the method depends on were met by the caller. For example, verify that argument values and/or types are as they should be for the method to work properly.

2. Postconditions: verify that execution achieves the expected result.

[8]W.E. Deming, "Out of the Crisis," MIT Center for Advanced Engineering Study, Cambridge MA 02139, 1989.

A somewhat contrived example of an internals test is the following fragment of the add:method of the Set class

```
@implementation Set ...
- add:anyObject {
        assert (isObject(anyObject));        // Verify that anyObject is an Object
        ... add the object
        assert ([self contains:anyObject]);//Verify that the add: worked right
}
```

The isObject() predicate is a C function that reports whether its argument is an instance of any class (e.g., whether the argument is certainly not a string or other pointer-based quantity, and is unlikely to be merely a large integer that happens to have an object's id as its value).

Carefully chosen white-box assertions provide a particularly cogent and readable kind of documentation. The preconditions describe what must be true to use the add: method, and the postconditions describe what the code will do in response.

The test procedures described at the beginning of this section do black-box testing. This means that the assertions do not appear inline with the code under test, but in a separate file. This reflects the fact that someone other than the programmer develops black-box tests, such as a quality assurance group, with the goal of examining the code's specification not from inside, as seen by the developer, but from the outside, as seen by the customer.

The software engineering community has only begun to explore the evolutionary path that might lead from a simple library of test procedures to the full-blown specification/testing technologies mentioned in this section.

This exploration will take years to settle down. The fact that white-box testing falls short of what is ultimately needed is no excuse for not using it aggressively today. Get into the habit of writing preconditions and postconditions in all of your code, if for no other reason than that it makes your own life so much easier when debugging. When your friends ask what all those assert macros are doing in your code, spread the gospel to them by saying they're a form of documentation that they know they can trust, because the compiler guarantees they are up to date with the code.

Perhaps by shifting gradually from the process-centered paradigm of an immature cottage industry, to the product-centered paradigm of manufacturing, we can make software engineering a mature engineering discipline, just as Blanchard, Eli Whitney, and John Hall did for manufacturing.

Optimization Techniques

Up until now, we have glossed over machine performance and focused on programmer performance. This section talks about two of the major performance optimization topics: the allocation of memory to hold instances and using a runtime lookup routine to bind selectors to the appropriate methods.

In open universe programming, most variables are of type id. This type is defined by the compiler as a pointer to a block of memory that may or may not have an existence that extends past the lifetime of the variable itself. But many examples of closed universe programming turn up in every project, and when you do know that a certain variable will hold only instances of a single class, you can exploit this information by using optimization techniques that Objective-C provides to trade flexibility for speed.

Static Binding

Performance tuning is a crucial part of the application development process. By running a profiler on an application, suppose that you discover that the following piece of code is critical to the performance of your application:

```
id strings;    // an OrderedCollection of strings
id currentStr; // the string from the collection being used.
int n;         // the number of items in the collection
n = [strings size];
while ( --n ) {
   currentStr = [strings at:n];
   [currentStr print];
   }
```

Since this code is sending the same message to a collection that you are sure will only contain instances of String, you might choose to optimize by statically binding all messages to the objects identified by the variables strings and currentString. You do this as follows:

```
OrdCltn *strings;
String  *currentStr;
```

This changes the code that the compiler generates for all messages involving those variables. Calls through the messager that would resolve the message binding at runtime are replaced by indirect function calls to the actual method. This applies only to variables typed in this new fashion (strings and currentString). Other places in your application that access Strings and OrderedCollections through variables of type id do so as usual, through the messager.

This puts the choice of binding mechanism in the hands of the consumer, rather than the producer, allowing producers to provide generic classes that the consumer can optimize as needed without having to change the producer's source.

Static Allocation

In both approaches, an object's private part is allocated from the heap, where it exists until you explicitly free it. Heap-resident objects have a lifetime that extends beyond the lexical scope (stack frame) that created them.

There are times, however, when you know that an object will exist only within the scope of a single stack frame. For those situations, you can specify that the object's private part be allocated on the stack, and not on the heap.

Suppose you are working with a window system that uses a Cartesian coordinate system to specify window size attributes. You might move all windows so that they staggered, like this:

```
{
id aPoint = [Point x: 0 y: 0];
id seq = [windowList eachElement];
while ( wnd = [seq next]) {
      [wnd origin:aPoint];
      [aPoint addXY:5];
      }
[aPoint free];
[seq free];
}
```

Since aPoint is needed only inside this compound statement, it makes sense to allocate its space on the stack. This way, aPoint will automatically be deallocated when it goes out of scope:

```
{
Point aPoint;
[aPoint x: 0 y: 0];
while ( wnd = [windowList next]) {
      [aPoint addXY:5];
      }
}
```

The compiler will generate code so that the object has a correctly set isa instance variable, but its other instance variables will be unknown until the [aPoint x:0 y:0] message sets them otherwise. The statically allocated instance behaves in the same way as a C structure would. This requires that a statically allocated instance must first be dereferenced in order to be passed in place of an id during a message send. However, once the receiver has gotten the message, it can't tell how objects passed as parameters were allocated. For example, if you wanted to send a message using a static instance of Point as a parameter:

```
Point aPoint;
aPoint.x = aPoint.y = 0;
[aWindow origin:&aPoint];
```

Public Instance Variables

Objective-C provides a special keyword, @public, that allows particular instance variables to be directly accessed just as C structure members can be accessed. For example, the interface declaration for such a Point class might be:

```
@interface Point {
     @public
     unsigned int x, y;
     }
@end
```

You may now use C's structure member access mechanisms to access the x and y instance variables directly. For example, the window staggering example might be done as follows:

```
{
Point aPoint;
aPoint.x = aPoint.y = 0;
while ( wnd = [windowList next]) {
     [wnd origin:&aPoint];
     aPoint.x = aPoint.y += 5;
     }
}
```

Areas to Watch

There are several concerns you should be aware of when using these optimization techniques.

1. As normally allocated, an object's lifetime persists beyond the lexical scope that created it. This allows one routine to create an object and then transfer ownership of that object to someplace else. The programmer is responsible for deallocating objects when they are no longer needed, and for insuring that deallocated objects are never referenced again. Some languages (not presently Objective-C) handle this issue with an automatic garbage collector as described in Chapter Ten.

2. Factory methods often override new to do some form of initialization. For objects that are allocated statically, this method will not be invoked, and the intended initialization will not be executed. If you intend to use static instances, you should establish the convention that all classes will implement an initialization method that can be invoked by either the new method, or directly by the consumer when static allocation is used.

3. One advantage of having a central messager function is that it provides a convenient place to implement advanced functionality such as remote messaging, persistent storage of objects, etc. Both static binding options bypass the message routine and therefore will not take advantage of the message function's amenities.

Summary

This chapter describes the concepts most used by a supplier of object-oriented functionality. It shows how objects are constructed of one part private to the object and another that is shared with all other instances of its class. Loosely speaking, the private part contains the object's data, and its shared part contains its methods.

Both parts of the object are modified by inheritance, by concatenating information from each superclass in two different ways. The private part is formed by concatenating the instance variables declared in its class onto those variables declared in each superclass. The shared part is formed by linking shared parts together such that methods defined in the current class are concatenated in front of methods declared in each superclass.

Classes are the unit of modularity in an object-oriented system. Programmers define them and the compiler turns them into Software-ICs. Each Software-IC contains a factory object that the linker assembles into an application, and these produce instances as directed by messages sent from the application. The programming language provides syntax for defining new classes, declaring instance variables, and defining instance and factory methods. Inside a method, a hidden formal argument, self, is constantly engaged behind the scenes, providing that crucial link between a method and the object's instance variables.

These concepts, working together, put reusability at the center of the programming process. Encapsulation raises firewalls around the objects within a system, so that if they change, other parts of the system can remain unchanged. Inheritance does the converse, by spreading decisions implemented in generic classes automatically to each of their subclasses. The net effect is making libraries of reusable code, called Software-IC libraries, a central feature of the system-building shop.

| Six

DependencyGraph Exercise

Object-oriented programming can help to put reusability at the fore-front of a programmer's work. But it can't do it alone unless an information network is provided to help consumers discover useful code quickly and to understand how it applies to their needs. This chapter describes how these information networks are used and explores one by using it to build a small application, DependencyGraph.

This application will be developed by reusing two substrate classes, Set and String, and defining two new ones that are potentially reusable in other applications, Graph and Node. During the process, a number of documents will be consulted to learn about the code that is being reused, and several others will be produced that help to describe the new code to others. The application is developed at this point in the book (before important foundation classes have been discussed) to introduce this vital network.

The final section capitalizes on this application's small size to measure the costs and benefits of this style of programming. The application is redeveloped using conventional programming techniques, and the differences in development time, execution speed, and program bulk are described.

Information Networks

While I was in graduate school at the University of Chicago, our Computer Science Department was still using a computer that had been designed and built several years earlier using discrete components throughout, the Maniac II. Building this computer was a major undertaking and not likely to be repeated again. Nobody builds computers that way any more because

105

the effort that they spent to assemble a single transistor in one bit in one of the Maniac-II's arithmetic registers now installs an entire computer on a chip.

The hardware industry quickly learned how to reduce development effort by building large reusable components, and they now do it successfully and routinely. The result is the well-known exponential increase in hardware cost-effectiveness. But the software industry has not learned how to do this nearly so routinely. As Figure 6.1 shows, during the same period that my friends in hardware were doubling their output year by year, I was progress-

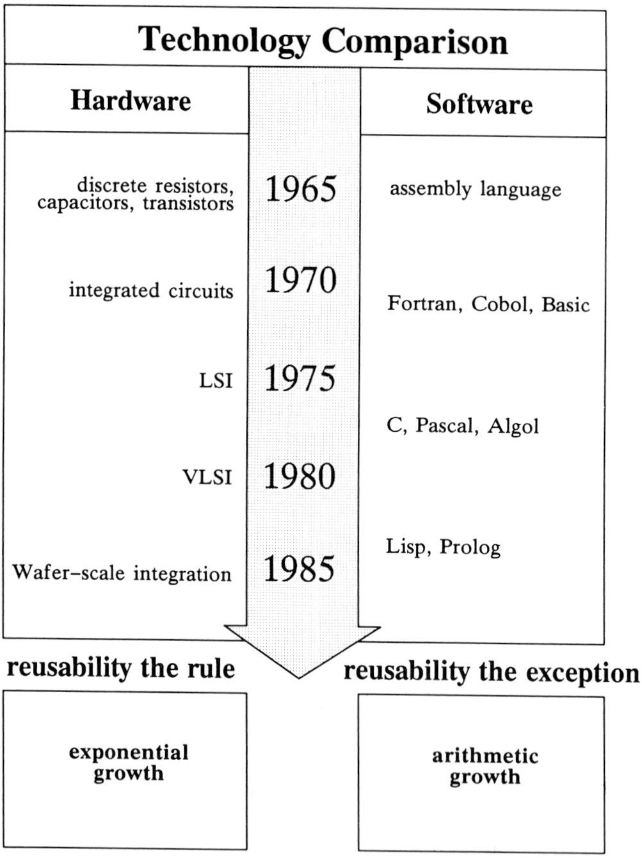

Technology Comparison		
Hardware		**Software**
discrete resistors, capacitors, transistors	1965	assembly language
integrated circuits	1970	Fortran, Cobol, Basic
LSI	1975	C, Pascal, Algol
VLSI	1980	
Wafer–scale integration	1985	Lisp, Prolog
reusability the rule		**reusability the exception**
exponential growth		**arithmetic growth**

Figure 6.1. Reusability in hardware versus software. During the last twenty years, hardware engineers learned to cope with building blocks whose size and complexity roughly doubles each year, producing geometric growth in what an individual designer can accomplish. Software engineers have only attained arithmetic growth because only their tools have changed, not the unit of modularity.

ing from assembly language to FORTRAN to C to Lisp. I gained productivity at each stage to be sure, but arithmetic growth always lags behind exponential growth in the long run.

In spite of the potential advantages of reusing code, most programmers are still exceedingly reluctant to do so. The most common objection is "I could rewrite it faster than I could learn it," and no wonder, considering the investment that programmers usually make in describing code for reuse. By expecting code to be application dependent; i.e., to be discarded after its current application, it isn't worth the trouble to document internals nicely. The cycle feeds on itself. It usually *is* easier to rebuild from scratch than to wade through the usual low-budget excuses for code level documentation.

Once code is reusable beyond its current application it becomes an asset; one to be conserved, publicized, learned about, and even bought and sold quite independently of its current application. Reusable code lives on indefinitely because its life is not dependent on the specific application that spawned it. With value comes the willingness to spend effort on not just commenting it and not just documenting it, but on actively marketing it with all the promotional vigor seen in the hardware industry today. Programmers have a lot to learn from the pioneers who built a thriving industry around reusable hardware components. For example, reflect on the fact that what programmers call documentation, the hardware industry calls advertising.

This chapter will describe an information network for communicating about reusable code. Suppliers use it to publicize their efforts, and consumers use it to discover potential solutions, to determine whether they meet the need, and to learn how to apply them to the problem at hand. The network is modeled after the information network that the hardware industry uses to help electronic component suppliers communicate with their consumers—an interlocking collection of blueprints, catalogs, specification sheets, and reference manuals, supplemented by informal channels like meetings, design reviews, and brainstorming sessions. Newcomers learn how to use the more technical information in the network by attending lectures, tradeshows, and conventions, and even before that, universities, colleges, and schools.

Although this book will emphasize a paper-based network, electronic versions are possible too. Much of the importance of Smalltalk-80 is in providing a sophisticated, well thought out, and highly acclaimed online implementation of most of the documentation tools described here. Later, after I have shown how a paper-based network is used, I will demonstrate a similar browser for Objective-C. But electronic implementations do have several limitations not shared by paper, since suppliers of reusable code must communicate with consumers, whether or not they share the same machine or even work for the same company.

Catalogs

Hardware design shops maintain a store of information about the universe of components that are available for potential use in the products of that shop. For example, an electronics shop might keep a file cabinet of specification sheets for the components they use routinely, organized according to type. A folder, Power Supplies, contains sheets describing power supplies, perhaps subdivided into categories: High voltage, High current, 5-volt, and so on. This catalog is a communication channel connecting the consumers and suppliers of electronics components. The consumers use it to learn about components that can be bought instead of built and the suppliers use it to tell consumers about their products.

This catalog is a powerful system-building tool. It is one of several channels that, working together, bring the talents of literally thousands of skilled individuals to bear on making the electronics shop's product a success. It is a highly specialized, low-noise, structured communication channel through which different individuals with interests that seldom coincide exactly can cooperate effectively while fulfilling their own self-interest. It provides a controlled way of communicating about functionality that can be bought, and about the interface specifications that the functionality requires.

Figure 6.2 is a catalog showing the Software-ICs used in this book. The catalog shows few details because it is primarily a summary of information that is provided separately in specification sheets that describe each Software-IC fully.

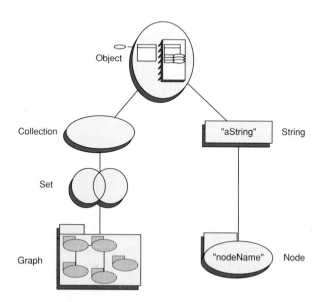

Figure 6.2. Software-IC catalog. Each icon represents a class, many of which have subclasses. The Graph and Node classes, to be developed in this chapter, are represented as subclasses of Set and String, respectively. Set is one of several subclasses of a class called Collection.

Specification Sheets

A specification sheet is the minimum acceptable level of documentation. Without this, a class is not reusable because no mechanism has been provided for potential consumers to learn about its capabilities. Specification sheets are terse and to the point, because they are used by experts in a hurry; trained engineers who appreciate a concise technical vocabulary. Each one focuses on a single component, not on a specific application of the component. They assume knowledge not only of object-oriented programming, but often of other library components as well. They always assume that inheritance and messaging are fully understood, and that the reader will actively apply this understanding while reading. For example, the class catalog conveys that Set is a subclass of Collection, and Set's specification sheet will assume that the reader knows, or is prepared to discover on his own, the full implications of this. Although Set will inherit the variables and methods of each of its superclasses, this will not be mentioned unless inheritance applies in some unusual or nonobvious manner.

Appendix A provides specification sheets for the classes discussed in this book along with instructions for how to use them. Printed on the front of every sheet is an extremely important metric, the maturity index. This is the supplier's way of telling the consumer how likely the class is to change over time. I know of no way to measure this index quantitatively, but the rating is so important that it should not be left out while one is sought. It is a way of facing up to reality and admitting that nontrivial software matures over time, moving from infancy to maturity to senescence. Without this index, both parties can be harmed; the consumer by becoming dependent on immature software, and the supplier by becoming committed to a bad early decision while software is still immature. The maturity index of the classes in Appendix A is "relatively mature," which signifies that they have been used in many diverse applications and found to hold up under stresses that could not have been predicted in advance. When a class has been used in only one application its maturity index is immature.

Engineering Know-how

Specification sheets seldom stand alone, because they will be read only once the value of their component has been made clear through some other communication channel. Their narrow focus and their orientation toward experts makes them nearly useless for presenting a library so that a newcomer can understand how to use it. Specification sheets assume that the reader already has engineering know-how; a fluid understanding of encapsulation, inheritance, and the basic architecture of a class library. For example, no specification sheet would point out that [aSet storeOn:"aFileName"] works for sets since that is documented in the specification sheet for Object which Sets inherit automatically.

Newcomers need more help than this, so specification sheets must also be backed up by tutorials which describe how a group of classes work together.

This level of the information channel has no specific name because there are so many and they are so diverse. Tutorial documents, of which Chapters 7 and 8 are examples, play a part, but even these depend on background information that some potential consumers will not possess. This book plays a part, as do courses, magazine articles, advertising, and trade shows.

Informal discussions and presentations are an unusually important channel, particularly for conveying detailed technical information within a system-building group, and this is where software blueprinting makes its most important contribution. A software blueprint is a picture that shows the significant parts of an object. These pictures are not formal design notations in the usual sense because blueprints are relatively poor at describing how things work. They are used the way that hardware engineers use theirs; to show how applications are built from their component parts.

Objective-C Browser

The Objective-C Browser (shown in Figure 6.3) automates the information network by letting you focus on the information, rather than on the mechanics of finding it. A browser is a tool for learning about objects and classes, reusing classes, and maintaining them.

The Objective-C Browser provides several different views into a library of classes. It lets you explore the contents of a class library in a top down fashion, starting with classes and moving toward the actual source that implements methods. Or, it lets you see how classes interrelate by providing cross-reference information. It will even provide analysis information that shows how the members of a class library might interact with each other at runtime.

Consider what it would cost to obtain this information without a browsing tool. For example, to locate the source for some method in a particular class, you would have to find the class and scan its source for the method of interest. If the method is not found, then you would repeat the search in the superclass, and so forth. This detailed mechanical work is the downside of an object-oriented language. It's also the type of mechanical work I would prefer to have done for me when learning about object-oriented programming for the first time.

Browsers are an important tool for enabling component reuse. You use the browser to explore what's available in a class library to see if it provides components you need. For instance, suppose you are developing an application to manage a list of items. You might use the browser to search for components to manage lists and to explore likely candidates in greater detail. If you can't find a single class that completely covers the requirements, you can broaden your search to see if there is a series of components that together would solve the problem. You might check for interrelations between classes (through cross-referencing) to see how the classes work together.

Finally, the browser helps to develop and maintain reusable software components. For example, if you were to develop a new software component, you could search a current library for classes that *almost* fulfill the stated require-

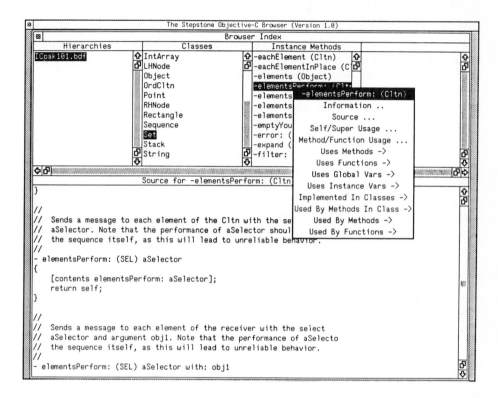

Figure 6.3. The Objective-C Browser. Each small window displays detailed information about the selected item to its immediate right. The larger window is used to display source code and analysis information. This figure shows the browser being used to display the source for the "elementsPerform:" method in Set that was inherited from the Collection (Cltn) class. The popup menu lists additional information that is available for the "elementsPerform:" method.

ments and extend them to accomplish the desired behavior. The browser could be used to verify that the extensions obey class protocols, and that new methods are named to preserve the messaging protocols of the existing class library.

The DependencyGraph Application

Now you are ready to begin exploring this network while using it to build a small application, DependencyGraph. As the design proceeds, a number of information sources will be consulted and others will be produced. At the end a pair of new Software-ICs will have been created that could in principle be stored in the library along with documents that were largely created while the code was being developed. This does not happen automatically, so the final Software-ICs will still be quite immature; both code and documents will need considerable work before they qualify as truly reusable. This chapter cannot trace all the steps because these classes will have been used in only a single application and are therefore immature and quite likely to need changing before they can be reused in other applications. But I will describe the earliest, formative stages and several places where mistakes can be avoided that would guarantee nonreusable results.

A graph is an arbitrarily connected collection of nodes, like a tree but with no prohibition against multiply referenced nodes or circular connection paths. A dependency graph is a graph in which the connections leaving each node indicate that the source node depends on the target node in some manner. For example, the nodes in a dependency graph could represent the subroutines defined in some program, and the arcs leaving each node could represent the subroutines called by the corresponding subroutine. A graph analysis tool might be used to determine nodes that cannot be reached via any path starting from a program's entry point, thereby locating coding errors or wasted space.

The problem is to build a program that constructs a dependency graph in memory and then prints those nodes that can be reached and those that cannot, starting from any given initial node. It should also report the nodes that have been referenced but never defined. The incoming data is formatted like this:

```
main initialize compute terminate
initialize openInputFile
compute phaseOne phaseTwo
terminate closeInputFile closeOutputFile
phaseOne
phaseTwo phaseOne
phaseThree compute terminate
```

The first word in each line defines the name of a node and any remaining words on names the nodes referenced from that one. The program produces[1]

```
Reachable from main:
    terminate phaseTwo closeInputFile closeOutputFile
    initialize openInputFile main compute phaseOne
Not reachable from main:
    phaseThree
Undefined nodes:
    closeInputFile closeOutputFile openInputFile
```

Design Phase

Different programmers approach a design problem in different ways. Programmers with an engineering or scientific background tend to decompose problems according to the actions that must be performed, while data pro-

---

[1]In a production version the lists should be sorted and greater attention should be given to formatting. These niceties have been omitted for simplicity, and the output is presented in random (hashed) order.

cessing people tend to decompose first according to entities. For example, a FORTRAN programmer would probably think in terms of first reading the file (to build a graph), then processing the graph (to build lists of reachable, unreachable, and undefined nodes), and finally printing the respective lists (to produce the output file). A COBOL programmer would probably do the inverse, first building the graph (by reading the input file), then the three kinds of nodes (by scanning the graph), and finally the output file (by printing the nodes).

The first point of view is procedure centered and the second is data centered. Object-oriented programming introduces a third possibility in which data and procedure are treated simultaneously as subsidiary thoughts within a master concept, object. This point of view is like the data centered one in focusing primarily on the entities involved in the computation, but different in that the procedural part of the problem is expressed inside the elements of the design.

Blueprinting

Two classes of objects can be identified in the problem statement, one to represent the graph as a whole and another to represent the nodes inside the graph. So two classes will be developed, one named Graph that will have only a single instance, and another named Node which will have many instances; one for each unique name in the file.

These are design decisions that could be recorded in a design document. A graphical blueprint shown in Figure 6.4 is such a document and is one of many ways that a code supplier communicates with a community of potential consumers, using pictures instead of words when that helps to communicate effectively. This blueprint shows that the application involves a graph object composed of nodes that are further cross-linked internally.

A blueprint does not describe everything about a design. While blueprints are relatively good at representing the entities involved in a problem they are relatively poor at representing procedures; how entities change over time. Nor do they describe details such as how graphs will be implemented. They have nothing to do with how a user interface might look. They only describe the things that matter most to a potential client of this work. They represent a supplier's effort on a single page, at about the level of detail that would be appropriate to show to a board chairman, or to a computer-naive customer. Their primary use is presenting a design to other team members during the earliest design states and establishing a set of standard blueprinting icons for use later should these components appear in larger designs.

Decide Interface to Consumers

Once the design has been decomposed into entities and icons chosen for each, the next step is to decide what each entity should do. I find it helpful to adopt the consumer's point of view at this stage and record decisions in

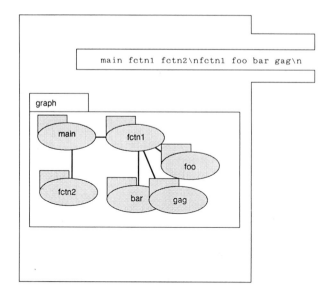

Figure 6.4. Blueprint for a software application. The focus during this initial phase is deciding what must be done, deferring the question of how to later in the implementation phase. The first step in designing a new class of object is to give it a name and a face; an icon that will represent objects of that class in other design documents. Shown here is the document describing an instance of Graph.

the form of code fragments that demonstrate how each component in the design would be used.

There are two ways to think about the code that parses the file into tokens and assembles these to build the graph object. Should the file (thought of as an object) compose characters into tokens and send them in messages to the graph? Or should the graph send messages to the file requesting it to deliver each new token? In principle, the choice is arbitrary. In practice, it is not because additional information is available. If the Graph and Node classes can be kept clean of all I/O code, they can in principle be reused in other applications, so parsing and all other I/O related matters are kept out of the reusable classes and on the file side of the boundary.

Just because it is convenient to think of the file as an object doesn't mean that it has to be implemented as one. Reading characters and breaking them into tokens is one of the things most base languages do quite well, so the consumer-supplier line will be drawn at the point where tokens have been collected into a buffer. A token could represent either the name of a node to be defined in the graph or the name of a node that is referenced by this one, depending on whether the token is first on a line or not, so the graph must support two different actions; the action of defining a new node, and the action of adding a reference to the most recently defined node. It seems logical that the graph should be responsible for defining new nodes, but should it also be responsible for creating references between nodes? Is adding a reference to a node graph's business, or a node's business?

This time the decision is really arbitrary since no I/O is involved. Therefore, we decide that the newly defined node, rather than the graph, will be responsible for managing its own references. The graph must somehow provide its consumer the id of each newly defined node so that he can direct messages at it

```
// Action to define a node named nodeName
definition = [graph defineNode:nodeName];

// Action to add a node to the reference list of node
[definition addReference:[graph addNode:nodeName]];
```

This code fragment is an example of another way of documenting design decisions, by writing samples that show how the consumer will use the class being designed.

This fragment has introduced three additional methods: defineNode: and addNode: for Graph and addReference: for Node. New nodes will be defined by requesting a graph to defineNode: with the name of the new node in the argument, nodeName. Nodes may be referenced before they are defined, so a different message, addNode:, is used to create them in the graph while marking them so that they can be distinguished from properly defined nodes. Both methods return the id of a node whose name matches nodeName, creating one by that name if it is not in the graph already.

These two lines of code pin down how nodes and graphs will be used by their consumer. Now let's switch to the supplier's side and design the two classes mentioned there. An easy way of capturing decisions about a class at this stage is to create a stub file for each one. During the design state the stub files describe only interfaces, not implementations. For example, the class name is described, but not the superclass, because inheritance is an implementation matter, not a design matter. Only method names appear in the file at this time, because these define the class's interface. The goal is to decide and record only what the objects must do, not how they will do it. The design stub for the Graph class just lists the messages used in the stub that shows how the consumer would use this class:

```
@implementation Graph ...
// Add a new node to the graph
- addNode:(char*)aNodeName { ... }

// Add a new node and mark it defined
- defineNode:(char*)aNodeName { ... }
```

And similarly for node's addReference method

```
@implementation Node
// Add aNode to my set of references
- addReference:aNode { ... }
```

That completes the protocol (the set of methods) used in building a graph, leaving the methods for printing the nodes that can be reached, and those that cannot, from a given starting node. Methods for printing the nodes that have been referenced but not defined will also be needed. A simple recursive printing loop cannot be used because graphs can loop back upon themselves and put the program in an infinite loop. But this can be solved by dividing the printing into two parts. The first part works like a community being infected by measles, starting with one member and then spreading to each neighbor, but only if the neighbor has not already been infected. Once the infection phase finishes, everyone that could be reached (or not reached) from the initial infected member can be determined from who has the measles.

This will be done with a mark method in each node. Nodes respond to mark by first determining whether they have been marked already, ignoring the message if so. Otherwise they mark themselves by setting a flag in an instance variable and send mark to each neighbor. An isMarked method is added also to allow the flag to be tested in the final printing loop.

```
@implementation Node { BOOL² isMarked; }
// If this node is unmarked, mark it and propagate mark to neighbors
- mark { }

// Reply whether this node is marked
- (BOOL)isMarked { }
```

Finally a way is needed to report nodes that were referenced but never defined. This can be handled by adding one more bit to indicate whether this node has received a define message, plus two methods to set and test this bit.

```
@implementation Node { BOOL isMarked, isDefined; }
- define { isDefined = YES; return self; }

- (BOOL)isDefined { return isDefined; }
```

These methods are not mentioned in the original example of the consumer's code because the example addressed only how graphs are built. Now a more involved example is needed to show how graphs can be marked and printed.

```
demoGraph() {
    id dependencyGraph, node;
    dependencyGraph = [Graph new];

    // Build a graph
    node = [dependencyGraph defineNode:"main"];
    [node addReference:[dependencyGraph addNode:"functionA"]];
```

²BOOL, and other symbols including STR, YES, and NO, are discussed in Appendix A. They are simple C extensions that are defined in a standard header file, objc.h. BOOL is a variable that holds a boolean value. It is implemented as typedef char BOOL. YES and NO are boolean values, implemented as #define YES (BOOL)1 and #define NO(BOOL)0. STR is the type of any variable used as a C string, implemented as typedef char *STR.

```
[node addReference:[dependencyGraph addNode:"functionB"]];
node = [dependencyGraph defineNode:"functionA"];
node = [dependencyGraph defineNode:"functionB"];
[node addReference:[dependencyGraph addNode:"functionA"]];

// Mark nodes reachable from "main"
[dependencyGraph mark:"main"];

//Print reachable nodes
for (sequence = [graph eachElement]; node = [sequence next];)
    if ([node isMarked]) printf(" reachable node=%s\en", [node str]);
}
```

Retrospective: Object-oriented Design

It is time to stop and comment on what has been going on. The design is now complete enough for coding to begin, but the feel of this design seems different. The greatest difference is that the solution domain and the problem domain both consist of the same entities, graphs and nodes, without the usual need to map problem domain concepts into data structures and procedures. Furthermore the usual concern with programming details is missing. For example, memory allocation has never been discussed even though this problem is replete with variable-length entities. The focus has been on what must be done, not how, leaving how for the implementation phase. Only the interfaces have been considered, and each one has been documented as soon as identified. A number of documents have been produced, each one aimed at the specific needs of several kinds of consumers.

1. Graphic documents have been produced for those who need only a general overview of the design.

2. Code samples have been produced that show how a consumer would use each class.

3. Stub files have been produced that show the class and method names of each class, thus defining the interfaces between that class and the rest of the system.

There has been no discussion of how graphs and nodes will be interfaced with the outside world. In particular, no thought has been given to how the input file is parsed, or to how the results will be formatted, because these matters are nearly always application specific and should never appear in code that is to be reused. Reusable classes should only provide hooks onto which external logic can hang application-specific printing logic.

Implementation Phase

The only object-oriented principle that has been applied until now is encapsulation; the aid to using an object-oriented system. Inheritance has not been mentioned because inheritance is an aid to building systems; an implementation issue, not a design issue. But now as implementors, both inheritance and encapsulation will be used because implementors are both consumers of a preexisting library of reusable Software-ICs and the supplier of new additions to the library.

Software-IC Library

A Software-IC library is an ordinary binary library. It may well contain conventional subroutines, but it primarily contains Software-ICs. The library is organized as a generalization-specialization hierarchy with generic classes at the root and specialized ones at the leaves. Each Software-IC is described in specification sheets that provide the highly compressed technical information that an expert needs to use a given component. Specification sheets for the major Software-ICs to be used here are provided in Appendix A.

These sheets are written for experts, not newcomers, and the background information to use them effectively will not be presented until Chapters 7 and 8. Until then you'll proceed as an apprentice hardware designer might, by following a veteran's advice. "If I were you I'd make the Graph class a subclass of Set, and Node a subclass of String."

That String[3] could be useful for handling named nodes is hardly surprising. But why Set? The catalog does indicate that a set is a kind of collection and graphs are certainly collections of nodes. Sets and graphs are also alike in that they must both reject duplicate entries. In this case two nodes are duplicates if their names are the same. Comparing two entries for identity must surely be application-dependent, so how could the Set supplier avoid wiring in assumptions that would be violated by most of his potential users?

Set's specification sheet (Appendix A) reveals that Sets have capabilities that make them almost ideal for the problem at hand. The Set supplier built in no assumption about how entries should be compared, since this is apt to vary between applications. For example, testing two strings for equality involves comparing each of their characters, but comparing other kinds of objects might need totally different logic. The Set supplier used dynamic binding to push this responsibility onto the entries themselves. Sets expect that every entry will support a method to determine whether the receiver and the argument are equal, in whatever manner is meaningful for that kind of receiver. Each entry must also support a hash method to compute an index that is used to reduce the number of comparisons, thus trading space to gain speed.

If you'll check the String specification sheet in Appendix A, you'll find that it already provides the needed isEqual: and hash methods, and that it tests equality by comparing characters one by one and it computes a hash code by computing an integer from the same characters. By building the Node class as a subclass of String, nodes will automatically inherit the logic needed to behave correctly as set members, and by building Graph as a subclass of Set, Graph will automatically inherit nearly everything it needs to manage named collections of nodes.

---

[3]The capitalization convention used to distinguish instance names from class names in source code is hard to adhere to stringently in straight narrative text, and is therefore relaxed. When the distinction between class and instance matters, it will be spelled out explicitly, as in "the class, Set" or "the set instance, aSet."

This seems like the right track, so its time to start coding. Begin by fleshing out the stub files (created during the design phase) with the inheritance decisions that have just been made. Graph will be a subclass of Set:

```
@implementation Graph:Set
- addNode:(char*)aCharPointer { ... }
- defineNode:(char*)aCharPointer { ... }
- mark:(char*)aNodeName { ... }
```

and Node will be a subclass of String

```
@implementation Node:String { BOOL isDefined, isMarked; }
- markAsDefined { ... }
- addReference:aNode { ... }
- mark { ... }
- (BOOL) isMarked { return isMarked; }
```

Nodes are first of all Strings, but they differ by having two additional boolean variables, isDefined and isMarked, and they recognize four additional methods. The method, markAsDefined, sets the variable isDefined. The mark method sets the variable, isMarked, and then propagates the mark to this node's neighbors. The isMarked method reports the status of the isMarked bit.

This is fine so far, but a major piece of the problem has been overlooked. No thought has been given to keeping track of references between nodes. This could be repaired by declaring an array of node identifiers for each node, but there is no way to decide how big an array is needed. Most nodes will reference only a few other nodes, but some might reference hundreds. Must hundreds of words be allocated in every node just to handle the few odd cases?

A solution is already at hand, because sets are a kind of collection and collections have elastic boundaries; they grow automatically to hold as much as you put in them. Each node can use a Set to keep track of the nodes it references, with the added benefit of automatically removing nodes that are referenced more than once by the same node. Repairing this oversight is merely a matter of adding one more instance variable, references, which identifies a set of nodes referenced from the current node. This allows the addReference: method to be fleshed out as follows, using the add: method documented in Set's specification sheet:

```
@implementation Node:String { BOOL isDefined, isMarked; id references; }
// Create a new node
+ new { return [[super new] initialize]; }

// Initialize the references variable with a set
- initialize { references = [Set new]; return self; }

// Add anotherNode to the set of nodes referenced from this node
- addReference:anotherNode { [references add:anotherNode]; return self; }
```

This overrides the inherited factory method, new, to ensure that the instance variable, references, is initialized with a new set whenever each new node is created. But this can be improved further because some nodes have no references at all, yet this implementation creates a set for each one. Recall that the main loop creates a node for each word in the input file but many of these nodes are immediately freed when they are filtered through the graph. It would be better to delay creating that set until it cannot be put off any longer. Therefore the new and initialize methods are discarded and replaced with

```
@implementation Node:String { BOOL isDefined, isMarked; id references; }
// Add anotherNode to the set of nodes referenced from this node
- addReference:anotherNode {
    if (references == nil) references = [Set new];
    [references add:anotherNode];
    return self;
}
```

That leaves the mark method. Testing whether the current node has been marked is no problem. But it needs to send a mark method to each of its references, and it is unclear how to do this. Set's specification sheet mentions no way of looping through its contents one by one. In fact it mentions that the elements in a set are organized by hashing, and this suggests that there is no well-defined order to loop over.

It would be unwise for set's supplier to publish some workaround for looping over set members for today's hashed implementation of the Set and risk loosing the opportunity to reimplement them in some other way in the future. This problem is not specific to sets, but applies to collections of all kinds. Therefore the solution is not special to sets, but to all collections. Set's specification sheet does not even mention the solution directly other than in this cryptic suggestion

To enumerate the members of a set, see Sequences. Or use one of the collection conversion routines documented in Collection. Sets enumerate their elements in random order.

The solution is not described in Set's specification sheets because these sheets always assume that the reader is aware of inheritance and inheritance can make capabilities described elsewhere available to the problem at hand. You are expected to also read and understand Collection's specification sheet, where several potential solutions are discussed. The following one is chosen:

```
// Mark myself and my dependents as reachable.
- mark {
    if (isMarked == YES) return nil;
    isMarked = YES;
    [references eachElementPerform:@selector(mark)];
    return self;
}
```

The eachElementPerform: message takes a selector as its argument. The receiver of this message can be any kind of collection, and it implements it by sending its argument (a selector) to each of its members in turn. The expression @selector(mark) is a way to obtain the selector code of the mark message at compile-time.

The Graph Class: Graph.m

The final implementation for the Graph class is remarkably brief. It has only three methods:

```
// Dependency Graph
#import "objc.h"
#import "Graph.h"
#import "Node.h"

@implementation Graph:Set {}
// Add a new node
- addNode:(STR)aCharPointer
    { return [self filter:[Node str:aCharPointer]]; }

// Add a new node and define it
- defineNode:(STR)aCharPointer
    { return [[self addNode:aCharPointer] define]; }

// Mark the given node (and all nodes referenced by it)
- mark:(STR)aNodeName
    { return [[self addNode:aNodeName] mark]; }
@end
```

The addNode: method creates a new node by using the node factory method, str: (inherited by Node from String), and then uses the method, filter: (inherited by Graph from Set) to discard the new Node if an older one by that name is already in the graph.

Node class: Node.m

The Node class is nearly as concise:

```
// Node in graph of named nodes
#import "objc.h"
#import "Node.h"
#import "Set.h"

@implementation Node:String
  { BOOL isDefined, isMarked; id references; }
// This node references anotherNode.
- addReference:anotherNode { extern id Set;
  if (references == nil) references = [Set new];
  [references add:anotherNode];
  return self;
}
```

```
// Mark myself and my dependents as reachable.
- mark { if (isMarked == YES) return nil;
  isMarked = YES;
  [references eachElementPerform:@selector(mark)];
  return self;
}
// Mark myself as defined
- define { isDefined = YES; return self; }

// Reply whether I'm reachable or defined
- (BOOL)isMarked { return isMarked; }
- (BOOL)isDefined { return isDefined; }
@end
```

Driver routine: mGraph.m

The Node and Graph classes are the potentially reusable parts of this application. What remains is application-specific code concerned with interfacing the reusable parts with the external world. The DependencyGraph program has at least three important interfaces:

1. Input: Reading the file that contains the symbolic representation of the graph.

2. Output: The file produced by the analysis can be thought of as a symbolic representation of the reachable, unreachable, and unreferenced nodes described by the input representation.

3. Command: The command line that triggers execution of the program will generally contain additional information that must also be parsed.

The following driver program implements the first two of the three interfaces:

```
#import "stdio.h"
#import "objc.h"
#import "Graph.h"
#import "Node.h"

id graph, lastNode;
extern STR root;
char yytext[BUFSIZ];    // lexical buffer

doGraph() { id sequence, node;

  //Build the graph by reading the input file
  graph = [Graph new];
  yyparse();

  // Mark all nodes reachable from root
  [[graph addNode:root] mark];

  // Print reachable nodes
  sequence = [graph eachElement];
  printf("Reachable from %s ", root);
  while (node = [sequence next])
    if ([node isMarked]) printf("%s ", [node str]);
  printf("\n");
```

```
// Print unreachable nodes
[sequence toFirst];
printf("Not reachable from %s: ", root);
while (node = [sequence next])
  if (![node isMarked]) printf("%s ", [node str]);
printf("\n");

// Print undefined nodes
[sequence toFirst];
printf("Undefined nodes: ");
while (node = [sequence next])
  if (![node isDefined]) printf("%s ", [node str]);
printf("\n");

[sequence free];
}
#define DefAction(yytext) lastNode = [graph defineNode:yytext]
#define RefAction(yytext) [lastNode addReference:[graph addNode:yytext]]
#include "Syntax.c"
```

The # define and # include statements (at the end), and the function call, yyparse() (near the beginning), implement the input side of this application's interface to the outside world. The file, Syntax.c, is shown in Appendix B. It contains C code that parses tokens from the input file and performs one of the macros, DefAction or RefAction, according to whether the token was first on a line. The printing statements implement the outgoing interface. The command line interface is implemented in an additional file (not shown), which parses command arguments and calls doGraph().

The Browser Revisted

Now that you have seen how an application can be built via paper specification sheets, lets see how a browser would help. While developing the Dependency Graph application, the browser helped retrieve information about the Node and Graph classes that would have been very difficult to get with a paper-based solution. For example, Figure 6.5 shows the browser being used to gather cross-referencing information concerning which methods, system wide, send the define message. Only one method does this, the defineNode: method in the Graph class. To learn this fact, the browser had to understand the call graph of the entire system—something you'd not want to try with paper. It's for this type of detail work that the browser proves its worth.

Figure 6.6 shows a second example of the browser being used to "flatten out" the inheritance hierarchy and to show a class as a whole. The browser knows each of Graph's superclasses and can draw a complete picture of the instance variables and methods, showing the Graph class as if it had been written without inheritance. Each instance variable and method is annotated on the right with the name of the class that it was inherited from enclosed in parentheses.

There is good news and bad news about the ability to view classes in this manner. The good news is that it is easy to see all the methods Graph defines

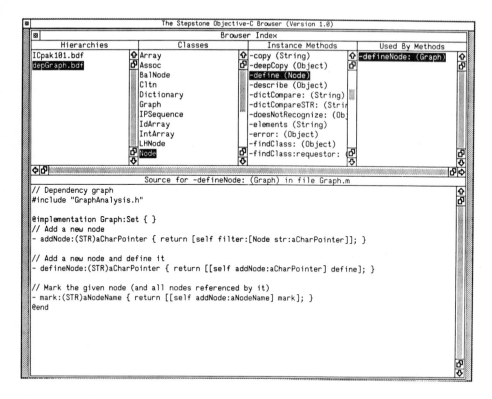

Figure 6.5. Cross-reference information for the define method in Node. This figure shows the browser being used to display which methods reference the define method from the Node class.

or inherits from its superclasses. The bad news, as discussed in Chapter 5, is that there is no indication as to which of these methods are meant to be private.

Of course, this is exactly the information that is contained in the specification sheets we used to develop the Dependency Graph application. That is why it's necessary to work with both the browser *and* the paper specification sheets when developing an application from reusable libraries.

Measuring Costs and Benefits

In spite of the apparent complexity of this application, the effort to build it was remarkably small. Only a small amount of code was written, and the difficult parts (the hashing and memory management logic, for example) were sidestepped completely by simply acquiring them from a library. The heart of this application was only 37 lines of code, and even this was built in such a way that it could be returned to the library. The application-specific

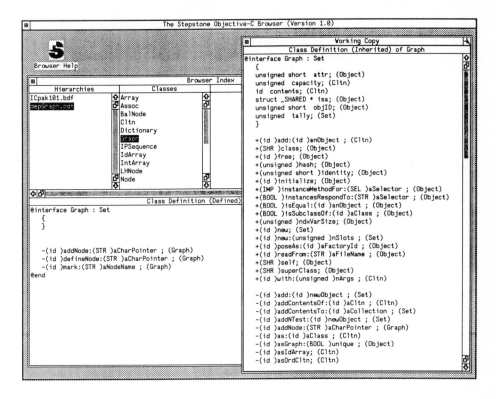

Figure 6.6. A flattened view of the Graph class. The figure shows two views of the method and instance variable definitions inside the Graph class side by side. To the left, only the methods defined in Graph class are shown. The right side shows the Graph class flattened by adding to the actual definition all the methods and instance variables that are inherited.

logic was neatly separated into three files which together contributed an additional 95 lines.

These benefits can be highly significant especially when applied to projects more complex than this one. But what price has been paid in achieving them? Glib statements like, "These benefits do not come for free, nor are they particularly expensive," are easy, but they hardly settle the real and valid concerns programmers have about the machine efficiency of object-oriented programming. The following section will answer these concerns by building the same application again, this time avoiding messaging, so that costs and benefits can be compared directly.

Some applications cannot be solved without dynamic binding, but this is not one of them. From the beginning we knew that graphs contain only nodes and that the dependency list of a node will only contain other nodes. But object-oriented code retains the flexibility to adjust should such a change be encountered downstream, for example, if requirements change over time. Machine efficiency could be improved by eliminating this flexibility. The question is, by how much? And how much development time would it cost to gain this improvement?

This section attempts to answer these questions. Of course, this is a tiny experiment on a laboratory specimen, not a clinical study of a commercially important system. But this is no excuse for ignoring data as it becomes available. The DependencyGraph application is small enough that redeveloping it using conventional programming techniques was an affordable option; a luxury that is seldom available in larger, albeit far more interesting, systems.

Although I'll describe the new implementation as hand coded, it was not actually developed from scratch. Instead, it was produced by making the following transformations to the object-oriented version:

1. A C include file was created to declare each of the data types as most C programmers would; i.e., as structures instead of objects.

2. The Graph and Node classes were transformed into two C files, graph.c and node.c. The symbol table logic (which did not appear before because it was acquired automatically from the library) was implemented in a separate file of C functions, set.c.

3. Each message expression was replaced with code written in conventional C language. In many cases message expressions were replaced with function calls, but in others statements were expanded inline.

4. Each occurrence of the type id was replaced with one of the data types declared in the include file.

5. C functions were written to handle operations that were previously inherited. For example, the methods of lower-level classes, like String and Object, were handled as a C programmer would, sometimes by implementing them inline and sometimes by calling a function.

The purpose of this mechanical translation was to reduce labor. Otherwise the goal was to duplicate the coding style I normally use in C. No special coding tricks were used to bias the results one way or the other, but obviously this is an uncontrolled aspect of this experiment. The source is shown in Appendix B. Overall, the effect of the transformation was to increase the interdependency between modules such that each class that impinges on another now states that dependence explicitly in the source rather than by leaving it to the messaging routine to resolve at run-time. Except for how binding is accomplished, the algorithms, parameter settings, and overall layout should be precisely identical.

Source Bulk Comparison

It was not possible to measure development effort or development costs directly. However, source bulk can be measured easily, and will have to serve as an estimate for development effort. Table 6.1 presents file sizes as reported by the word count (wc) program.

Table 6.1
Source Bulk

	Lines	Words	Bytes	Filename
	26	104	705	Node.m
	13	58	415	Graph.m
Object-oriented	37	131	1024	mDriver.m
	19	46	371	GraphAnalysis.h
	95	339	2515	Total
	88	272	1832	node.c
	16	60	385	graph.c
Hand-coded	36	125	991	cDriver.c
	112	460	3067	set.c
	52	160	1070	gr.h
	304	1077	7345	Total
	36	157	923	Syntax.m
Miscellaneous[1]	31	145	890	main.m
	67	302	1813	Total

[1]This category contains the parsing logic and startup routines that are shared between both implementations. These routines contain test scaffolding that has been excluded from the source bulk comparisons.

The object-oriented version was developed in 95 lines of code, and the conventional version 304 lines; a factor of 3.2 times larger (Figure 6.7). The set class accounted for most of the difference (112 lines), although the extra header file, gr.h, contributed 52 lines. The node class was also noticeably bulkier.

Qualitatively the hand-coded version took noticeably longer; days instead of hours, and was far more difficult to develop than even the bulk measurements suggest. Most of the design effort, and almost all of the testing and debugging, was spent developing the hashing algorithms in the set class (file set.c). Even though I started with a well-debugged object-oriented version, a number of minor bugs crept in and each one had to be chased down with the aid of debuggers and test harnesses. The object-oriented version worked correctly the first time I tried it, but the hand-coded version required substantial debugging to get right.

In recompiling this code for the 1990 edition of this book, an astonishing result was obtained: The object-oriented version of the sample application ran significantly *faster* (25%) than the hand-coded version!

It turned out that one of the substrate classes (String) had undergone a series of performance enhancements involving low-level string manipulation. As a consumer of the String class, the dependency graph application ac-

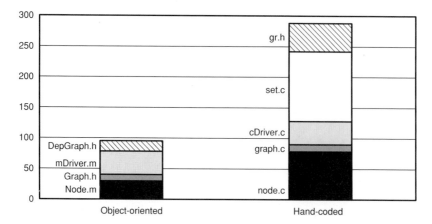

Figure 6.7. Source bulk (lines). Two solutions to the same programming problem, one using object-oriented programming and the other using conventional C coding practices. The conventional version required 3.0 times as many lines of code to develop. This is primarily because conventional programming does not allow code to be captured in libraries and reused to nearly as great a degree as does object-oriented programming.

quired all these performance enhancements automatically! The C version didn't, and ran slower as a result.

I then modified the hand-coded version to use the improved techniques. As expected, the hand-coded version once again outperformed the object-oriented version by the same margin as before, about 43%, primarily because of the extra overhead in message passing (as shown in the next chapter, this overhead is approximately 2.5 times that of a function call), and far slower than accessing memory directly with C expressions.

By changing how the String class performs to its specification, without changing the specification itself, the performance improvement was felt by consumers of string, without having to modify, *or even recompile* their code. This is another indication of the real benefit object-oriented technology brings to software developers through the ability to reuse code.

Binary Bulk Comparison

One way to measure memory utilization costs is to examine the sizes of each individual binary module. Notice that the files gr.h and Syntax.m no longer appear in Table 6.2 and Figure 6.8, because they have been incorporated into other files.

Roughly speaking, the sizes of the binary files tracks the source file sizes, although exceptions do appear. When the source sizes were comparable, as between mGraph and cGraph, noticeably tighter code was generated for the hand-coded version.

Table 6.2
Binary Bulk

	Text	Data	Bss[1]	Total	Filename
	256	288	8	552	Node.o
	200	240	8	448	Graph.o
Object-oriented	1016	312	8	1336	mDriver.o
	328	152	0	480	main.o
	1800	992	24	2816	Total
	440	8	0	448	node.o
	120	0	0	120	graph.o
Hand-coded	816	112	0	928	cDriver.o
	720	16	0	736	set.o
	312	154	0	466	main.o
	2408	290	0	2698	Total

[1]These figures are reported by the UNIX size program. The files were compiled for a Motorola 68020 CPU, using Sun Microsystems C compiler with the optimizer enabled. The text, data, and bss labels reflect instruction space, initialized data space, and uninitialized data space, respectively.

Execution Bulk Comparison

However when the total size of the two applications is compared, the hand-coded version is noticeably smaller (Table 6.3 and Figure 6.9).

The object-oriented version, at 74536 bytes, is significantly larger than the hand-coded one, at 7252 bytes; almost 10 times larger. This reflects additional code that was linked into the object-oriented version from the library.

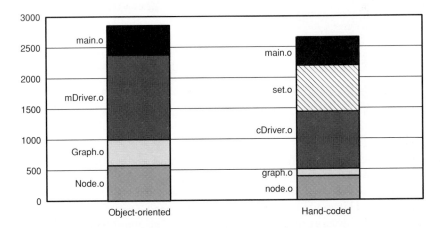

Figure 6.8. Binary bulk (text + data + bss). This compares the compiled sizes of the modules of the two solutions. It shows that object-oriented code is bulkier than conventional code by a very small margin.

Table 6.3
Execution Bulk

	Text	Data	Bss	Total	Filename
Object-oriented	36216	12504	25816	74536	mGraph
Hand-coded	4812	1416	1024	7252	cGraph

Part of the reason for the larger space requirements is that substrate classes provide more generality than is used by the application at hand. For example, the object-oriented version contains code for removing nodes, even though this application never uses this capability. However, Table 6.4 shows that the methods account for a relatively small fraction (20.6%) of the problem. Over one-third the space (38.9%) is functions referenced from code that might never be executed. For example, although this application never called the activation/passivation logic except during debugging (or the error handler for that matter), functions to support both occupy space in the application. The major space consumer (38.9%) is ordinary C functions that were linked into the application from references in low-level classes, particularly the Object class. The messaging routine is there also, but its size (384 bytes) is nearly negligible.

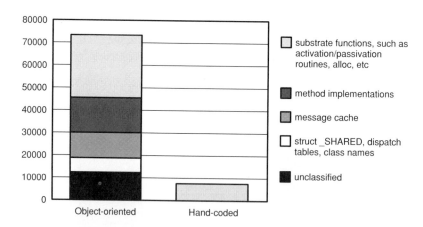

Figure 6.9. Execution bulk. When the two applications are linked to create a complete application, the hand-coded application is significantly smaller. This is primarily because inherited methods provided more generality than was needed in this application. This tends to make small applications larger than usual, but this may well be offset in large applications by the fact that inherited code is loaded only once and shared in many places, while conventional programming duplicates the functionality each time it is used.

Table 6.4
Space Allocation

38.9%	Functions (activation/passivation, object allocator, error handler)
20.6%	Methods
15.5%	Message cache
9.6%	struct __SHARED, dispatch tables, class names
15.4%	Unclassified

In other words, inheritance is no panacea. It can be costly in space for small applications that don't take full advantage of the library. However, most of the size penalty is incurred when the Object class is linked into the application, and size grows relatively slowly after that. Figure 6.10 and Figure 6.11 show that linking the Object class into an application brings in approximately 46K of supporting code.

With conventional programming, size grows linearly with functionality, since there is little opportunity to reuse code for multiple purposes. With inheritance, there is an initial price of approximately 46K as soon as the Object class is included, and size increases relatively slower thereafter. The 46K price resulted from including considerably more functionality into this application than was really needed. For example, Figure 6.12 shows a break down of the contents of the Object class.

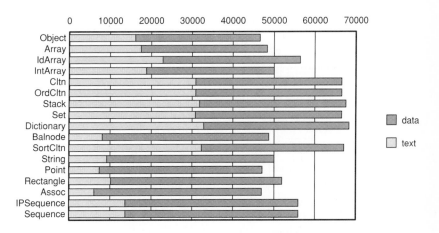

Figure 6.10. This figure shows how application size depends on which classes are included in the application. It was measured by building applications consisting of only a single class, plus any other classes and functions that it references. A 40K size penalty is incurred as soon as the Object class is loaded and size grows only slowly thereafter.

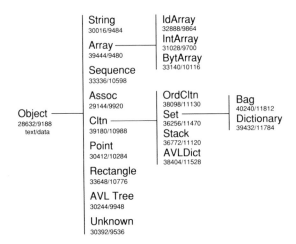

Figure 6.11. Linked size of one-class applications shown in a hierarchical format.

Execution Speed Comparison
The last measurement is execution speed, measured as the time to run each program on a standard test file of 1409 lines and 2767 words; approximately two words per line. The timing was done with the UNIX time program which reports the total elapsed time (real time), the time spent inside

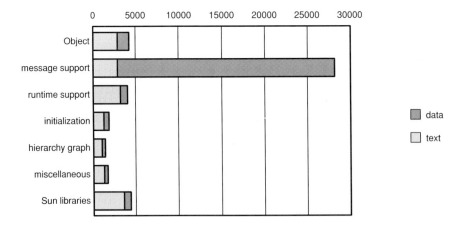

Figure 6.12. What's in the Object class? A breakdown of the 46K of space linked from the Object class. Note that the largest contributor is the memory used for message resolution caching.

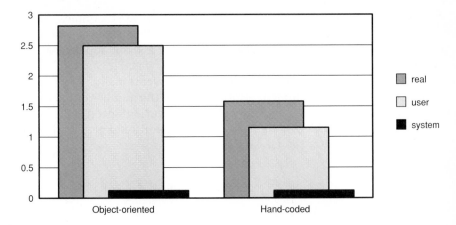

Figure 6.13. Execution time. The machine cost of object-oriented programming is measured by comparing the speed of the two applications for the same 1409 line test file.

the application (user), and the time spent inside the operating system on the application's behalf (system), in seconds (Table 6.5 and Figure 6.13):

This points out the advantage of hybrid languages over pure languages like Smalltalk-80. A large fraction of any application's execution time is spent on low-level operations like parsing bytes from the incoming text stream, computing hash values, comparing strings, and so forth. In a hybrid language these operations are done at full machine speed, while in Smalltalk they incur the full messaging treatment. Even though messaging is 2.5 times slower than a function call, the application does not run 2.5 slower because the application spends much of its time executing ordinary C code at full machine speed.

Table 6.5
Execution Time

	Real	User	System	Program
Object-oriented	2.8	2.5	0.1	mGraph
Hand-coded	1.6	1.2	0.1	cGraph

Summary

This chapter has described the information network that must surround any library that purports to be reusable. The network provides a number of resources for learning about large libraries of code, including software blueprints, catalogs, specification sheets, and tutorial documents, of which this book and particularly the chapters that follow, are examples. This chapter has also shown how the encapsulation and inheritance concepts of Chapters 4 and 5 are used in combination in building a small application. Finally, the cost and benefits of the new technology have been measured in comparison with the way such problems are solved conventionally. The benefit was a 320% savings in development effort (based on the number of lines of source code), and the cost was a 43% penalty in execution speed, and a memory penalty of 1028%. The last figure ignores an additional penalty in dynamic memory requirements, the isa link in every object.

| Seven

Foundation Classes

The syntax of a hybrid object-oriented language can be learned in minutes: one new type that identifies objects of any class, the message expression, and declarations for methods and classes. The semantics of messaging and inheritance are complex and take somewhat longer but even this is a matter of hours not days. But after these have been learned, one feels all dressed up with nowhere to go. The new syntax and semantics has only provided the language skills needed to begin learning a body of useful code.

Electronics engineers do not start out knowing how to apply complex chips in school. They do learn enough background to begin learning on their own, and knowledge of specific integrated circuits is acquired during years of hands-on experience. The preceding chapters only provided the know-how that is needed for the real work to begin; learning a library of useful classes.

Chapters 4 and 5 described the concepts used by suppliers and consumers of object-oriented functionality, and Chapter 6 provided some hands-on practice. But many threads are still dangling, because there has been no discussion of how the classes in the exercises really work. This chapter begins to set this right by introducing the most generic classes at the root of the inheritance hierarchy. It summarizes their capabilities and shows how they fit with other classes. It doesn't describe every method of every class since this is available in the specification sheets in Appendix A. Nor does it discuss every class in Stepstone's commercial class library, for this would require far too much space. Only a few classes are described, enough to show how larger libraries can be built and documented, yet small enough that you aren't swamped with detail.

The last section describes how the messager is implemented and presents figures for messaging speeds compared to function speeds. This section should be skipped on first reading, since it is primarily a reference for building messagers for other languages.

Overview

The classes shown in Figure 7.1 form the root of the inheritance hierarchy. They define how all objects will be implemented in computer memory. The Object class describes how named instance variables are managed for all classes, and the various kinds of Arrays add the ability to manage indexed instance variables of various types.

The Object class's position at the root of the inheritance tree means that all other classes inherit its capabilities. The Object class is an abstract class, which means that its contribution is not in the power of its instances, but in defining methods and variables that are used when inherited by subclasses. This doesn't mean that an abstract class cannot create instances because it can, just like ordinary nonabstract classes:

```
myObject = [Object new];
```

Array is abstract in an even more extreme sense. Although it can also create instances, the usefulness of doing so becomes increasingly questionable. Are

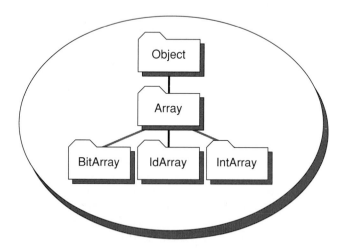

Figure 7.1. Foundation Library. These five classes describe how all objects will be implemented within computer memory. The object class specifies that objects will be implemented as a private part and a shared part, and the Array class adds the ability to manage indexed instance variables. The data type to be managed in these variables is determined by Array subclasses. Three of these are shown here.

these instances arrays of no type? Or arrays of any type? *Abstract* signals that the supplier didn't try to provide a clean answer for questions like these.

The Array class inherits the ability to manage named instance variables from the Object class, and adds the ability to manage indexed instance variables as well. Subclasses of Array support specific types in these variables. IntArrays manage indexed instance variables of type int, and IdArray manages indexed variables of type id. Other array subclasses, FloatArray, BitArray, and so forth, are not discussed because they can be added as needed by following the principles described for IntArray and IdArray.

Object Class

The abstraction to be implemented in the Object class has already been discussed in Chapter 5 and will only be reviewed here. The Object class defines the data structures and methods that implement objects as a private part that contains the object's variables and another part shared by all instances of that class. The parts are linked by a variable called the isa link, defining the memory model shown in Figure 7.2.

The Object class implements this memory model by declaring a sole instance variable, isa, that will be automatically inherited by all subclasses. The type of this variable is pointer-to-a-struct-__SHARED, where struct __SHARED declares the field layout of the shared structure.

```
@implementation Object { struct _SHARED *isa; }
```

The Object class defines a number of methods that provide access to an instance's private and shared data. It also defines a number of factory methods that will be inherited by the factory objects of all subclasses. For example, the method new is inherited by the factory object of every class. This provides a standard way to create instances of any class and it ensures that the isa variable is properly initialized whenever instances of any class are created.

Data Declarations

The Object class is strongly coupled to (1) the messager, which navigates the data structures defined here, and (2) code generation in the compiler, which allocates and initializes all shared structures. This section describes the information that the compiler captures at compile-time and preserves in the shared structure at run-time. A complete specification for the names and contents of each field is shown in Figure 7.3. The figure represents the entire structure produced by compiling the Graph class in Chapter 6, and then creating a single instance with [Graph new].

This figure represents the information that is preserved from compile-time to run-time and therefore the amount of functionality that can be implemented automatically by the substrate rather than manually by the programmer. It is not necessary to memorize the details of this figure. It is provided

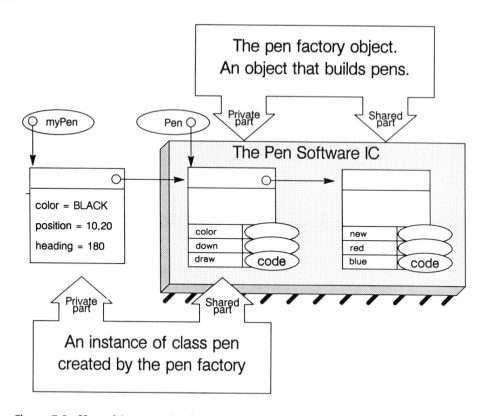

Figure 7.2. How objects are implemented in computer memory. Objects are identified by their address in memory. An object consists of a private part that contains its data, and a shared part that contains its code and additional data that is shared by all instances of the same class.

as a reference and to introduce fields that will be mentioned in the text that follows. You should keep the following points in mind:

1. Every object has a part that is private to itself and a part that it shares with all other instances of its class. The layout of the private part varies with the kind of object, subject to the restriction that the first word in its layout must identify its shared part. This pointer is called the isa link.

2. Every shared structure (struct __SHARED) is itself an object. Its first word contains an isa link to another struct __SHARED.

3. Every shared structure holds a dispatch table of methods, plus a link (cls-Super) to another structure from which it inherits additional methods.

4. Every shared structure records the size of its instances (clsSizInstance), encoded as the number of bytes required to store the named instance variables. Indexed instance variables are, of course, not included in this size since they are allocated at run-time.

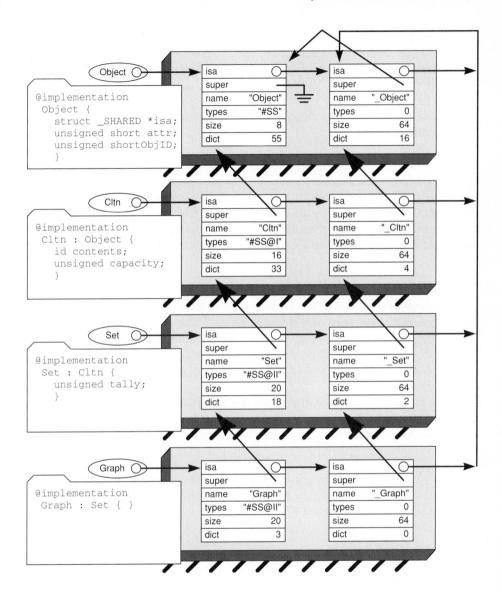

Figure 7.3. Memory model details. This shows the data structures declared by the Object class, and the way they are initialized by the compiler. It shows how source for the Object, Collection, Set, and Graph classes are transformed into C data initialization statements. The content of these structures is represented graphically, as compiled for the Motorola 68000.

5. Every shared structure also records the type of each instance variable, encoded as an array of characters, each character representing the type of consecutive named variables. This vector provides the information that drives power features, including automatic machinery that can convert objects into an ASCII representation for storage on files (passivation), and complementary machinery for reconstructing them again in memory (activation).

As an implementation detail, the dispatch tables are not declared within the shared structures, but are referenced through a pointer. This level of indirection avoids the need for the variable-length structures that would result if the tables were inside the shared structures. This makes it possible to implement factory variables (Smalltalk's class variables) as additional structure members, declared after the dispatch table pointer.

Allocation/Deallocation Methods

A basic responsibility of the Object class is establishing the machinery for creating and disposing of objects of any class. The shared part of its factory is inherited by all other factory objects, so the allocation machinery defined for the Object factory will be inherited by all other factory objects. Its factory method, new, implements the standard way of allocating objects of any class system-wide.

The instance methods of this class are inherited by all other kinds of objects, including factory objects. For example, the instance method, free, implements the standard way to deallocate objects of any class, system-wide.

+ **new**   To see how this single method works to create instances of (almost) any class in the system, follow the execution of the following statement using the data structures in Figure 7.3 as a guide:

```
myGraph = [Graph new];
```

The global variable, Graph, identifies the Graph factory as the receiver of the message, new. The messaging logic finds this message in one of the receiver's shared parts—the one that Graph inherited from the Object class. It dispatches control to the method, new, whose implementation is shown below.

```
+ new {
    id newObject;
    newObject = allocNilBlock(self->clsSizInstance, 0);
    newObject->isa = self;
    return newObject;
}
```

Table 7.1
Size of __PRIVATE for Graph

Member	Size (bytes)
struct __SHARED*isa	4
unsigned short attr	2
unsigned short objID	2
id contents	4
unsigned capacity	4
unsigned tally	4
sizeof(struct __PRIVATE)	20

Refer to Figure 7.3 in reading this code,[1] and keep in mind that the receiver of the message is always identified in the (hidden) formal argument, self. In this case the new message is being executed by the Graph factory object, so self points to the private part of the Graph factory. The method calls the allocNilBlock function to allocate a block of memory for the new object with an argument to specify how much memory to allocate. This argument is obtained from self->clsSizInstance. Use the figure to verify that this variable contains 20, the amount of memory needed to hold a graph instance. Table 7.1 is an example.

The method concludes by initializing the all-important isa variable and returning the id of the new object to the caller. What was until now an ordinary block of memory becomes a fully functional object, an instance of class Graph.

Notice how this outcome was influenced by (1) the object that acted upon the new message, and (2) information that was collected by the compiler and preserved in the factory object, Graph. The compiler built this object and initialized its instance variable, clsSizInstance, to indicate the physical size of its instances. The outcome of the message, [Graph new], was determined not by which class defined the implementation for message new, but by the object that performed the message.

The attr and objID variables are inherited by all objects from the Object class. The attr variable holds 16 bits, only two of which are used. The first indicates whether or not the instance has indexed instance variables, and the second indicates whether the instance's private data is allocated on the heap or the stack.

The objID variable is presently unused. It was added in anticipation of automatic garbage collection, where heap compaction might reposition ob-

---

[1]The code samples in this chapter have been rewritten to bring out essential features and hide unnecessary details. For example, allocNilBlock is named differently and called differently in the actual code. See the specification sheets for details such as this.

jects in memory. Since this would change the objects address, which many objects use as the basis for the hash code that Sets use to distinguish set members, this variable was to hold an address-independent hashing value.

Both are likely to be removed in future releases, assuming that we can isolate the impact on client classes.

- free   Since Objective-C does not currently provide automatic garbage collection, the programmer is responsible for deallocating objects once they are no longer needed. The id returned by the factory object may be used to access the new instance until the instance receives a free message. It then becomes illegal to access this instance further.

```
- free { isa = 0; deallocate(self); return nil; }
```

Zeroing the isa link before deallocating the object provides a kind of safety net to catch accesses to freed objects, should this occur before its memory has been allocated to some other object.

Dependency Graph Revisited

All Object class methods treat the object as a featureless block of memory. The new method creates a block of memory filled with nils, and free deallocates this block, without regard to its contents. This default behavior is often inappropriate, and so it is common to override one or both of these methods in subclasses.

The dependency graph application, for example, was designed as a UNIX process: it did its job quickly and promptly exited. Memory was cleared automatically, and garbage collection was a nonissue. But the Graph and Node classes implement algorithms that are in principle independent of this application, and could be used not only for finding wasted space in a program, but also for analyzing communication linkages between large cities, battlefield units, or supply/demand marketplaces. They are reusable, and should be usable in larger applications with little or no change.

This explains why the printing and parsing logic was kept in an application-specific module, mDriver.m, and not allowed to pollute the reusable code. Interface code is nearly always application-specific. The batch-oriented interface of Chapter 6 would be entirely inappropriate for tracking connectivity between battlefield units. Rapid and convenient change becomes crucial so the batch-oriented interface should be replaced with an interactive interface so that graphs could be maintained and edited online.

Techniques for building these interactive user interfaces will be discussed in Chapter 9. For now imagine that the Graph and Node classes have been provided with an interactive user interface and reused in an application that tracks connectivity between battlefield units. These units, and the communication linkages between them, come and go, and it is important to remove nodes and dependencies as well as to add them. It also becomes necessary to recover the memory each removed node occupied so that the application does not strangle from lack of memory after extended use. So long as there is no chance that an object is multiply referenced, it is straightforward to deallocate its memory. For example, the graph as a whole could be removed by giving it a custom-free method that knows that graphs contain nodes that can be freed safely when the graph is freed. The correctness of this method depends on the fact that nodes are referenced either from the graph or from other nodes in the graph, and that freeing a node does not free the nodes it references.

```
- free {
    [self freeContents];
    return [super free];
}
```

This implementation overrides the one that was inherited from the Object class and frees graphs by first freeing the member nodes and then freeing the receiver. Graphs inherit a suitable implementation for freeContents from Collection which simply sends free to each member of the graph. Then the graph deallocates itself using [super free] to access the inherited free method.

Utility Methods

The Object class defines an extensive repertoire of standard ways to determine things about objects of any class: Does it recognize this message? Is it an instance of this class? Of what class is it? And so on.

- class   This method replies the contents of the receiver's isa link. This quantity is variously known as the class of the receiver, the id of its factory object, and the memory address of its shared part. In Objective-C, these terms are synonymous.

```
- class { return (id)isa; }
```

- (STR)name   This method replies a pointer to a string of characters containing the name of the receiver's class. If the receiver is a factory object, the name begins with an underscore character.

```
- (STR)name { return isa->clsName; }
```

- (STR)str   This method replies a character string that describes this instance. Subclasses such as Strings override this to describe the bytes they contain. The default implementation provided here is

```
- (STR)str { return isa->clsName; }
```

- (int)size   The size method reports the number of elements in a collection or an array. It is defined in the object class to ensure that all other kinds of objects report their size as 0.

-(BOOL)isKindOf:(struct __SHARED *)aClass The isKindOf: message tests whether the receiver is an instance of aClass or any of its subclasses. For example, [someObject isKindOf:Object] is true for all objects, while [someObject isKindOf:Collection] is true for any kind of collection. The implementation is to compare aClass with each element in the chain of superclasses.

-(BOOL)isMemberOf:(struct __SHARED *)aClass This method reports whether the receiver is an instance of aClass itself; but not of its subclasses. For example, [someObject isMemberOf:Set] is true only if someObject is an instance of class Set, and false for an instance of Graph.

-(BOOL)respondsTo:(SEL)aSelector This method replies whether the receiver recognizes a specific message.

It is extremely important to keep in mind that these methods are inherited by objects of all classes. For example, use Figure 7.3 to determine what the following sequence of statements will do:

```
aGraph = [Graph new];
aSet = [Set new];
aCollection = [Collection new];
anObject = [Object new];
someObject = [[aGraph class] new];
if ([someObject isKindOf:Collection]) [someObject add:anObject];
printf("%s\n", [someObject name]);
```

Activation/Passivation
The methods discussed thus far demonstrate how compile-time information can be preserved and used at run-time to allow a single piece of code to serve many different uses. The single copy of the new and free methods serves not just the Object class, but all classes, except when the basic implementation is entirely inappropriate. The famous trade-off between generating more code and making it table-driven leans in favor of less code, more data. This section exploits this notion to its extreme and shows what can be done when the type of each variable is also available at run-time.

In every object's shared part is a field, clsTypes, that encodes the type of each of that object's named variables as a string of characters. The encoding is simple: i indicates int, s indicates short, @ indicates id, and so forth for all the C types that can be fully determined at compile-time. This encoding is a simple language for describing the type makeup of any contiguous block of memory, complete with provisions to handle complex types like structures and arrays. But its capabilities are finite, because it cannot deal with overlapped layouts (C unions) or noncontiguous memory (pointer constructs). This means the language cannot deal with the C types like int* (pointer to integer), primarily because there is no established convention for what this really means. How many integers? Terminated how?

This information provides the guidance system needed to automatically traverse any object's instance variables. This allows several powerful features to be implemented once and for all in the Object class, and inherited automatically system-wide. The simplest of these, a method called deepCopy, builds a duplicate of the receiver and all objects referenced from it, by traversing the graph of object references rooted on the receiver. But the power of these generic methods is most vivid in the readFrom: and storeOn: methods that together implement a capability known as activation/passivation:

Passivation builds a symbolic representation of any object as a file of characters.

Activation reconstructs an object from its symbolic representation.

The activation/passivation pair provides a way of moving arbitrary objects across computer addressing barriers (computing barriers). Passivation converts a graph of objects as they exist in dynamic program memory to a symbolic representation in a file, and activation does the inverse. These capabilities are automatically inherited by all objects so the feature is sometimes called automatic I/O or the filer mechanism.

For example, even though activation/passivation was not considered when the Graph and Node classes were developed, these classes inherit this ability without further attention by the programmer. The single statement

```
[graph storeOn:"aFileName"];
```

produces a file that represents the data content of the graph, sufficient that the object can be automatically regenerated in memory by the complementary activation message

```
graph = [Graph readFrom:"aFileName"];
```

The symbolic form is a file of records, one object per record. Object identifiers are encoded as record numbers, with other C types printed in a standard representation. The following sample was produced by the graph instance formed by running the sample input in Chapter 6:

```
#AsciiFiler i3
0 #Graph a2 i40 i10
40 #IdArray i40 $0 a3 a0 a4 a0 a0 a0 a0 a0 a0 a0 a0 a0 a0 a0 ...
10 #Node i9 i9 *9"terminate cl cl a13
11 #Node i10 i10 *10"initialize cl cl a14
8 #Node i7 i7 *7"compute cl cl a15
15 #Node i14 i14 *14"closeInputFile c0 cl a0
16 #Node i15 i15 *15"closeOutputFile c0 c1 a0
11 #Node il0 il0 *10"phaseThree cl c0 a16
5 #Node i4 i4 *4"main cl cl a17
9 #Node i8 i8 *8"phaseTwo cl cl a18
14 #Node i13 i13 *13"openInputFile c0 cl a0
9 #Node i8 i8 *8"phaseOne cl cl a0
0 #Set a19 i20 i2
```

```
0 #Set  a20 i20 i1
0 #Set  a21 i20 i2
0 #Set  a22 i20 i2
0 #Set  a23 i20 i3
0 #Set  a24 i20 i1
20 #IdArray  i20 $0 a0 a0 a0 a0 a0 a0 a0 a0 a0 a0 a0 a0 a0 a0 a0 ...
20 #IdArray  i20 $0 a0 a0 a0 a0 a0 a0 a0 a0 a0 a0 a0 a11 a0 a0 a0 ...
20 #IdArray  i20 $0 a0 a10 a0 a0 a0 a0 a0 a0 a0 a0 a0 a0 a0 a0 a0 ...
20 #IdArray  i20 $0 a0 a0 a0 a0 a0 a0 a0 a0 a0 a0 a0 a11 a0 a0 a0 ...
20 #IdArray  i20 $0 a3 a0 a4 a0 a0 a0 a0 a0 a0 a0 a0 a0 a0 a0 a5 ...
20 #IdArray  i20 $0 a0 a0 a0 a0 a0 a0 a0 a0 a0 a0 a0 a0 a0 a0 a0  ...
```

Passivation centers around an object that serves as a file table of contents. First it is initialized with the id of the starting object. Thereafter it sequences through its members, commanding each member that has not yet been processed to passivate itself to the file. The passivation logic uses the clsTypes information to determine how to deal with each instance variable, and the table of contents to determine the record number of any object that is referenced by the object that is currently being processed. Some references will be backward references to objects that have already been written, so their record number is known immediately. Others are forward references to objects that have not yet been written, so the table of contents simply assigns them a new record number and enrolls them as members so that they will be written once the writing process reaches this record number.

Notice that the passivation process saves only the private part of each object. The shared part is handled by writing the name of the class into the file. There would be no great conceptual difficulty to write the shared part into the file as well, perhaps even encoding methods as source to make the saved file machine independent. I decided against this, since it is usually simpler to just link shared information into each program in advance.

The activation/passivation machinery provides an automated way to convert arbitrary objects to a symbolic representation that can be stored in files, and an inverse transformation to regenerate objects given the symbolic representation. The symbolic representation can be transmitted between different processes, even those running on different machines. It allows objects to be stored indefinitely, in files or in databases, and reconstructed in memory later, and it is always available without foresight by the programmer. It is often used in debugging, because it can be aimed at absolutely any object to produce a readable symbolic representation of that object.

The machine-oriented flavor of the passivation format was determined by its heavy use in the compiler, but the format can be changed by simply replacing the passivation/activation routines. For example, it is possible for Objective-C programs to passivate objects in a format that Smalltalk's activation logic understands, and vice-versa. This creates some truly interesting possibilities that were alluded to briefly in Chapter 3. Objective-C programs coexist happily with most mainframe applications, including large scientific and commercial databases. These are often written in FORTRAN or COBOL, and they hide immensely valuable, often irreplaceable information inside some truly atrocious user interfaces. This information can usually be accessed from Objective-C, where it can be converted to objects of various classes and then passivated into a format that can be activated on a Smalltalk-80 system. This creates a bridge; the opportunity to choose the best of either computing world in routine scientific or commercial computing.

Comparing

The collection classes, particularly the Set class, assume that all members can rank themselves with respect to other members of the collection. Three basic comparison procedures are needed; compare:, isEqual:, and hash. These methods must behave consistently with each other and must therefore be reimplemented in parallel. If one is changed in a subclass, each of them should be changed to match.

In effect, Set has imposed a requirement on all classes system-wide, but one that cannot be met by providing a default implementation in the Object class. Comparing cannot be defined generically, because there is simply no general rule by which arbitrary things can be compared sensibly. This problem will recur time and again. The supplier of some generic class needs to enforce and document semantics for a set of messages, but lacks enough information to provide a meaningful default implementation. The convention in such cases is to document the required semantics and to provide a default implementation that merely generates an error message. The message warns that a subclass should have, but failed to, replace the implementation with a meaningful one. For example, although the semantics of these three messages are documented below, the implementation is to generate a subclassResponsibility error message as shown here:

```
- (int)hash { return [self subclassResponsibility]; }
```

- (int)hash   This method replies an integer whose value must be the same for all objects that reply YES to isEqual:. Collisions, or nonidentical objects that return identical hash values, are inevitable and are handled by the classes that use hashing. This method is used by classes like Set to spread different objects across a hashing arena, yet send identical objects to a consistent location. The search is refined from there by comparing each object in the collision pool via isEqual:.

- (BOOL)isEqual:anObject   This method replies YES if the receiver is equal to the argument.

- (int)compare:anotherObject   This method replies an integer less than, equal to, or greater than zero according to whether the receiver is less than, equal to, or greater than anotherObject.

- **(BOOL)isSame:anObject**   This method tests whether the receiver is identical to anObject (i.e., whether they are precisely the same object). The default implementation, return self == anObject, is never overridden.

- **(BOOL)notEqual:anObject**   This is the complement of isEqual:.

- **(BOOL)notSame:anObject**   This is the complement of isSame:.

Computed Selectors

Computed selectors are selector codes held in C variables, as opposed to being compiled directly into message expressions. They provide a way for selectors to be read from files or held in C data structures, and then accessed in message expressions. The compiler provides a special syntax, @selector(...), for initializing such variables, and the library provides dynamic functions that allow arbitrary C strings to be converted to selector codes.[2]

- **perform:(SEL)aSelector**   This method is implemented as __msg(self, aSelector).

- **perform:(SEL)aSelector with:anObject**   This method is implemented as __msg(self, aSelector, anObject).

- **perform:(SEL)aSelector with:firstObject with:secondObject**   This method is implemented as __msg(self, aSelector, firstObject, secondObject).

Error Handling

The conventional way for an object to signal an error is to send itself the message error:.

```
if (condition) return [self error:"cannot handle this"];
```

This prints a message describing the problem and terminates the program, so the return statement will never be executed. This default behavior is modifiable through techniques that are described in Appendix A.

The first argument may contain format control as documented for the C library function, printf. For example,

```
if (min > max)
    return [self error:"impossible condition: min=%d max=%d", min, max];
```

---

[2]The selector argument should be a selector code computed at compile-time by the @selector (...) feature of the compiler. However, if this conversion is not done, the substrate will perform it automatically. This is far slower because it involves searching the selector code tables dynamically.

The other methods are implemented in terms of error:.

- error:(STR)aCStr, ...;   This is the system-wide error handler. It signifies that a nonrecoverable error condition has been encountered elsewhere, and the receiver should do whatever it can to recover or terminate. The default implementation is to print an error message, print the stack of messages that led to the problem, and exit. This default is often overridden as described in Appendix A to allow the application to recover and continue.

- subclassResponsibility   The conventional way for an abstract superclass to insist that all subclasses provide a custom implementation for a method is to declare that method, and implement it as return [self subclassResponsibility]. If the method is (incorrectly) inherited by a subclass, a special error will be generated.

- doesNotRecognize:(STR)aMessage   The messager reports that the receiver did not recognize aMessage by sending doesNotRecognize: to the receiver. The default implementation is to send error: to terminate the process. Notice that overriding this message produces a class that recognizes all messages. This can be used to build a simple scheme for working with nonresident objects. For example,

```
@implementation ShadowObject:Object { id realObject; STR fileName; }
- doesNotRecognize:(SELECTOR)aMessage {
    if (realObject == nil) realObject = [ShadowObject readFrom:fileName];
    return [realObject perform:aMessage];
}
```

The instances of class ShadowObject are stubs that stand in for larger objects that normally reside on disk. If a shadowObject is ever accessed, it reads the real object into memory and thereafter retransmits all messages to the real object.

Array Classes

There are an arbitrary number of Array classes. All are subclasses of the abstract class, Array, which provides the ability to support indexed instance variables to the capabilities inherited from Object. Indexed variables are like named instance variables except that they are accessed by integer offsets instead of names. They occupy memory immediately after the object's named variables. Each subclass handles a different C type in these slots; IntArray holds ints, IdArray holds identifiers, and so on. All arrays inherit a single named instance variable, capacity, which records the number of indexed slots owned by each instance.

Although array factories do inherit the method, new, it makes little sense to allocate an array with no indexed instance variables. More commonly, the

message new: is used with an argument to indicate how many indexed variables are needed. The capacity of an array instance is determined when that
instance is created, so different instances can have different capacities. It is
not straightforward to increase the capacity of an array instance, because
this involves relocating it in memory and changing its id. This has drastic
consequences, since every reference to the array must be tracked down and
updated with the new address. This makes them sufficiently inconvenient
to work with that they are best regarded as low-level building blocks, used
primarily to build higher level classes that can hide this difficulty from user
code. For example, Chapter 8 will show how this is done in the Collection
classes.

Each array subclass provides a set of methods for accessing instance variables. For example, IdArray provides at: and at:put: methods for reading
and writing indexed variables of type id, and IntArray provides intAt: and
intAt:put: methods that read and write ints. These messages provide amenities to protect the conceptual integrity of the array abstraction, such as
checking that array offsets are valid.

However useful these protections may be, there are times when they must
be bypassed. Arrays are low-level classes that are often used to build higher
level classes like the Collection classes described in the next chapter. These
system-level classes could have been implemented using raw data structures
of the base language, thus bypassing Arrays altogether. This would simplify
common operations, but it would seriously complicate complex actions like
activation and passivation.

The pragmatic appeal of a hybrid programming language is that the safeguards can be bypassed by falling back on conventional programming techniques to penetrate the encapsulation when expedient. The following macro
definitions are an example of such an expedient. These macros are defined in
a header file that can be included by any file that needs to gain uncontrolled
and speedy access to an array's indexed instance variables:

```
#define IVCONTENTS(obj) ((STR)[(((id)obj) elements])
#define IVAFTER(obj) ((STR)(((STR)obj) + ((id)obj)->isa->clsSizInstance))
#define IV(obj) ((((id)obj)->attr&OBJC$M_HASIDXVARS)?IVAFTER(obj):IVCONTENTS(obj))
```

These macros are valid on any object identifier. They compute the address
just past the object's named variables by referring to the size information in
that object's shared part: obj->isa->clsSizInstance. For example,

```
STR p = IV(anObject);
```

initializes p with the address of the first indexed instance variable of anObject, allowing its indexed variables to be accessed at full machine speeds by
using pointer arithmetic. The technique requires care, because all safeguards
have been bypassed except the extremely limited ones available to any C
programmer. But it does provide a way of building exceedingly fast systems

that still benefit from object-oriented safeguards throughout most of their code. The sections that have been optimized in this way can always be automatically located with string search tools.

IntArray Class

IntArrays hold a fixed number of C integers. As for all arrays, it is inconvenient to increase an IntArray's capacity. In this sense, they are low-level building blocks out of which more congenial and powerful classes are constructed. For example, an OrderedCollection of IntArrays could be the starting point for building a spreadsheet.

IdArray Class

IdArrays are arrays whose indexed instance variables are of type id. They are used to build other classes that manage collections of objects, since they provide a way to manage arbitrary numbers of object identifiers. They are seldom used directly, because extending their capacity requires copying them to a new location in memory, thus changing their id (see the Collection classes in Chapter 8 for examples of how this limitation is controlled).

Messager

This section describes how the messager implements dynamic binding and presents some measurements on messaging speed in relation to the speed of calling a simple C function. Most readers should skip this section. The primary information of general interest is that messaging can be implemented in various ways to make various trade-offs of space versus time, and that the overhead ranges from 2 to 2.5 times that of a simple function call.

Consider any message expression, such as the unary expression:

```
if ([node isMarked]) ...
```

This statement compiles into a function call on the messager,[3] an ordinary C function named __msg. The message selector, isMarked, is compiled to reference a table slot containing the coded value of the isMarked selector.[4]

```
if (_msg(node, /*isMarked*/selectorCodeTable[48])) ...
```

[3]Message expressions of the form [super ...] compile into calls on a separate messager, __msgSuper. The two messagers are identical except for how they handle their arguments. In __msgSuper, the receiver argument references a shared part in which the selector search is to begin, and the object to receive that message is obtained from the caller's stack frame.

[4]For brevity, I have removed the typecast that informs C that this message returns a boolean instead of an object id. I have also omitted the compile-time logic involved in translating the selector name, isMarked, into the selector code stored in selectorCodeTable[48].

When C executes a function call such as this one, it pushes any arguments and the return address onto the call stack and branches to the function's entry point. In this case there are two arguments, the id of the receiver and the coded selector (the 48th value in the selectorCodeTable array):

```
id _msg(receiver, selector)
    id receiver;
    SEL selector;
{
    ...
}
```

First the messager provides several convenience features; printing message traces for debugging, intercepting messages to freed objects or nonsense addresses so that they do not crash the system, and so forth. Then the address of the C function that implements the selector for this receiver (the implementation) is determined as follows (see Figure 7.4):

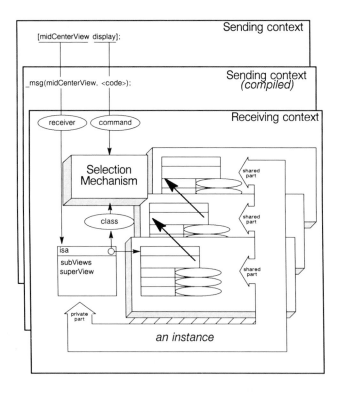

Figure 7.4. The messager provides the selection mechanism whereby an object decides how to implement its commands. The selection mechanism can be implemented in many ways.

1. The address of the receiver's shared part is obtained from the isa variable; e.g., receiver->isa. This quantity will be called the class code in what follows (it is really the address of the receiver's shared part).

2. The class and selector codes are used to determine the implementation; the address of the C function that implements this selector for this kind of object. Several ways of doing this will be described.

3. Control is transferred directly to the implementation address without changing the stack.

When control was passed to the messager, the caller allocated a new stack frame and pushed the receiver, the selector code, the arguments, and the return address onto it. This information is exactly where the target method expects it to be, if the messager could simply cover its tracks and jump directly to the target method. This is not possible in C because a global goto operation is needed, whereas C only provides a function call (which changes the stack). The global goto can be accomplished, however, by expressing it as a function call in C (e.g., JMP(implementation)) and turning the function call instruction (JSR) into a goto instruction (JMP) by editing the C compiler's output file. The overhead of a function call is paid only once when entering the messager, and transferring control to the implementation involves a negligibly small overhead—the time to execute a simple jump instruction.

The second step is the heart of the selection mechanism and central to the whole dynamic binding machinery. This step transforms a class/selector pair to produce a single output, the address of the implementation to be used in step three. This transformation can be implemented in several ways that make various trade-offs between space and time.

The slowest technique is the most economical in space because it uses no information beyond that held in the Software-ICs. The implementation for each message is determined by searching for the selector in the dispatch tables of the linked list of shared structures. Although there is no space overhead, the time overhead is not only substantial, it is also proportional to depth of inheritance. This is usually intolerable because it can inhibit speed-conscious developers from using this powerful tool.

The fastest technique is shown in Figure 7.5. It involves using additional space attached in each shared structure. Each table lists the implementation of each of the messages recognized by this kind of object, indexed by the selector code. This table reduces all three steps to a single line of code:

```
JMP(receiver->isa->selectorTable[selector]);
```

This scheme is exceedingly fast, although slower than a simple function call by the time needed to execute the statement shown above. If the time to call an (empty) function of a single argument is 1.0, the time to send a unary message with this technique is slightly less than 2.0. In other words, about half the messaging time is spent passing control to the messager, and about that much again is spent executing the selection logic. However, the space

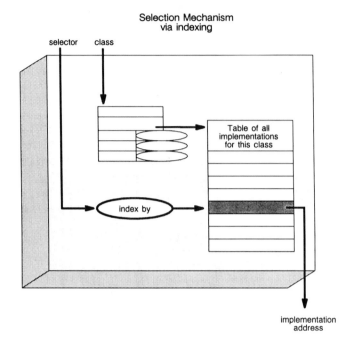

Figure 7.5. Messaging implemented via indexing. The fastest implementations of messaging trades space to gain speed by holding a fully expanded table in the shared part of every instance containing all messages that might be sent to that instance, indexed by the message selector.

required by those tables can be large enough to be troublesome. For example, an application with 20 classes and 200 different selectors would tie up 4000 words in these tables, not to mention the space in the original dispatch tables (which are no longer used).

Between these extremes is the compromise implementation shown in Figure 7.6. This solution allocates a fixed amount of space to a message cache that is shared by all classes. The cache is a table of two fields, one containing a marker that encodes a class/selector pair, and the other the implementation address for that class/selector combination. The slots are indexed by hashing the class and selector codes, a very fast operation. To find the implementation address for a given class and selector, the messager computes and hashes the class and selector codes to produce a cache index, verifies that the cache slot at this index is valid for this class and selector by examining the marker stored in that slot of the cache, and if so branches directly to the implementation address held in that slot. If the marker is invalid, the cache slot must first be refreshed by using the exhaustive search algorithm.

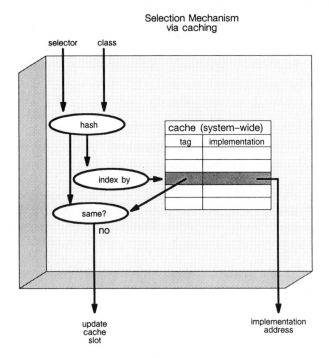

Figure 7.6. Messaging implemented via caching. Caching strikes a compromise between space and speed by dedicating a fixed amount of space to a global cache. A cache slot holds an implementation address and a marker that signifies which class and selector pair yield that implementation. When the marker does not agree with the current class/selector pair, the cache slot must be recomputed, for example, by reverting to a full search.

    The performance of this scheme is remarkably good, given that the logic is still written in C for portability and retains a number of convenience features for printing message traces and trapping messages to freed objects, strange addresses, and the like. The time to send a message with a valid cache is about 2.5 times greater than the overhead of a C function call, and the cache hit ratio for typical applications is over 95%.

    Even faster schemes are possible, but they generally involve eliminating the messager in favor of expanding the selection logic at the call site. I've never gone to this extreme because this would eliminate the possibility of amenities like message tracing. For example, the fastest schemes eliminate the messaging function by having the compiler generate the entire selection mechanism inline, like this:

```
(*receiver->isa->selectorTable[selector])(receiver);
```

This removes the time needed to push the selector onto the stack and other inefficiencies associated with saving/restoring registers in the messager.

Summary

The Foundation category contains the Object and Array classes. They establish the fundamental abstraction of an object-oriented system by defining how the object concept is mapped onto computers. The Object class determines how the named instance variables of any object are managed in memory, and the Array classes modify this abstraction to add support for indexed instance variables.

Several implementations of messaging have been presented to show how messaging speed is not absolute but depends on how much space can be allocated to messaging. Some implementations are nearly as fast as function calls but use large amounts of memory. Some use no additional memory but are considerably slower. Caching provides a compromise, a middle of the road solution that allows a bound to be set on both space and time.

| Eight

Collection Classes

his chapter describes the important group of classes that manage collections of various kinds, particularly two collection classes that have been used time after time in this book—Set and OrderedCollection. Every single method in every class will not be covered here since the details are available in the specification sheets in Appendix A.

The primary emphasis, however, will be on demonstrating how a hybrid object-oriented language can be used to develop code that must be simultaneously reusable and highly machine-efficient. Message-based encapsulation is a tool, not a panacea, and there are times when it should be laid aside in favor of conventional programming techniques. Although the collection classes could certainly be developed without violating the encapsulation dogma in any way, it is useful to do so here to demonstrate how the bridge between object-oriented programming and conventional pointer-based programming is crossed in practical work.

| Collections

The common property of all collections is binding arbitrary numbers of member items into units that can be dealt with as a whole. Almost anything that has a varying number of discernible parts is a collection, including not only high-level application domain concepts like FileFolder, AccountsReceivable, GradeBook, or SchoolBus, but also implementation domain concepts like List, Stack, Queue, SymbolTable, and Dictionary. These collections can be built in turn on lower level abstractions that correspond to familiar data structures like linked lists, trees, and arrays.

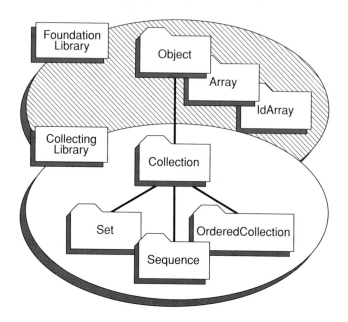

Figure 8.1 Collection library. The collections to be described in this chapter.

Ultimately, at the root of this tree of abstractions is the most generic notion of Collection, the bare concept independent of how collecting might be implemented on a computer. All collections share certain properties yet differ in others. For example, all collections allow members to be added without limit, stretching as needed to accommodate the number that have actually been added. All collections can report how many members they contain, and they all support a property called enumeration, which means to loop over the members one by one. Collections also provide for removing elements and for reporting whether the collection contains a member that matches various externally supplied criteria.

Figure 8.1 shows the collections to be discussed in this chapter. An abstract class, Collection, defines a standard message interface that will be preserved across all collections. For example, collections of all kinds will recognize add:anObject to mean add an object into the collection, and remove:anObject to mean remove this object.

Each specific kind of collection will have its own specific differences. OrderedCollections maintain their members in the order they were originally added, while Sets discard duplicate additions and maintain their members in a random, hashed, sequence. This makes OrderedCollections useful for maintaining linear sequences of things, while Sets are most useful for building structures in which things can be looked up by name very quickly like SymbolTables, Dictionaries, and PasswordFiles. Collections always bear some basic similarities to each other, but there can be fundamental differences also.

For example, it is reasonable to speak of the third element in an OrderedCollection, but not in a Set. Those collections that maintain an ordering of their members may support additional methods such as firstElement and lastElement to provide their first and last members and sometimes at: to access specific members, but these methods will not be available for collections that do not maintain such an ordering, like Set.

Collection Class

All collections must expand on demand to handle arbitrary numbers of other objects. This ability was missing in the IdArray class, since the maximum capacity of an array must be provided when each array is created, and collections must avoid this trait. Any good book on data structure design will suggest a wealth of structures that serve for this. Singly or doubly linked lists are a definite possibility, as are arrays, trees, etc. The IdArray class has already been discussed, so it will be used throughout this chapter.

Collection will be a subclass of Object with two additional variables, contents, that identifies whatever subsidiary data structure is chosen, and capacity, that identifies the size of the subsidiary data structure:

```
@implementation Collection: object {
    id contents;
    unsigned capacity;
}
```

Declaring the contents variable at this level does not commit the subclasses as to the kind of object that will be referenced there. The two subclasses discussed in this chapter will be based on IdArrays, but this will not always be the case. A class as generic as Collection must not commit its subclasses to a specific implementation strategy and must make it possible to define subclasses that cannot be implementable with an array-oriented data structure. A collection that keeps its members in alphabetical order might, for example, be best implemented as a height-balanced tree instead of an array.

In practice, however, this requirement is balanced by other needs. For example, some of the Collection class methods to be presented may seem to violate this requirement, sending messages that could only work for IdArrays. These methods are written to assume the implementation strategy used by most of its subclasses so that they can share a single copy of these methods, and the invalid methods are simply overridden in those subclasses that do not use the strategy that Collection assumes.

Allocation/Deallocation

Collections inherit the capabilities of their superclass, Object, including even complicated ones like activation/passivation. Collection's specification sheet (given in Appendix A) describes three factory methods for creating a new instance of a collection, including one method, new, which was also defined in Collection's superclass Object. It is worth a moment to consider why the method new had to be overridden in Collection, and what impact the way it is implemented has on collections that inherit from it.

We have talked about the advantages of polymorphism earlier in this book. It is very important that a supplier of a class respect the intended meaning of methods that might be found in its superclasses. For example, suppose that a subclass of Collection, such as OrderedCollection, is created by:

```
myCollection = [OrderedCollection new];
```

It is reasonable for the consumer of OrderedCollection to expect that messages to myCollection will work correctly, even if the collection is empty. Unless the method, new, has been explicitly overridden in either the Collection class or the OrderedCollection class, the instantiation logic described in the previous chapter will simply allocate a block of memory long enough to hold the named instance variables, zero it, initialize its isa link, and return its address as the id of the new object. The contents variable of this block will contain zero, not an IdArray, and if this is not attended to by every method that accesses this variable, a crash can result.

The collections to be discussed here allocate space for storing members when they are created. As a consumer, you will have the choice of using a default size, or specifying a starting size, based on your knowledge of how the collection will be used. Either way, the use of the method new does what you would expect from your knowledge of the method new in Object, it creates a ready-to-use instance of the collection class you specified.

+ **new**   The Collection class overrides the new method inherited from its superclass Object to provide a consumer with a collection of default size. It creates the named instance variables, including the isa link, by invoking the new method inherited from its superclass. It then delegates the responsibility for initializing its instance variables to a method named initialize. Finally, it returns the address of the new collection.

```
+ new {
    return [ [super new] initialize ];
    }

- initialize {
    contents = [IdArray new];
    capacity = [contents size];
    return self;
    }
```

+ **new:(unsigned)nElements**   If the number of members in a collection is known in advance, some overhead can be saved by allocating enough space for them all in advance. This is allowed for in the special method, new:nElements, whose argument describes how much space should be allocated. It works just like the new method, except is uses a separate initialization routine.

```
+ new:(unsigned)nElements {
    return [ [super new] initialize:nElements ];
    }

- initialize: (unsigned)nElements {
    contents = [IdArray new:nElements];
    capacity = nElements;
    return self;
    }
```

- free   When a collection is deallocated it also deallocates its captive data structure, but not the members of the collection themselves (it is seldom safe to deallocate things that were originally passed in as arguments, such as collection members).

```
- free {
    if (contents) [contents free];
    return [super free];
}
```

At first, it might seem wasteful to incur the overhead of separating the creation of the instance variables from their initialization. After all, the only classes that inherit from Collection are used to hold objects of type id. But suppose it became necessary to construct a collection of integers in an application you were writing. You know that an IntArray class exists and that it works like the IdArray class. Maybe there's a way that you can modify Collection to work with IntArrays instead of IdArrays. This is where you find the separation of creation from initialization making its payoff.

Instead of having to implement an IntCollection class entirely from scratch, you only have to inherit from Collection and override the initialize and initialize: methods as follows:

```
- initialize {
    contents = [IntArray new]; // instead of IdArray
    capacity = [contents size];
    return self;
    }

- initialize: (unsigned)nElements {
    contents = [IntArray new:nElements];
    capacity = nElements;
    return self;
    }
```

Managing Size

The Collection class also implements the methods necessary to allow a collection to grow and shrink as necessary. In order to do this, the collection must keep track of the size of its contents. Since the IdArray containing the contents of the collection is private, there are a number of options available.

1. The collection could request the array to report its capacity each time a new member is to be added.
2. The collection could retain the capacity of the array in a local variable, spending space to save the time required to send a message.
3. The collection could drop the messaging protocol entirely and access the array's capacity variable directly from the base language.

All three of these options are legitimate possibilities that make different kinds of trade-offs. The first optimizes space at the expense of speed, the second optimizes speed at the expense of space, and the third optimizes space and speed at the expense of coupling this class to implementation details recorded in another class, IdArray. In the case of Collection, the second option of keeping a local variable with the capacity of the IdArray array was chosen over the other two. The first option was not attractive, since it would place a heavy performance burden on system-level classes that would be used heavily, and the third solution is not particularly attractive since it removes a safeguard that the wise programmer normally leaves in place.

- expand   This method is used by subclasses of Collection to indicate that the size of the object holding the contents of the collection must grow. In the process of telling the contents to grow, the capacity instance variable is updated also. Methods can then use the capacity instance variable to check on the size of the array that holds the collection.

```
-expand {
    [contents capacity: capacity += capacity];
    return self;
    }
```

The remaining methods of this class introduce no new concepts, so I refer you to the specification sheet in Appendix A for further details.

Sequence Classes

A common operation on collections of any kind is to loop through the members one by one, an activity known as enumeration. However, collections will be implemented in very different ways, and this could require that the consumer use a different scheme for each one. This would be highly undesirable because it would expose to the consumer's code how each kind of collection is implemented and make them depend on implementation matters that might change over time. It would be far better to encapsulate enumeration in the Collection class so that enumeration works the same for all collections.

The details of how to enumerate the members of any collection is hidden from the user in a parallel hierarchy of classes called Sequences. To enumerate the elements of any collection, the consumer requests the collection to provide a sequence appropriate to that collection and uses it like this:

```
id sequence, member;
sequence = [anyCollection eachElement];
while(member = [sequence next])
    ... operate on member ...
[sequence free];
```

Each collection subclass implements the message eachElement to create an instance of a Sequence. Sequences deliver the members of their collection one at a time in response to the message, next. Whenever a radically different kind of collection is defined, such as for example, a collection based on linked lists instead of IdArrays, its developer overrides the eachElement method to return a kind of sequence that knows how to do this properly. In general, there are as many kinds of sequences as there are different data structures for building collections.

Sets and OrderedCollections are both based on IdArrays, so they share a common sequence class that knows how to sequence through the slots of an IdArray. This class implements enumeration by maintaining an integer in an instance variable, and scans from this offset to find the next non-nil array element.

This simple technique works well and is superbly efficient, thanks to a small cache that helps avoid allocation/deallocation overhead when creating and releasing sequences. But it is not as powerful as the block mechanism described for Smalltalk-80 in Chapter 3.

Imagine that you need to perform some arbitrary application-specific operation on each member of a collection of rectangular screen regions, such as determining the first one beneath the position of the cursor. This can be done with sequences, but it is unwieldy and leads to bulky code:

```
id member, sequence;
sequence = [rectangularRegions eachElement];
while(member = [sequence next])
    { if ([member includesPoint:cursorPosition]) ... }
[sequence free];
```

The usefulness of blocks is that they allow the operation part of this loop (the compound statement part of the loop) to be passed directly to the collection which applies the block to each element in turn, like this:

```
rectangularRegions do: [ aMember | aMember includesPoint:cursorPosition ifTrue: ... ]
```

Blocks are difficult to support completely in languages that are based on hardware stacks, but restricted implementations are not impossible. Blocks are one of the major enhancements under development for Objective-C.

OrderedCollection Class

OrderedCollections maintain their elements in the order in which they were added. They provide methods for adding (add:), removing (remove:), and enumerating (eachElement), and also for choosing and replacing elements at specific locations in the collection (at: and at:put:).

This section will describe how OrderedCollection works. OrderedCollection inherits the implementation assumptions already made for collections through its superclass Collection; in particular, the instance variables and methods that create and manage the array that contains the contents of the collection. OrderedCollection then augments what has been inherited from Collection by defining one new instance variable (firstEmptySlot) that holds the offset of the first empty slot in the array and several additional methods (at:put:, add:, remove:, and eachElement) that manage the contents of the ordered collection. The consumer uses these methods to modify the contents of the collection, so that the assumption about the location of the firstEmptySlot made by OrderedCollection will always be valid.

In discussing Collection, we mentioned several options for maintaining knowledge about the capacity of the IdArray. At that time, we decided that the performance of a Collection when using a local variable for storing the size of the IdArray was adequate, and therefore it wasn't necessary to violate the encapsulation of IdArray by accessing its size variable directly. There are times, however, when the safeguard of encapsulation can and should be removed in order to increase performance.

For example, we have an important piece of knowledge from Chapter 7 concerning how IdArrays store their contents that would be very useful to exploit in building the OrderedCollection class. We could use this information in methods that add (at:put:) to the OrderedCollection to directly index into the array of id values, as opposed to having to send a message every time a particular value of the IdArray was needed. Again, the costs of removing safeguards by directly accessing IdArray's internal structures are weighed against the need for performance in a heavily used system-level class, and this time we decide the benefits outweigh the cost. A penalty will have to be paid if IdArray is ever changed, but the gain may exceed the risk in this case.

The safeguard is removed by simply reverting to the ordinary programming style that was used before all this newfangled talk of encapsulation. We simply aim a pointer at the IdArray's private memory and have at it using C pointer expressions:

```
typedef struct { id isa; short attr, objID, capacity; id*contents;}IDARRAY;
IDARRAY *gropeHandle = (IDARRAY*) contents;
id *elems = gropeHandle -> elements;
```

The typedef statement describes the memory layout of an IdArray, and the second statement typecasts the id held in the OrderedCollection's instance variable, contents, to the type, structure pointer, in the local variable, gropeHandle. Or equivalently, the local variable can be dispensed with by writing the typecast operation in-line, like this:

```
id * elems = ((IDARRAY*)contents) -> elements;
```

However, this would hardwire the structure of IdArray instances directly inside OrderedCollection's source, and there would be no automatic way to find it if IdArray ever does change. Accordingly, Objective-C provides some syntactic help in generating the correct structure member information automatically. It is used like this:

```
typedef struct { @defs(IdArray); } IDARRAY;
```

The @defs(IdArray) statement triggers Objective-C to generate the structure member declarations from the IdArray class automatically. The ((IDARRAY*)contents) typecast can be ugly when it is used a lot, but it can be hidden inside the following macro definition:

```
#define FIRST (anIdArray) ((IDARRAY*)anIdArray) -> elements
```

-at: (unsigned) anOffset put: anObject   Given these declarations, the at:put: method can be implemented as follows:

```
-at: (unsigned) anOffset put: anObject {
  id *member, temp;

  if ( anOffset != firstEmptySlot ) checkOffset (anOffset);
  if ( anObject == nil ) return nil;
  if (anOffset == capacity ) [self expand];
  temp = FIRST[(contents)anOffset];
  FIRST[(contents)anOffset] = anObject;
  if ( anOffset == firstEmptySlot ) firstEmptySlot++;
  return temp;
  }
```

The first statement checks the offset and makes sure it is valid. The check-Offset()macro will generate an error: message to self if anOffset is out of bounds. The second statement ensures that nils will never be inserted into the middle of an ordered collection, since this would invalidate assumptions made by other methods such as size. The third statement insures that if a member is to be added to the end of the collection, sufficient space remains in the IdArray to hold it. This is accomplished by comparing the index of the current slot with the local variable that keeps track of the size of the IdArray, and sending the expand message as necessary. The fourth and fifth statements use the shortcuts discussed above to preserve the original value located at anOffset (so it can be returned) and replace it with the value in anObject. The sixth statement increments the firstEmptySlot variable if anObject has been added to the end of the collection.

- (int)size   The remaining methods of this class are implemented in obvious ways. For example, collections all provide a size method to report the number of members, and this is implemented as follows.

```
- (int)size { return firstEmptySlot; }
```

Set Class

Sets are collections that automatically discard duplicate entries. They are often used for building tagged structures like symbol tables. In Chapter 2 sets were used to count the number of unique words in documents, and in

Chapter 6 they provided the backbone for a graph analysis application. Sets differ from other collections in blocking attempts to add a new member when a matching member is already in the set. This, and the fact that they add, remove, and locate members extremely quickly, makes sets useful in any application that requires fast table lookup.

The UniqueWords example in Chapter 2 is typical of how sets are used. A set, uniqueWords, was used to hold a table of the words that had been read thus far, and each new word involved determining if that word was already in the table. Had this table been implemented with another kind of collection, like OrderedCollection for example, this would have involved comparing the new word against every existing member of the collection and performance would degrade as the size of the collection increased.

Sets implement adding in such a way that the time to add a new member is nearly independent of the size of the set. This is done by storing elements in an IdArray at offsets that are some random function that the member computes on its contents. If two members compute the same index, there is a high probability that they have the same contents. This is not a certainty, of course, because different contents can always produce the same hash value, producing what is called a collision. The hash value is used solely to collect the entries that might be identical into pools that have a probability of being identical. The final decision is made by a full-blown comparison.

Normally the pools stay small so the full comparison must be done on many fewer members than had hashing not been used. But as the memory fills, entries begin to compete for the available slots and collisions become more and more likely. Eventually performance degrades to worse than had hashing not been used at all. Therefore sets watch for this and acquire more space early, before performance begins to degrade noticeably.

This strategy can be implemented by using an IdArray as the memory arena. An additional instance variable, tally, will be used to keep track of the number of elements in the set. The size method provided by IdArray could have been used for this, but this would be slower because it involves counting non-nil elements in the array.

```
@implementation Set : Collection { int tally; }
- (int)size { return tally; }
```

In implementing the add: method a number of possibilities exist for how to handle collisions. Entries that have collided at a slot could be stored outside the table by linking them into chains, or they could simply be stored in some other slot chosen in one of several ways, the simplest of which is to take the next adjacent slot. As far as the set itself is concerned, chaining is simpler and has better statistical properties,[1] but it requires that space be

---

[1] See Donald Knuth, *The Art of Computer Programming Volume 3, Sorting and Searching,* Addison-Wesley, 1975.

available in each member for linking the collision chain together. This might be the way to go in a specialized application, but this would be an intolerable restriction for a general-purpose class like Set to impose on every other class in the system.

Open addressing does not have this problem because all storage occurs inside the table space itself. Additional space must be allocated whenever the arena gets more than about 80 percent full. The precise ratio at which expansion should occur should be tunable so it will be defined in a macro, EXPANSIONPREDICATE.

```
#define EXPANSIONPREDICATE() self->contents == nil \ /4
    || (self->tally >= ((3 * CAPACITY(self->contents)) ))
```

This macro is TRUE when the tally exceeds three-quarters the capacity, guaranteeing that sets will expand soon enough that the collision pools stay small and rarely coalesce with neighboring pools.

- addNTest: newObject   The implementation uses the findElementOrNil method to indicate where newObject belongs in the set. The findElementOrNil method returns the address of a slot which will contain either (1) a reference to an existing member that matches newObject, in which case a duplicate entry situation exists, or (2) an empty slot (containing nil) into which newObject can be added. If nil is returned the tally is incremented and the slot is assigned the value of newObject. This method returns newObject if it was added to the Set, or nil, if newObject was already a member of the set.

```
-addNTest: newObject {
  id *member;
  if (newObject == nil) return nil;
  member = [self findElementOrNil:newObject];
  if ( *member == nil ) {
      tally++;
      return *member = newObject;
      }
  else
      return nil;
  }
```

- filter:newObject   The filter method does exactly the same thing as add:, but it provides for a slightly different mode of use. The add: method either adds an element returning nil, or it returns the element if it could not be added. It never changes the element being added. By contrast, filter always returns the id of a set member. This member will be the newly added one if no duplicate existed already, or it will be the old member that duplicates the argument. In this case the argument will be freed. The filter: method is often handier to use than add: because of this. For example, using filter: instead of add: would have repaired the memory allocation inefficiencies in the Unique-Words application in Chapter 1. It was used in the DependencyGraph example in Chapter 6 for the same reason.

```
-filter: newObject {
   id *member;
   if (newObject == nil) return nil;
   member = [self findElementOrNil:newObject];
   if ( *member == nil ) {
       tally++;
       return *member = newObject;
       }
   else {
       if (newObject != *member ) [newObject free];
       return *member;
       }
   }
```

- **expand**   Expanding a set's capacity involves assigning every element
to a different location in a new larger arena. A simple way to do this is to un-
hook the old IdArray, replace it with a larger one, and then tell the old one to
add its contents to the receiver, which is now empty but with a much larger
capacity. The specification sheet for IdArrays describes a method,
addContentsTo:aCollection, that does precisely the right thing, so:

```
#define EXPANSIONAMOUNT CAPACITY(contents)*2
#define INITIALCAPACITY 10
- expand {
   if (contents) { id oldContents = contents;
       contents = [IdArray new:EXPANSIONAMOUNT];
       tally = 0;
       [oldContents addContentsTo:self];
       [oldContents free];
   } else contents = [IdArray new:INITIALCAPACITY];
   return self;
}
```

The [oldContents addContentsTo:self] message commands the old members
to send a sequence of add: messages to this set to assign each old member
to new locations in the expanded arena. Finally the [oldContents free] method
returns the old IdArray to the free memory pool.

- **(id*)findElementOrNil:anElement**   The findElementOrNil method returns
the address of a slot in the arena. The slot will contain either the id of an
element that duplicates the argument, or it will contain nil, indicating that
the set contains no duplicate. It does this quickly by having the element
compute its hash code, thus determining the beginning of a pool that might
contain the element. The method scans through the pool having each pool
member compare itself with the new element via [poolMember isEqual:an
Element]. The search fails when a nil is found.

```
// Determine address of slot containing either anElement or 0
```

```
-(id*)findElementOrNil:anElement

    {
        register int n; register id *now, *end; id *begin;
        if (tally*2 >= capacity) [self expand];
        n=capacity;
        begin = FIRST(contents);
        now = begin + ([anElement hash] % n);
        end = begin + n;
        for (; n--; now++) {
            if (now >= end) now = begin;
            if (*now == nil || [*now isEqual:anElement])
                return now;
        }
        return (id*)[self error:"findElementOrNil() failed"];
    }
```

Again, I'll describe this statement by statement for those unfamiliar with C language:

```
register int n; register id *now, *end; id *begin;
```

Since this method will probably be time-critical, the C compiler is directed to use machine registers for certain variables. The loop counter, n, and two array slot pointers, now and end, will be used every pass through the loop, but the other, begin, is not stored in a register because it will only be used once (when now wraps around). The extra speed of this reference won't repay the cost of saving and restoring a register.

```
if (tally*2 >= capacity) [self expand];
```

All methods that add to the contents of set, do so through the findElementOrNil method. Therefore, this method is the logical place to isolate the logic for managing expansion of the set.

```
n = capacity; begin = FIRST(contents);
```

This sets up to begin the loop, by loading n with the capacity of the array and begin with the starting address of the arena.

```
now = begin + [anElement hash] % n; end = begin + n;
```

The first statement initializes a slot pointer, now, to the beginning of the pool, and the second records the end of the entire arena. The offset of the pool from the beginning of the arena is determined by requesting anElement to provide its hash code, and this integer is reduced to fit the arena size by using the C modulus operator, %.

```
for (;n--; now++) { ... } and if (now >= end) now = begin;
```

These statements work together to move the variable through the entire arena, starting at the beginning of its pool and wrapping to the beginning of the arena when now $> =$ end. Unless the internal exit is taken, every slot in the arena will be considered once and only once. The internal exit will always be taken, because all sets will contain at least one nil element.

```
if (*now == nil || [*now isEqual:anElement]) return now;
```

Finally, the nub of the matter. If the contents of the current slot (*now) is nil, or if [*now isEqual:anElement] returns YES, return the address of that slot. Otherwise the loop will exit eventually on a slot that does meet this condition.

```
return [self error: ...]
```

This validates the assertion that all sets will have at least one, and ideally many more, nil slots, by generating a hard error if the loop ever terminates.

- remove:oldObject Removing elements from a set is more complicated than adding them, since emptied slots must be either marked in some distinctive manner or removed by packing the rest of the collision pool to eliminate the empties. Since no new object-oriented techniques are involved, the code for removing elements is not presented.

Combining

Given this backbone logic, the complete functionality of sets can be added quickly. For example, the union of two sets is a set of the members contained in both. This can be implemented by creating an empty set and then adding both sets to it:

```
- union:aCollection {
    id theUnion = [isa new];
    [theUnion addContentsOf:self];
    [theUnion addContentsOf:aCollection];
    return theUnion;
}
```

The only subtlety here is the [isa new] message. This might have been coded instead as [Set new], but this would mean that subclasses who inherit this method would always get sets as unions, not the subclass. However, referencing isa explicitly in this manner is a shortcut. A better implementation would be to replace [isa new] with [[self class] new], since this does not rely so directly on how the Object class implements its memory model.

The difference of two sets is a set containing the elements of the first, minus those of the second:

```
- difference:aCollection {
    id diff = [isa new];
    [diff addContentsOf:self];
    [diff removeContentsOf:aCollection];
    return diff;
}
```

And the intersection of two sets is a set containing only those elements that occur in both.

```
- intersection:aCollection {
    id tmp, union = [self union:aCollection];
    [union removeContentsOf:tmp=[self difference:aCollection]]; [tmp free];
    [union removeContentsOf:tmp=[aCollection difference:self]]; [tmp free];
    return union;
}
```

These implementations are optimized for simplicity, not for efficiency. The primary goal is to get something working in as simple a fashion as possible, and to optimize only if profiling proves the implementation to be a bottleneck.

Summary

This chapter and the previous one describe a class library of only eight classes in all. These eight classes provide enough functionality to support everything else discussed in this book. The four collection classes were built from capabilities defined in the four classes of the previous chapter, and this layering process can be continued indefinitely to build ever larger capabilities.

This chapter has also demonstrated how the encapsulation principle can and sometimes should be violated to meet sufficiently stringent performance constraints. The implementations described in this chapter use C's pointer-handling abilities freely to gain complete control over the internal structure of their captive IdArray instances. In the judgment of the programmer who developed these classes, this liberty was called for, and the programming language supported him in putting this decision into practice.

| Nine

Iconic User Interfaces

Computers are being bought and used today like typewriters, automobiles, or kitchen stoves, and purchasing decisions are increasingly made by novices who know little and don't care to learn about computers, software, or their idiosyncracies. In this computer-as-appliance market, customers want to use computers, not to learn about them, and the user interface is becoming a dominant factor that can make or break sales.

The user interface has become fashionable, and we're awash in self-righteous sermons and marketing hype about the glories of "user friendly" systems. But it is still hard to find pragmatic information about how to actually build them, and especially hard to find out how to avoid crippling development costs while doing so. Therefore, this chapter will skip the usual discussion of whether, or why, iconic user interfaces are better, and concentrate on how to build them. It describes an architecture composed of the following three layers:

1. The application layer is composed of models, a catchall term that stands for whatever is used to implement the application. A model can be an object, a global variable, a value computed by a function, or even a hardware device.

2. The presentation layer is composed of objects called views. Views implement an interface between the user and the models, ideally according to some coherent user interface style. This chapter emphasizes the desktop metaphor, a user interface style in which views behave like pieces of paper that overlap on a desktop.

3. The virtual terminal level is a library of graphics functions that provides

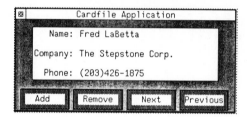

Figure 9.1. An iconic user interface for a telephone list program. The user interface can be used to view and maintain a list of people and their contact information.

a hardware-independent way for the application to draw things, mapping virtual terminal operations into operations on some physical display device. This level is well established today, as it is the level supported by systems like X Windows and the Macintosh toolbox.

The architecture will be demonstrated by building an iconic user interface for a simple telephone list program. This program, *cardfile*, replaces the paper version commonly found on office desks with the iconic version shown in Figure 9.1. The user interface is based on ICpak 201, a library of Software-ICs that Stepstone provides to implement a particular user interface style. The use of a common library such as ICpak 201 will ensure that different applications built by different programmers will exhibit a consistent user interface style across multiple hardware platforms.

Once I've described the demonstration application, the costs and benefits of developing the user interface using object-oriented technology will be discussed. As you might expect, the hardware cost of using an iconic interface (measured, for example, by the amount of memory required to run it) is higher than a conventional textual interface. However, our goal is human productivity. The cost of developing the iconic interface (measured, for example, by lines of application-specific code) will turn out to be remarkably small. This is not an attribute of the iconic interface style (this style is inherently more difficult than developing a command-based interface), but an attribute of the object-oriented technology used to build it. This suggests that object-oriented programming and its ability to preserve large quantities of reusable code in libraries could radically alter the cost factors that have made iconic user interfaces prohibitively expensive to build routinely.

Object-oriented Languages and Iconic User Interfaces

Although iconic user interfaces and object-oriented programming are usually discussed as connected topics, the connection is actually indirect and not immediately obvious. An iconic user interface does not have to be built in an object-oriented programming language, and an object-oriented programming language need not be used on a high-resolution graphics terminal. Command-oriented applications can be built in Smalltalk-80 or Objective-C as readily as in C or COBOL. So why *are* iconic user interfaces sometimes called "object-oriented"? Why are these topics so intertwined? Does the connection go any deeper than the fact that both are so prominent in influential systems like Smalltalk-80?

One reason is that both use information hiding to reduce surface area between suppliers and consumers—of an application, on the one hand, and of a Software-IC, on the other. An object-oriented programming language encapsulates data with the operations on that data inside a well-defined tangible interface, the object. An iconic user interface uses the same principle to associate data with the operations that can be applied to the data managed in an application. The same principle that reduces the surface area between programmers serves to decrease the amount that a novice must learn to use an application.

A different reason is that object-oriented programming is unusually suitable for the kind of programming involved in building iconic interfaces. For example, I will soon show how object-oriented programming makes it possible to build user interfaces in much the way that artists build animated movies, by drawing images onto pieces of transparent acetate and positioning the layers with respect to one another. Inheritance allows the basic abstraction of a transparent acetate sheet to be implemented in a generic class, Layer, and then varied by using inheritance in much the way that an artist uses paint, scissors, and glue.

A final reason is that iconic user interfaces are far more complex than command-oriented interfaces, making it more important than ever to control complexity, provide reusability, and encapsulate change. The very appeal of the iconic style is in building a bridge between two worlds that differ in even the most fundamental laws of space, time, and physics:

1. Computer space is a linear, equally reachable arena, in which real world concepts like boundary, distance, ownership, or interaction have no meaning.
2. Computer time is high speed and sequential, while real time proceeds independently and concurrently for all objects.
3. Physical concepts like conservation of space and mass have no meaning in the computer. It can create (and destroy) important objects with blinding speed.

Iconic user interfaces are so popular because they project an intermediate world onto the screen, an illusion that physical laws of geometry, time, and physics remain intact in this application. For example, in the desktop illusion the user's objects behave like pieces of paper in three-dimensional space, so as to exploit highly developed spatial reasoning skills in organizing files by putting them where he can find them instead of giving them a unique name. Some iconic systems even preserve physical laws like conservation of matter in illusions like "To create a document, tear a sheet from the stationery pad. To destroy one, move it to the trash can. Destroyed documents can still be retrieved there, until you empty the trash."

User Interface Architecture

Behind all the hype and glitter, an exciting thing is happening as system developers begin to understand how to routinely build systems that consumers find genuinely easier to use. This understanding has not yet gelled into a consensus; that will obviously take years. But a new architecture is being discovered that is analogous to the one that is now used routinely to build time-sharing systems.

It is difficult to determine this architecture's origins because it has not been discussed in a widely accessible way. I first encountered it by reading Smalltalk-80 source code, where it is called the model-view-controller paradigm (MVC). It's interesting that even though Smalltalk-80's user interface is based totally on this paradigm none of the early Smalltalk literature discussed this architecture in detail. My own early ideas were refined during discussions with Trygve Reenskaug at the Norwegian Central Institute, who originated the MVC concept during an extended visit to Xerox PARC, and with Larry Tesler at Apple Computer, who exploited many of the same ideas in the Lisa and Macintosh development environments.[1]

UNIX applications are based on a one-dimensional abstraction, the bytestream. This abstraction is excellent for driving computer devices, but relatively poor for transmitting information to people. By contrast the new architecture is based on two-dimensional abstractions like points, rectangles, and rectangular images called bitmaps. These abstractions are implemented by the lowest of the three architectural layers shown in Figure 9.2.

1. *Application level:* This level implements the functionality of the application, without concern for how the functionality will be interfaced to the user. The components of the application level are called models because the functionality of most applications is to model some aspect of reality. Models are slaves of the user interface. They avoid holding information about the user interface because the presentation layer may be detached and replaced at any time. Models are always referenced from views—seldom the inverse. (However, see the discussion of dependents on page 194).

2. *Presentation level:* This level interfaces a specific application to a specific class of user. The components in the presentation level are views, each of

[1]Kurt Schmucker, *Object Oriented Programming on the Macintosh*, Apple Press, 1986.

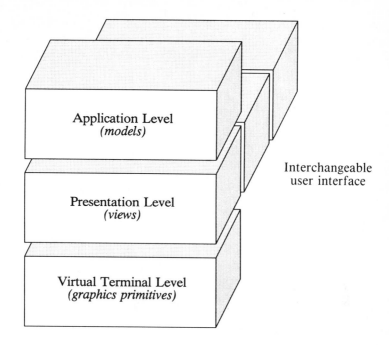

Figure 9.2. User-interface architecture. The user interface architecture consists of three levels between the operating system and the user. The application layer is composed of objects, called models, that implement the application's functionality. The presentation layer is composed of objects, called views, that implement a user interface to the application's models. The presentation layer is detachable, so different layers can be provided to suit the needs of different users. For example, one can provide a debugging interface for the programmer, another can provide an editing interface for the clerks, and a third can print a summary report on the lineprinter for the manager. The virtual terminal layer is a graphics library that provides device independence for the other layers.

which implements a user interface to a specific model in the application level. A given model may well have many different kinds of users, so there will in general be many different views to serve their diverse needs. For example, one presentation layer might provide fancy editing on a high-resolution terminal, another might print hardcopy reports about the model on a lineprinter, and a third might support low-level debugging for an expert programmer.

3. *Virtual terminal level:* This level implements a device-independent interface between the presentation layer and some class of hardware graphics devices. For brevity, only high-resolution raster-oriented graphics devices

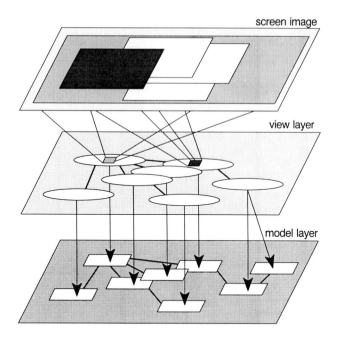

Figure 9.3. Relationship between models and views. Models hold the information to be interfaced to the user, and the views implement the user interface. Control resides in the user, not in the application. The application is the slave of the user interface, not the other way around. The presentation layer contains pointers into the application level, not the inverse. This allows the presentation layer to be detached and replaced as needed.

will be discussed here, even though the architecture can be modified slightly to apply to vector terminals, hardcopy terminals, and alphanumeric terminals (glass teletypes). This layer will not be discussed in any great detail here to focus on the relationship between the application and its user interface.

Views interface a model with a user via a device, such as a graphics terminal and a mouse. The view references the model to obtain data, formats the data, displays it to the user, receives commands from the user, and commands the model as to what to do next. Views generally hold pointers (ids) to their model, but the converse is never true.[2] Models are completely passive and never hold information that could make them dependent upon any particular presentation layer. They hang suspended from the presentation level by pointers in much the way that circuit boards are connected to test equipment with a bed-of-nails testing jig (see Figure 9.3).

---

[2] This is an overstatement to reinforce a point. See the discussion of dependents on page 194.

Cardfile

The rest of this chapter applies the user interface architecture to building a program, Cardfile, that exhibits an iconic user interface. This exploration will introduce concepts in the order in which questions would arise to a newcomer, but not in the neatly layered organization defined by the architecture. The discussion proceeds first horizontally to describe each of the architectural layers, and then vertically to show how the various layers were built and used in this application.

The cardfile program is a simple application to demonstrate how the user interface architecture implemented in ICpak 201 can be used to build iconic user interfaces. Cardfile's user interface, shown in Figure 9.1, provides:

- Push buttons for adding and removing cards from the file.
- CardLayers for editing the name, company, or telephone number.
- Menu selections for quitting or moving the cardfile application.

For example, to enter the name, company, and telephone number of a new contact, you click the "Add" button to create a blank card. Once several cards have been created, the "next" and "previous" buttons can be used to cycle through the list. You can close the cardfile application into an icon by clicking on the close box in the upper left corner of the window. To exit the application, select "quit" from the Cardfile Menu, and the application will prompt for confirmation. This application uses the activation/passivation mechanism discussed in Chapter 7 to keep a permanent copy of the list on disk.

ApplicationLayer

The model layer for this application is very straightforward, consisting of two objects that model their real world counterparts: a Card object for holding a name, company, and telephone number; and a CardFile object for maintaining a collection of Cards. Figure 9.4 shows the class hierarchy that does this.

The Card class defines three instance variables: name, company, and phone. An instance of Card initializes these to hold empty String instances that contain the information for that Card. The CardFile class defines no new instance variables, and inherits most of its behavior from its superclass OrderedCollection. It only defines methods to manage the collection of cards as if it were a circular OrderedCollection.

An important reason for designing the separation between models and views carefully is that it allows the activation/passivation procedures discussed in Chapter 7 to be used to save and restore session results in a nearly automatic fashion. Transient graphic information is held in the views, and models hold no references to this information. The models only represent permanent information that must be saved across invocations of the application. By adhering to these rules, the permanent information can be preserved

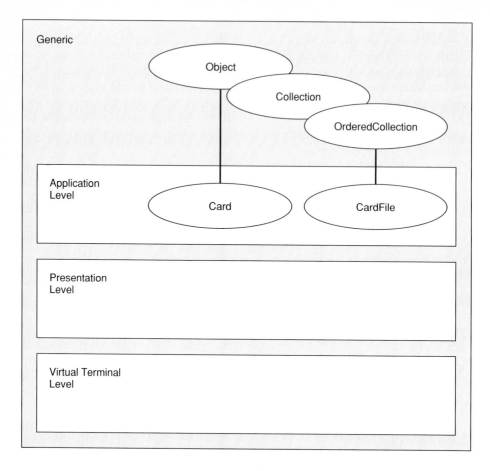

Figure 9.4. The cardfile application consists of a main routine (not shown), which creates a single instance of class CardFile. This instance holds a collection of cards that corresponds to a simple telephone list. The user interface allows cards to be created, edited, and removed.

across invocations by simply commanding the model to passivate itself in a file:

```
// Passivate the cardfile for the next session
[cardfile storeOn:"cardfile.data"];
```

and restored at the beginning of each new session by reactivating the model from the file.

```
// Activate the cardfile from the previous session
if (!(aCardfile = [aCardfile readFrom:"cardfile.data"])) aCardfile = [Cardfile new];
[aCardfile activate];
```

If a file (cardfile.data) exists in the current directory, it is assumed to contain a passivated cardfile instance. This statement reactivates the cardfile by parsing the file, storing the id of the newly created instance in the variable, aCardfile. Otherwise, a new, empty cardfile, is created.

Virtual Terminal Layer

This work is based on the virtual terminal layer on which ICpak 201 is based, called earthbase. Since portable graphics libraries have been covered in numerous articles and books,[3] I shall cover earthbase only briefly to focus primarily on the user interface architecture as a whole.

Earthbase is an Objective-C graphics primitives library modeled after the Smalltalk-80 graphics primitives. It supports a virtual terminal abstraction on any platform so that applications can be platform independent. User interfaces are constructed by using existing classes off the shelf, or by customizing them (through inheritance) to do a specialized task not included in the library already.

The graphics primitives in earthbase implement a uniform virtual terminal. From the point of view of a user, the virtual terminal exists inside one of possibly multiple windows on a hardware manufacturer's terminal, such as the SUN platform I've used in this book. The virtual terminal's interface to the application is the same on other platforms. The main task when Stepstone ports ICpak 201 to new platforms is to port earthbase to the target platform.

Presentation Layer

After deciding on a virtual terminal and an application, isn't everything in hand to just get on with the job and start building things? Absolutely not. Certainly, many applications have been built in this way, and even some outstanding ones. But neither of these layers provides anything to ensure that the user interface for this application is consistent with interfaces for other programs. Forging ahead at this point is certain to produce chaos; a random grab bag of applications with absolutely no consistency that a user can depend on to guide him in learning a new application. Building a user interface on top of a virtual terminal is like building a roof directly on a foundation without first designing the walls. It can be done, but it violates important architectural and practical principles. No one will be happy with the result.

The primary job of an interface library is to ease the construction of presentation layers that help their user reason about the behavior of an application, generally by encouraging him to draw analogies with real world

---

[3]I particularly recommend "A Survey of Graphics Standards and their Role in Information Interchange," Peter R. Bono, Graphics Software Systems, *Computer Magazine*, page 63, October 1985, published by IEEE Computer Society.

experience. This chapter describes a user interface library that exploits the metaphor of pieces of paper on a desktop. This metaphor was pioneered at Xerox PARC in systems like InterLisp and Smalltalk-80, and is now routinely used in commercial systems including Xerox's Star, Apple's Lisa and Macintosh, and others too numerous to mention.

The library helps a programmer build a user interface in the same way that a roll of transparent acetate, stencils, scissors, glue, paint, and brushes help an artist build an animation. The artist cuts conveniently sized sheets of acetate, draws images on them, positions them with respect to underlying sheets, and on occasion moves them with respect to one another to obtain effects like movement of a figure against a static background.

The Layer Software-IC implements the roll of transparent acetate. Its factory object produces rectangular sheets, and these can be changed in size, positioned with respect to their background, and removed from one background and attached to another, and any layer can serve as background for any others. Since frontLayers might be attached to any layer, together they form a tree in which every layer provides background for each of its frontLayers.

The relationship between a background layer and those attached immediately to it is implemented in a data structure called the layer hierarchy. This data structure provides a consistent framework in which all graphic operations are performed (Figure 9.5). For example, a layer's coordinates are expressed with respect to the origin of its backlayer and the system translates them to absolute screen coordinates automatically. Furthermore, all graphics generated by a frontLayer are automatically clipped at the margins of its backLayer. The layer hierarchy implements the three-dimensional aspects of the desktop metaphor by managing its list of frontLayers as an ordered collection where position in the collection indicates the distance of that layer from the user. This visual priority information is necessary to maintain the illusion that layers overlap each other in three-dimensional space and to decide the order in which user generated events are interpreted and by which layers.

Conceptually, events are generated at the tip of the cursor and penetrate the stack of layers until acted upon and consumed by one of the layers beneath the cursor's tip. By convention, the background layer responds to all events, absorbing events that are not handled elsewhere and implementing standard default menus for one or more mouse buttons.

Transparent acetate is not very exciting until it has been modified with paint, stencils, and glue. This is done by defining layer subclasses that inherit the acetate abstraction of the layer class, changing it to produce an application-dependent user interface. Figure 9.6 shows how a user interface is composed of a number of overlapping layers.

The background for the window as a whole is handled by an instance of FrameLayer which is covered by three sublayers of radically different sizes. When the FrameLayer factory method created this instance, it created the three sublayers and positioned them to cover it completely. This is particular

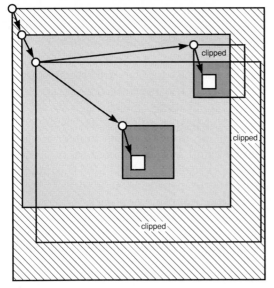

- FrontLayer origins are measured relative to the origin of their BackLayer

- FrontLayer images are clipped at the margins of their BackLayer

Figure 9.5. Relationship between backLayers and frontLayers. The backLayer defines the visual background for its frontLayers; the origin of their coordinate system, and a boundary beyond which frontLayer-generated images will not appear on the screen.

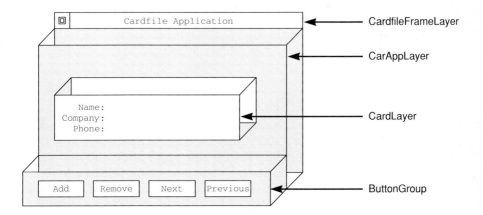

Figure 9.6. How subclass modify the transparent acetate abstraction. The Layer class defines the transparent acetate abstraction. The CardfileFrameLayer class modifies this abstraction to define acetate that is painted with a particular image and which responds to the cursor in a particular way. Several other subclasses are shown, and each modifies the acetate abstraction in its own particular way.

to this kind of layer. Layers can have any number of sublayers, and each can be any size. This can be seen in the application layer of the FrameLayer. This layer has been constructed using several layers, which in turn are constructed using several layers, and so on.

Some of these layers were developed specially for the cardfile application, but most of them were acquired directly from the user interface library. This is important, because it ensures that all applications that use this library will exhibit a consistent user interface. StringLayers will look and behave the same, because they *are* the same. Although an application builder could in principle invent his own nonstandard StringLayer if he chose to, in practice this will occur only if the standard one is really unsuitable for this application. Otherwise the standard one will be used because it is already in the library and it works without effort on the programmer's part.

This architecture is very similar to the one used in Smalltalk-80, with one exception. Smalltalk's presentation layer consists of not one, but two, class hierarchies. The outgoing leg of Smalltalk's user interface is handled by a hierarchy of views much like the ones discussed here. But the incoming leg is implemented by a separate hierarchy of classes, Controllers, that provide the logic for parsing cursor and keyboard actions with respect to the view to control the application. My approach differs in that each layer is responsible for managing both of these channels. The need for the separate controller hierarchy is unclear and is the topic of spirited debate even within the Smalltalk-80 community.[4]

The advantage of having each view support a complete user interface is that it is far easier to describe and understand. But this scheme may have the disadvantage of insufficient generality to accommodate differences such as one-button versus three-button mice. It is hard to predict the extent to which differences of this kind require an additional architectural layer, or whether they can be handled through routine use of the flexibility that does exist already (e.g., inheritance, encapsulation, and virtual terminals).

A Tour of the Cardfile User Interface

The discussion until now has described the function and structure of each architectural layer one at a time. Now I'll shift to describing how this architecture was applied in building the cardfile application and how parts of the user interface library work. Rather than describing this in a horizontal, one layer, at the time manner, I'll adopt a more vertical order of presentation, describing things in the order in which they occur when the program is executing. Methods will be introduced in a piecemeal fashion, so their class will be indicated by preceding each method or method group with the class name

---

[4]Personal communications with Alan Borning, Trygve Reenskaug, Glen Krasner, and Larry Tesler.

as follows:

```
@implementation ClassName ...
```

Since this section provides an overview of the generic classes in ICpak 201, those who are only interested in the Cardfile application may prefer to skip the next two sections on first reading.

The transparent acetate abstraction is implemented in the Layer class:

```
#import "UserInterface.h"
@implementation Layer:LayerMedium {
        id backLayer;
        id frontLayers;
        BOOL visible;
        id controller;
        id clipList;
        }
```

In addition to inheriting from LayerMedium, Layer also inherits from Disp-Medium, DispObject, Quad, and Object. Although we won't discuss these classes (DispObject, DispMedium, LayerMedium, and Layer) in detail, they support the virtual terminal abstraction beneath all of this work. For example, DispObject is the superclass of any object that can be displayed, and DispMedium is a superclass of any object that can be displayed on. For example, a Bitmat is a DispObject that can be displayed on a DispMedium like Window. Since Layer is a subclass of both, layers can be used both as writing surfaces and as paint.

Each layer is attached to another that provides its background. Each may also serve as background for other layers. This relationship is managed in the pair of instance variables, backLayer and frontLayers. The frontLayers variable is initialized with an OrderedCollection when the Layer is created, and both are subsequently managed as to maintain the backLayer/front-Layer hierarchy as a doubly linked tree. This hierarchy controls such things as visual priority, the order in which views overlap the screen. The controller also uses it to determine the sequence in which user actions (mouse clicks) are interpreted by the stack of sublayers beneath the cursor's position.

One of Layer's superclasses that provides an important set of behaviors is Quad. Layer inherits from Quad the instance variables:

```
PT origin;
PT extent;
```

These instance variables define a rectangular shape that is described in terms of its origin and the length of its sides. Layer also inherits from Quad a set of behaviors for changing its size, and positioning itself relative to other objects that inherit from Quad.

Quad uses a C structure defined in a geometry package, geom.h, to manage its properties. The point declaration, PT, type in this package is:

```
typedef struct { short x,y; } PT;
```

The Layer class implements the behavior of a sheet of transparent acetate. For example, it provides size changing behavior in an extent: method that allows the acetate to be cut to any rectangular size. This method ensures that size changes interact meaningfully with subsequent behaviors like clipping and interacting with user-generated events. The Layer class also provides positioning behavior in an origin: method that allows the layer to be positioned with respect to its backLayer. This method ensures that repositioning interacts meaningfully with subsequent behaviors like displaying (both of itself and its frontLayers), the way events interact with the layers, and so forth. Finally, it provides behaviors for creating layers and rearranging their attachments to each other; e.g., detaching them from one layer or attaching them to another.

This base abstraction is changed by defining subclasses that override one or more of this class's methods (see Figure 9.7). For example, subclasses commonly override the transparency attribute by overriding the method, displayLayer, to draw a specific image. The user-interface library contains many subclasses like this already, and these help to define a standard user-interface style. Any specific application will generally involve additional layer subclasses to support the needs of that specific application.

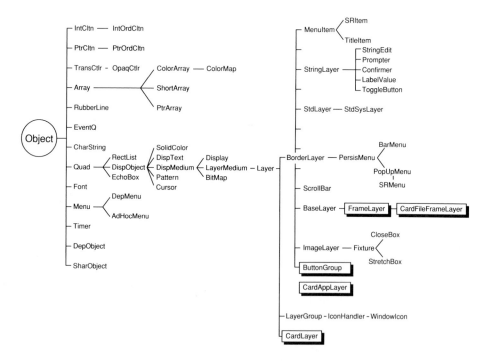

Figure 9.7. Presentation level class hierarchy. The inheritance hierarchy of ICpak 201 is shown with the classes added for the Cardfile Application (highlighted).

The complete presentation layer of the cardfile application is shown in Figure 9.7. Only the four classes inside the highlighted box are specific to this application. The others are generic layers provided as part of the user-interface library.

Generic Application

The user-interface library also contains a simple but ingenious tool first described to me by Larry Tesler of Apple Computer Corporation. A generic application is merely an intact, fully functional application, complete with user interface, but whose application level is trivially small. By compiling and running this degenerate application, a programmer can discover what the consistent user interface should look like without being distracted by a complicated application. The source to the generic application is given in the user interface library documentation to define a starting point for studying the library.

```
// genericApl.m - the generic application

#import "stdio.h"
#import "FrameLayer.h"

main( argc, argv )
    int argc;
    char *argv[];
    {
    id frameLayer, model;

    parseArguments( argc, argv );

    // initialize the ICpak201 GUI
    init201();

    // Create the application layer (window system window)
    frameLayer = [FrameLayer origin:pt(10,10) extent:pt(500,500)];

    // build application model
    // model = [ApplicationModel new];

    // pass application model to the application layer
    // [frameLayer applicationModel:model];

    // pass control to the application layer
    [frameLayer controlStart];

    // clean up prior to exiting
    }

parseArguments(argc, argv) {

    ...
    }
```

The generic application is a complete program that when compiled produces a user interface complete with titleLayer, closebox, and pop-up menus.

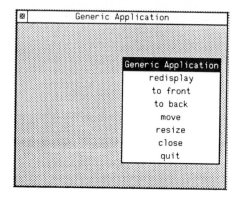

Figure 9.8. The generic application. The generic application implements a user interface to a nonexistent application (i.e., an application that does nothing at all). Its purpose is to demonstrate the standard user interface, and to provide a starting point from which to build specific applications.

Its user interface already works and demonstrates the consistent user interface that the programmer should retain in building a real application. The generic application is certainly simple, but it is an effective system-building tool nonetheless. It enforces a standard, not by making other interfaces hard, but by making the standard interface easy. It works not by putting up barriers, but by defining a line of least resistance. Figure 9.8 shows the screen image produced by running this application.

This figure shows an image of three parts: the title layer, a fixture for closing the application into an icon, and the application layer area. Also shown is the standard application menu that can be used to manipulate the size, position, etc., of the application window. Specific applications are created by customizing the generic application, often by simply replacing the generic FrameLayer with one that performs a specific task.

The generic application uses a single instance of the class FrameLayer as its main presentation layer. The FrameLayer class is a specialization of the BaseLayer class in ICpak 201 that will highlight several important methods used when creating an application.

The FrameLayer class provides a protocol for creating instances that invoke a series of default methods. This protocol is actually an extension of the Layer protocol. FrameLayer overrides the initialize method that Layer guarantees will be generated each time a new instance of any subclass is generated.

```
@implementation FrameLayer : BaseLayer
    {
    id appModel, closeBox, titleLayer, appLayer;
    }
```

```
-initialize {
   [super initialize];

   [self borderWidth:2];
   closeBox = [CloseBox client:self];
   titleLayer = [StringLayer str:[self defaultTitleSTR]];
   [titleLayer borderWidth:2];
   appLayer = [self defaultAppLayer];

   [titleLayer attachTo:self];
   [closeBox attachTo:titleLayer];
   [appLayer attachTo:self];

   return self;
   }
```

This initialize method creates the necessary fixtures for the generic application. It sends several messages to establish that the application will have a title and an application layer. You can override these methods to create a new application. The following default methods are defined in and used by the FrameLayer class:

```
-(char *)defaultTitleSTR {
   return "Generic Application";
   }

-defaultMenu {
   return [ [super defaultMenu] assignSTR:[self defaultTitleSTR] ];
   }

-defaultAppLayer { return nil; }

-(BOOL)defaultExitCheck {
   return [Confirmer askSTR:"Exit the Application ?"];
   }
```

Once the initialize method has created these sublayers, they must be positioned. This is done by overriding the Layer protocol methods. The extent: method is overridden in FrameLayer to resize its frontLayers when the size of its backLayer changes:

```
@implementation FrameLayer ...

-extent:(PT)ext {
   [super extent:ext];
   [titleLayer origin:[self origin]];
   [titleLayer extent:pt(ptX(ext),17)];
   [closeBox origin:[titleLayer origin]];
   [closeBox height:[titleLayer height]];
   [appLayer origin:[titleLayer bottomLeft]];
   [appLayer extent:pt(ptX(ext),(ptY(ext)-17))];
   return self;
   }
```

There are two distinct ways in which the extent: method specified the new sizes for its frontLayers. The first way was to specify a value representing a physical coordinate in space as in the message:

```
[titleLayer extent:pt(ptX(ext),17)
```

The second way was to use a logical coordinate of another layer to position relative to, as shown in the message:

```
[closeBox height:[titleLayer height]];
```

The FrameLayer also provides a method for placing the application into a read-evaluate-dosomething loop:

```
@implementation FrameLayer ...

-controlStart {
    [self setVisible:YES];
    [myCursor beCursor];
    [Cursor cursorOn];
    do {
        keepControl = YES;
        while( keepControl ) {
            [EventQ readEvent];
            if ( ![self processEvent])
                [self perform: event.selector];
        }
    } while( ![self defaultExitCheck] );
    [cursors.Xeq beCursor];
    [Cursor cursorOff];
    return self;
}
```

In summary, you create a user interface for an application by creating a layer subclass with all the subparts, linking them together, and then starting the application. This control style, known as a *push* type control, is opposite from the traditional pull style where the program prompts the user for some input, waits until the input arrives, and then processes it. The push style has an application waiting until the user specifies something to be done. The program might then have a dialogue with the user to gain more information, before processing the user's request. The user controls the application, not the other way around.

Initialization

The first step in building a specific application is to copy the generic application and modifying it to meet the needs of the new application.

```
// cardfileMain.m - the generic application

#import <stdio.h>
#import "CardfileFrameLayer.h"
#import "CardFile.h"
```

```
static char cardfileStr[] = "cardfile.data";

main( argc, argv )
   int argc;
   char *argv [];
   {
   id frameLayer, cardfile;

   parseArguments( argc, argv );

   // initialize the ICpak201 GUI
   init201();

   // Create the application framework (window system window)
   frameLayer = [CardfileFrameLayer new];

   // build application model
   if ( (cardfile = [CardFile readFrom:cardfileStr]) == nil )
      cardfile = [CardFile new];

   // initialize framework with application model
   [frameLayer applicationModel:cardfile];

   // pass control to the FrameLayer
   [frameLayer controlStart];

   // preserve the contents of the cardset for next time
   [cardfile storeOn:cardfileStr];
   }

parseArguments( argc, argv )
   int argc;
   char *argv[];
   {
   }
```

The CardFile application uses the activation/passivation machinery discussed in Chapter 7 to save the results of each editing session and to restore them for the next invocation. If no passivated model exists, the cardfile factory object is used ([cardFile new]) to create a cardfile instance.

Defining Application-specific Layers

The layers discussed so far are generic layers provided in the user interface library. Significant applications usually involve a number of application-dependent layers. Four are needed here:

1. CardfileFrameLayer adds cardfile specific details to the generic application's FrameLayer by overriding several methods that CardFrameLayer inherited from its FrameLayer.

2. CardAppLayer implements the application-specific part of the user interface to an instance of CardSet. This class will be used in the CardfileFrameLayer as the applicationLayer. It is responsible for creating and managing the interactions between the CardLayer and the ButtonSet fixture.

3. CardLayer implements the user interface to instances of the Card class. It displays an instance of card for modification through generic string editing layers that are provided by ICpak 201.

4. ButtonSet implements the four button fixture used to view and manage the card set.

The first item to be created is the CardfileFrameLayer. It provides a way to customize the cardfile application without having to reimplement a lot of standard functionality.

```
@implementation CardfileFrameLayer : FrameLayer
  {
  }

  +(PT)defaultOrigin { return pt( 10, 10); }
  +(PT)defaultExtent { return pt(360,160); }

  -defaultMenu {
    id idMl;
    idMl = [Menu str:[self defaultTitleSTR] ];
    [idMl append:[Menu str:"move"
      selector:@selector(moveFromUser) receiver:self]];
    [idMl append:[Menu str:"quit"
      selector:@selector(controlTerminate) receiver:self]];
    return idMl;
    }

  -(char *)defaultTitleSTR {
    return "Cardfile Application";
    }

  -(BOOL)defaultExitCheck {
    return [Confirmer askSTR:"Exit the Cardfile Application ?"];
    }

  -defaultAppLayer {
    return [CardAppLayer new];
    }

@end
```

One of the overridden methods, defaultMenu, is responsible for returning the instance of the application's logical menu. The code shown here uses a very basic form of menu, without features like child menus, mixing icons with text, etc., since these features aren't needed in the demonstration program. Although we have specified a selector-receiver pair that will comprise a message when the user selects a particular item from the menu, we haven't specified how that choice will be presented to the user. ICpak 201 makes a similar distinction between the logical layout of a menu and its physical representation to the one described here between models and views, so that there is a firm separation between what a menu does and how it is presented to the user. In the case of the cardfile application, the menu will be formatted as a popup menu.

As the CardfileFrameLayer is being created, an instance of CardAppLayer is also created, which in turn creates an instance of CardLayer and ButtonSet:

```
@implementation CardAppLayer : BorderLayer
    {
    id cardLayer, cardFile, buttonGroup, currentCard;
    }

    -initialize {
       [super initialize];

       [self insideColor:colors.Blue];

       cardLayer = [CardLayer new];
       [cardLayer attachTo:self];

       buttonGroup = [ButtonGroup new];
       [buttonGroup attachTo:self];
       [buttonGroup onReceiver:self];

       return self;
       }
```

CardAppLayer is a superclass of BorderLayer in order to acquire an opaque background (remember that Layer is transparent) for the application layer. One more point worth commenting on is the message to self with the argument colors.blue that sets the background color to blue. The include file "uil.h" defines a C structure with a set of default color values. These values are always present on color systems, and each earthbase maps them to reasonable patterns on monochrome systems. This moves the burden of picking default colors onto the virtual terminal.

The final two custom classes created for the cardfile application use preexisting components from the user interface library heavily.

```
@implementation CardLayer : Layer
    {
    id card, background, nameLV, companyLV, phoneLV;
    }

    -initialize {
       [super initialize];

       background = [BorderLayer extent:pt(300,80)];
       [background attachTo:self];

       nameLV = [[LabelValue labelSTR:nameLVStr] maxValueSize:20];
       [nameLV borderWidth:0];
       [nameLV attachTo:background];
       [nameLV addDependent:self];

       companyLV = [[LabelValue labelSTR:companyLVStr] maxValueSize:20];
       [companyLV borderWidth:0];
```

```
[companyLV attachTo:background];
[companyLV addDependent:self];

phoneLV = [[LabelValue labelSTR:phoneLVStr] maxValueSize:20];
[phoneLV borderWidth:0];
[phoneLV attachTo:background];
[phoneLV addDependent:self];

return self;
}
```

The CardLayer class uses the Layer class as its parent since it needs a transparent back layer for the front layers that it creates and attaches to itself. The CardLayer creates four front layers, including three LabelValues, attaches them in a specific order, and then establishes the dependencies between the different instances of LabelValue and itself. The LabelValue class is defined in ICpak 201. It supports a user interface for editing strings with the keyboard and mouse.

Dependencies between Layers

The ICpak 201 class, DepObject, provides behavior for managing dependency relationships between objects. DepObject installs itself via the poseAs: mechanism (discussed in Appendix A) at runtime, so its methods are inherited by all objects in the system.

For example, CardLayer's initialization routine creates three instances of LabelValue (a class that manages the editing of Strings) and then registers itself as a dependent by sending the addDependent: message to each LabelValue with itself as the argument.

```
-initialize {
    [super initialize];
    nameLV = [[LabelValue labelSTR:nameLVStr] maxValueSize:20];
    [nameLV borderWidth:0];
    [nameLV attachTo:background];
    [nameLV addDependent:self];

    companyLV = [[LabelValue labelSTR:companyLVStr] maxValueSize:20];
    [companyLV borderWidth:0];
    [companyLV attachTo:background];
    [companyLV addDependent:self];

    phoneLV = [[LabelValue labelSTR:phoneLVStr] maxValueSize:20];
    [phoneLV borderWidth:0];
    [phoneLV attachTo:background];
    [phoneLV addDependent:self];

    return self;
}
```

By convention, whenever a model changes its internal state, it will announce [self changed]. The method changed, which the model inherits from DepObject, will broadcast an update:because: message to each of its dependents. For example, changing the contents of the LabelValue results in a [self changed] message being sent. In the case of CardLayer, the update: because: method has been overridden to take appropriate action when one of its LabelValues change:

```
-update:idObj because:(SEL)aSel {
   [super update:idObj because:aSel];
   if ( idObj == nameLV )
      [card name:[nameLV valueAsStr]];
   else if ( idObj == companyLV )
      [card company:[companyLV valueAsStr]];
   else if ( idObj == phoneLV )
      [card phone:[phoneLV valueAsStr]];
   return self;
   }
```

The final part of the user interface to be constructed is the ButtonSet fixture:

```
static char *addBtnStr    = "  Add   ";
static char *removeBtnStr  = " Remove ";
static char *nextBtnStr    = "  Next  ";
static char *prevBtnStr    = "Previous";

@implementation ButtonGroup : Layer
   {
   id addBtn, removeBtn, nextBtn, prevBtn;
   }

-initialize {
   [super initialize];

   addBtn = [PushButton str:addBtnStr];
   [addBtn attachTo:self];
   [addBtn onSelector:@selector(addCard)];

   removeBtn = [PushButton str:removeBtnStr];
   [removeBtn attachTo:self];
   [removeBtn onSelector:@selector(removeCard)];

   nextBtn = [PushButton str:nextBtnStr];
   [nextBtn attachTo:self];
   [nextBtn onSelector:@selector(nextCard)];

   prevBtn = [PushButton str:prevBtnStr];
   [prevBtn attachTo:self];
   [prevBtn onSelector:@selector(previousCard)];

   return self;
   }
```

The ButtonGroup consists of four PushButtons that the user can select to move through the list of cards. Once again, each button is created, attached to the ButtonSet's layer, and then initialized with a selector to perform when the button is pressed. Fixtures, like menus, also have the property of isolating the presentation to the user from the definition of the action to be performed when the user selects the fixture.

Until now, nothing has been displayed on the screen, other than that the cursor's shape has been changing to reflect what is going on. For example, the main routine changed the cursor to an eyeglasses shape while the model is being read from disk ([readCursor display]), and to an hourglass shape while the view hierarchy is being assembled ([waitCursor display]). These behaviors are provided by the Cursor class, a member of the virtual terminal layer.

Cutting and Fitting

Layers are displayed on the screen as a side effect of passing control to the user in the [frameLayer controlStart] message. The event queue mechanism is part of the virtual terminal layer of ICpak 201 and was initialized as part of the call to init201(). During this initialization, the virtual terminal is told about the events that are of interest to this application and a function that will be called whenever one of these events occur. The only events that will be discussed here are cursor button events and events regarding changes in the virtual terminal itself.

Recall that the virtual terminal is implemented inside a window supplied by the workstation vendor's window manager. Whenever one of these base windows change shape or is covered or uncovered by another window, the virtual terminal redraws itself to repair the newly exposed area. The event handler triggers this by first resizing the topmost layer to the new size of the window (in case the user has changed the size of the window), then commanding the top layer to redraw itself.

When a new application starts to run, its event queue is initialized with a windowChangedSize event. This ensures that the application automatically sizes its user interface to fit the window before presenting the interface to the user. Sizing is generally handled by the extent: method inherited from the Layer class but a few layers override this message, for example, those that must stay completely covered (tiled) by their sublayers. CardAppLayer, for example, is tiled by two sublayers, so it overrides the extent: method to first change its own new extent and then command each of its sublayers to change their origin and extent to tile the available screen precisely:

```
@implementation CardAppLayer...

-extent:(PT)ext {
    [super extent:ext];
    [cardLayer origin:[self origin]];
    [cardLayer extent:pt(ptX(ext),((ptY(ext)*75)/100))];
    [buttonGroup extent:pt(ptX(ext),((ptY(ext)*25)/100))];
    [buttonGroup bottomLeft:[self bottomLeft]];
    return self;
    }
```

Adding Paint to Transparent Views

So far a view hierarchy has been created and linked to its models, and the screen origin and extent of each view has been determined. But nothing will be drawn on the screen until the display message arrives at the top view, to produce the image shown in Figure 9.9.

Before delving into how the display logic is implemented, review the responsibilities that every layer has for its frontLayers:

1. Each backLayer is responsible for displaying any visual image that should appear as background for its frontLayers. If the background layer is transparent, no action is needed.

2. Each backLayer is responsible for defining the coordinate system for its frontLayers. The position of a frontLayer is never specified in absolute screen coordinates, but relative to the origin of its backLayer. This makes it simple to move a layer since it ensures that all frontLayers move with the backLayer.

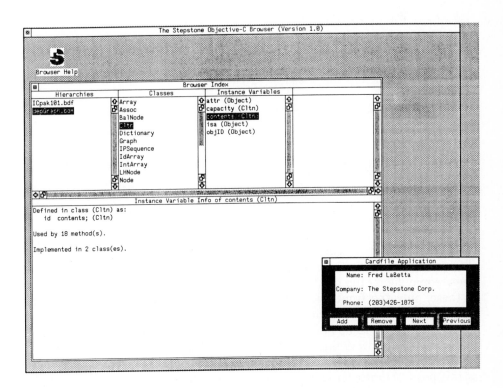

Figure 9.9. When the application passes control to the event handler, the topmost view is sized to fit the window and commanded to display itself. Until the display command is issued, nothing is drawn on the terminal.

3. Each backLayer is responsible for clipping any images generated by the frontLayer to the backLayer's margins.

These basic requirements are accomplished in the Layer class. Layer uses a protocol such that a subclass of Layer is only concerned with displaying its contents, and not the contents of its backLayer or frontLayers. This includes correctly managing the clip list and coordinate systems for layers that are in front of it.

The message [someLayer display] tells the layer to draw itself. Each layer does this by sending displayLayer messages to itself and then sending display to each frontLayer in turn. The frontLayers then follow the same steps until all of the Layers in the hierarchy have been displayed.

If a subclass of Layer wishes to do something special when the layer is redrawn, it can override the paintBackground and/or the displayLayer method. For example, CardLayer wants the part of itself not covered with the card data to be transparent. It does this by overriding the -displayLayer method:

```
@implementation CardLayer...

-displayLayer {
    [super displayLayer];
    [background center:[self center]];
    [nameLV topLeft:[background topLeft]];
    [companyLV centerLeft:[background centerLeft]];
    [phoneLV bottomLeft:[background bottomLeft]];
    return self;
    }
```

Responding to Events

The logic that generates the graphic image on the screen is now intact, but this is the easy part. The effort spent getting to this point is small compared to the effort of making the model responsive to user commands. But the user-interface library provides support for this as well.

The layer hierarchy controls the dispatching of events in such a way that the user's illusion of a three-dimensional iconic interface is maintained. Some objects may lie on top of other objects, and if the mouse is clicked over one of these, only the front one should respond. Some events are reserved for global effects, so events can be allowed to percolate through the stack of overlapped layers to be handled eventually by the background window. The background window defines a standard meaning for each possible event.

Events are generated at the tip of the cursor and penetrate each layer at this position until acted upon and consumed by one of them. For example, with the cursor positioned as in Figure 9.10, events will be considered by the LabelValue that is managing the model for Name first. Unless consumed there, it will be considered next by the CardLayer managing the Card as a whole (the white area in the center), and if not consumed there, it will be

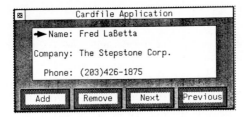

Figure 9.10. Associating events and layers. Events emerge from the tip of the cursor and are examined by each layer they penetrate between the user and the background. Layer intercept events by defining a message corresponding to the event's name, and consume them or not according to the boolean value returned from the message. Unconsumed events are dealt with and consumed by the FrameLayer, which defines a default meaning for each event.

processed and absorbed by the CardfileFrameLayer that underlies all of the layers.

The application sleeps inside the operating system awaiting one of the kinds of events that the graphics primitives library declared interesting. The user generates events by pressing one of the mouse buttons.[5] This awakens the event handler, and it obtains the event from the queue by calling get-Event. This function places the event in a globally accessible structure and annotates it with a message selector that indicates which event has occurred. Then it dispatches the event to the background view by executing [self processEvent].

The top view, FrameLayer, inherits the necessary methods from Layer.

```
@implementation Layer ...

- (BOOL)processEvent {
    int i;
    extern id _msg();
    PT ev;
    ev = event.origin;
    /* see if our outer bounds contains the event (w/o messaging) */
    // recall that origin is really the outsideOrigin
    if ((visible) && (X(ev) >= X(origin))
                  && (Y(ev) >= Y(origin))
                  && (X(ev) < X(origin)+X(extent))
                  && (Y(ev) < Y(origin)+Y(extent))) {
        /* first try my frontLayers */
        if (frontLayers)
            for (i = [frontLayers size]-1; i >= 0; i--) {
                /* sent to Layer to traverse the tree*/
                if ([[frontLayers at: i] processEvent])
```

[5]Other classes of events, such as keyboard events, are not discussed here.

```
                    return YES;          /*event consumed by frontLayer */
           }

       return NO;          /* we don't contain the event point */
     }
```

Notice the similarity with Layer's display logic. Both work from the back to the front (toward the user) to manage the layer hierarchy in accordance with the origin and extent of each view. If the layer does contain the point, it will send processEvent to each of its sublayers. Eventually, some layer (the one nearest the user) will execute [self perform:event.selector], commanding itself to respond to the specific kind of event.

By default, layers are transparent and ignore events. This default is implemented in the Layer class:

```
= Layer ...
- (BOOL)rightButtonDown { return NO; }
- (BOOL)leftButtonDown { return NO; }
- (BOOL)middleButtonDown { return NO; }
```

To create a layer that is sensitive to any particular event, a layer overrides the appropriate event method to return YES or NO according to whether the event should be considered by other layers in the background. For example, CardfileFrameLayer defines a rightButtonDown method to guarantee that the right button will always pop up a standard system menu no matter where it is pressed. Establishing such system-wide conventions is one of the primary responsibilities of the topmost layer, and is one of the ways that layers like CardfileFrameLayer help to ensure a consistent user interface.

And On and On . . .

This discussion has compressed a lot of details into a small space, but it has covered but a fraction of the capabilities needed in a comprehensive class library. I've not described how the strict box-within-a-box clipping strategy that the layer class provides as a default is overridden when, for example, handling pop-up menus and other kinds of layers that must cross their back-Layer's margins. Describing the ParagraphLayer class and associated topics like the advantages of having only a single text editing class to learn, how this class accomplishes text editing, how font changes are made, and how hardcopy is produced, could easily involve as much discussion as the simple classes presented here. And I've not even mentioned classes that implement various kinds of menus, choice boxes, verifiers, and so forth.

But I must close the tour at this point with one final observation. Inheritance and encapsulation definitely help to develop code of this nature, but they do complicate the task of describing how the code works to a newcomer. Conventional programs have a flat structure that can be presented in a straightforward front to back order. But object-oriented code is as three-dimensional as a termite nest and just as hard to describe on the printed page.

To some extent, the problem stems from paper-based technology and can be corrected with electronic means like browsers and interpreted languages. Correcting this problem is one of the reasons that Stepstone developed the Objective-C browser, and is exploring other technologies, such as interpreters.

Summary

I have covered a lot of ground in this chapter, and have still barely scratched the surface of a remarkably deep and complicated topic. The primary conclusion is an extremely optimistic one. The combination of object-oriented programming, the user interface architecture, and the libraries described in this chapter does radically reduce the amount of code that must be written to build iconic user interfaces. Table 9.1 shows the Cardfile application was written in only 392 lines of code in all, of which only 287 lines were user interface code. Based on code bulk alone, there seems to be reason to hope that iconic user interfaces might someday become as common as conventional scrolling interfaces are today.

The key contribution of the new architecture is to make it possible to define a number of important tools, the most basic one being a comprehensive Software-IC library. This library defines a standard, consistent, user interface that can be attached to multiple applications with reasonable programmer effort.

However, the cost of building these libraries is not small, and the difficulty of describing what they do and how to use them is high. The generic application idea does help, but it does not completely solve the problem of how to describe highly nonlinear code to newcomers.

Table 9.1
Cardfile Application Source Bulk

	Lines	Words	Byte	Filename
User Interface	79	134	1633	CardAppLayer.m
	80	184	2088	CardLayer.m
	41	86	894	CardfileFrameLayer.m
	87	256	2394	ButtonGroup.m
	287	660	7009	Subtotal
Model	54	117	1001	Card.m
	51	119	966	CardFile.m
	105	236	1967	Subtotal
	392	896	8976	Total Application

| Ten

Different Tools for Other Jobs

The hybrid object-oriented language discussed in this book, Objective-C, has a specific set of strengths and weaknesses that derive from the following assumptions:

1. All objects reside in a single address space and can be identified uniformly by memory address. This assumption is inappropriate if objects must also reside on disk or on other machines on a network.

2. The lifetime of an object is controlled by the programmer, not by the system. This becomes increasingly difficult as the complexity of the application increases and as duration of execution increases. The job becomes increasingly impossible as object lifetimes approach infinity in moving to disk.

3. Messaging is synchronous: the sender waits while the receiver computes.

This chapter sketches some different implementations that relax one or more of these restrictions. These modifications capitalize on the ability of the object concept to provide a uniform framework for working with highly distributed, extremely smart systems in which the machine takes on much of the work now carried out in painstaking detail by programmers. Of course, this makes the machine work harder and the resulting decrease in machine efficiency will only be worthwhile if the extra programmer freedom is actually needed in the problem at hand. The frustration, and the challenge, is that the need for so many of these advanced features turn up simultaneously in the systems that are being dreamed of today.

Heap Compaction and Automatic Garbage Collection

The implementation of Objective-C discussed in this book[1] identifies objects by their memory address. This keeps efficiency high enough that programs can benefit from Software-IC technology without crippling degradation in machine performance. For noninteractive batch-oriented applications, garbage collection and heap compaction are often an unneeded luxury because memory will be released automatically when the application terminates. Long-running interactive applications must, however, protect the user's data from crashes caused by:

1. Running out of memory because the available space is fragmented into tiny chunks, each too small to hold the next object. Plenty of free memory might exist, but only in tiny units, each too small to hold the new object.

2. Running out of memory because objects that are no longer needed were not released. Objects that are no longer referenced from any other part of the system are unused, wasting space.

3. Releasing some object and then accessing the freed space after the space has been assigned to a new purpose.

The designer faces a strategic decision here. Leaving memory management to the programmer frees machine resources for useful work, and the savings can be substantial. But the cost in programmer efficiency is also large:

1. Productivity suffers, because each decision to release any object requires that the programmer know the rest of the system sufficiently to guarantee that this object will never be accessed again. This increases the surface area of the interfaces between members of the programming team enormously.

2. Reliability suffers, because testing can never reliably guarantee that no future path of execution will access a freed object.

3. Reusability suffers, because conventions about which objects own other objects, and are thus responsible for freeing them, won't necessarily apply when they are exported into new environments.

4. Source bulk increases, because memory management cannot be coded into reusable subclasses. For example, container classes like Set and Ordered-Collection cannot automatically free their contents when they themselves are freed. Reusable container logic must always assume that their contents are also referenced from elsewhere.

---

[1]A version that does perform automatic garbage collection has been built and is being tested.

As program complexity increases, these problems eventually get out of hand. Especially in experimental programming environments that emphasize rapid prototyping, notably Lisp, Smalltalk-80, and even Simula, automatic garbage collection and heap management become absolutely essential.

Object Tables

Objective-C identifies objects directly by their address in memory. As the program executes, identifiers are repeatedly copied as messages and function calls copy arguments onto activation records and assignment statements copy identifiers into local variables, instance variables, C external variables, and even machine registers. If the address of an object ever changes, every one of these variables must be changed to reflect the new address.

One reason for changing the address of an object is to relieve the memory fragmentation that can result as an application creates and deletes objects of random sizes. Over time the pool of free memory becomes fragmented into hundreds of tiny free areas separated by valid objects. Plenty of free space remains but no individual free area is large enough to allocate the next object. The system cannot proceed unless the good objects are packed to squeeze out the useless holes. This operation, called heap compaction, repositions every good object in memory, and every identifier that references these objects must be located somehow and changed.

Compacting a heap is easy, but finding and updating every reference to repositioned objects is not. This is especially true in a hybrid language like Objective-C, where object references might be hiding anywhere—in global variables, in stack frames (C local variables), hardware registers, etc.

Although other approaches exist, the simplest one is to design the implementation such that objects cannot spread into such hard-to-reach places. For example, many interactive object-oriented systems include an additional level of indirection to make object identifiers address independent. Instead of identifying objects by their memory address, they are identified by their offset in a table of all objects called the object table. The table slot provides the address of the object's private part and often other information as well

```
struct OTB { struct _PRIVATE *addressOfPrivatePart; ... } ObjectTable[MAX];
```

This extra level of indirection makes heap compaction and other operations (such as resizing IdArrays) easy, because the table contains the only copy of the object's address. Also it takes fewer bits to store an index than a pointer, and a smaller identifier width can reduce memory requirements substantially. Messaging speed can be slightly higher because the cache indexing logic becomes simpler when class object identifiers are consecutive numbers instead of pointers.

However, these potential gains are offset by the extra computations needed to reference instance variables. Where self->anInstanceVariable once sufficed,

```
ObjectTable[self]->addressOfPrivatePart->anInstanceVariable
```

is now necessary. Therefore it may be worthwhile to forgo the space advantage of defining identifiers as object table indices and implement them as object table slot pointers

```
self->addressOfPrivatePart->x
```

Once all memory addresses are collected in one easy-to-find place, heap compaction becomes a matter of scanning the table and moving the good objects to one end of memory to pack out the holes. As each object is moved its object table slot is adjusted to reflect the new address. This compaction process is generally triggered when memory allocation fails because of insufficient memory. Compaction potentially changes the address of all objects, making it unwise to hold any memory addresses in user code, especially during a function call that might allocate memory and thereby trigger heap compaction.

The object table introduces a number of new possibilities, and even a new point of view about the object memory model. For example, since all objects have an isa link, why not move this into the object table and think of the table slot as the object itself? From this point of view the system consists of a large but fixed number of objects, each the same size and having the same fields:

```
struct OTB {
    struct _SHARED *addressOfSharedPart;
    struct _PRIVATE *addressOfPrivatePart;
    ...
}
```

Such objects would allocate and manage memory by attaching any amount they need in their addressOfPrivatePart instance variable. The depth of an object table establishes the number of active objects the system must support at any given time, and its width (the number of fields per slot) establishes the services the table can support. If only heap compaction is supported the slots would be of width two. If the system supports automated garbage collection, additional fields are used to hold reference counts and the like. If the system allows multiple objects to be active concurrently, additional fields will be used to hold the execution status of temporarily inactive objects. Virtual object systems (in which objects live primarily on disk but move into memory temporarily when they are accessed) use additional slots for staging bits, disk addresses, etc.

Automatic Garbage Collection

By changing to address-independent object identifiers it becomes possible to reposition objects without constantly worrying about invalidating an identifier. But this does not provide automatic garbage collection, for this involves automatically determining when objects are no longer reachable.

There are a number of ways of doing this, and I will only mention two approaches at opposite ends of the spectrum of possibilities.

Mark and Sweep

In the mark and sweep approach the system runs at full speed, not bothering to rid itself of garbage until memory is exhausted. This triggers a two-pass garbage collection procedure. The mark pass traces all reachable objects and marks them as not-garbage. The sweep pass removes the garbage. An additional heap compaction pass may or may not be invoked as well.

The mark process starts with some initial object that is known to be reachable, for example, the global symbol table object. This object is marked reachable, perhaps by linking it into a list of reachable objects with a word reserved for that purpose in the object table. This is repeated for each object that can be reached from this one, and so forth, recursively. Heap compaction is a separate pass, and may or may not be run after every sweep.

The advantage of the mark and sweep algorithm is that it allows the system to run at full speed until garbage collection is really needed. And it reliably tracks down all garbage, even the circularly linked groups of objects that cause problems with other schemes. The disadvantages are that the collection process can trigger at inopportune times, a nuisance in an interactive system, but absolutely intolerable if the system is controlling real-time machinery. By postponing the garbage collection work, the work accumulates, and garbage collection delays can become long. There are technical problems as well, in that the recursive procedure requires memory, which is by definition in short supply when the procedure is started.

Reference Counting

With incremental or reference counting schemes, the system never runs at its full potential, but it never stops completely either. It spreads the garbage collection overhead more or less evenly over time. Reference counting is based on having the programming language keep track of how many references point to each object. For example, every assignment statement must decrement the reference count of the object that the target variable used to point to, and increment the count of the object it now points to. When each function exits, its local variables leave scope and the objects they point to must be de-referenced. The inverse occurs on each function call, since formal arguments generate new references. When an object's reference count is decremented to zero, it is removed and the reference counts of all objects it refers to are decremented, and so on recursively.

The language-level support can be provided straightforwardly, even in a precompiled hybrid language like Objective-C. The precompiler must determine each condition that can modify the value of an identifier variable and generate function calls to handle the reference count operations. For example, assignment is handled by replacing assignment statements of the form

```
anIdVariable = aValue;
```

with a function that accomplishes the same effect. The function also decre-
ments the reference count of the object that was pointed to before the assignment and increments the reference count of the new one.

```
idAssign(&anIdVariable, aValue);  // generated code
```

Function arguments can be handled similarly, replacing each call of the form

```
aFunction(anIdVariable);  // source statement
```

or

```
[anObject aSelector:anIdVariable];  // source statement
```

to read instead

```
aFunction(idReference(anIdVariable));  // generated code
```

or

```
_msg(idReference(anObject), /*aSelector*/..., idReference(anIdVariable));
```

Virtual Object Memories

Why not allow objects to live primarily on disk, and load themselves into
memory only when they're needed? The appeal of removing the usual barrier that separates what goes on in high-speed memory and disk is obvious.
Large systems are generally too large to fit in memory, and in any event,
volatile memory was never intended for long-term information storage.

How Big Is Global?

In this book to date, the address space of a given process determines the
range of identifier uniqueness. Although a UNIX user may well own more
than one process, the identifier in one process has absolutely nothing to do
with the identifier in another. Each process is an isolated world, immune to
external influences except for information that the process actively reads for
itself via pipes, files, and signals.

These restrictions make Objective-C's automated activation/passivation
support unusually valuable, because it provides a way to move objects between processes, by converting the object to a symbolic representation that
can be transported in a UNIX byte-stream. The activation/passivation process translates identifiers represented as addresses into identifiers represented as record numbers. This is expensive and not very general, but at
least it does retain a clearly defined protection domain across which errors
cannot propagate. If one process crashes, little harm is done.

Alternatively, suppose the identifier concept is changed to identify all objects owned by a given individual, thus allowing the individual's processes
to communicate directly. This is the rationale of integrated programming

environments like Interlisp-D and Smalltalk. Instead of separating tools by UNIX process firewalls, all tools are integrated into a single process. This process is generally the entire central processing unit (CPU) of a personal workstation, so that all objects are identified within the addressing limits of this CPU. Some of these environments (e.g., InterLisp) are supported by virtual memory hardware to reduce the amount of real memory needed to address all these objects. Still others (e.g., most Smalltalk-80 implementations) insist on real memory. In either case the user preserves work by writing out all of memory periodically, building a checkpoint from which the system can be restored if things go awry.

This change does expand the range of uniqueness, but not nearly enough to satisfy those who want to build systems that encourage cooperative use of the system by allowing objects to be exchanged much as we exchange paper in an office. In an integrated system like Smalltalk, my objects have nothing to do with your objects. The objects live in different worlds, separated by the same computing barrier but one notch further out. This problem regresses infinitely. The range of uniqueness might be defined to span all the objects on a large shared disk so teams can share objects conveniently, but this excludes the marketing department down the hall who are on a different disk. Should the range of uniqueness be expanded to encompass them? How about workers on a local area network? If so, what about the branch office in Denver? What about the national sales force? The planet?

Capability Addressing

Range of uniqueness is not even the toughest snag that expanded identifier schemes run into. Every time the addressing range is expanded, there is a greater chance of accident or design damaging ever increasing amounts of information. If a UNIX process or a personal computer crashes, the only harm is to the information in that process. Crashing an InterLisp or Smalltalk process destroys everything that has been accomplished since the last checkpoint. The same dangers exist as the range of an errant identifier increases, spreading the danger of harm in ever widening circles.

The danger is especially acute because until now an object identifier contains no provision for restricting access to the object. As soon as addressing becomes possible outside an individual's private arena, it is crucial to be able to publish identifiers of useful objects while simultaneously restricting the things that might be done with them.

By enhancing what we've called an identifier to include a set of access restrictions, a more powerful concept called a capability is born.[2] A capability is an object identifier with restrictions on what the owner can do with it. The restrictions are called access rights, and they restrict the operations that may be performed on that object. For example, the access rights can be

[2]Henry M. Levy, *Capability-Based Computer Systems*, Digital Press, 1984.

thought of as a list of the messages that the owner of the capability is allowed to send to this object.

Each user, program, or procedure in a capability system has access to a list of capabilities. A program cannot access an object unless its capability list contains a suitably privileged capability for the object. Therefore, the system must prohibit a program from directly modifying a capability, for if this were allowed it could forge access to any object in the system by changing the identifier and access rights fields.

Concurrency

For many, including Alan Kay, the greatest appeal of the object-oriented concept is in escaping the strictly sequential mold of conventional computer architectures. The very idea of objects communicating by messages evolved from Kay's dream of little independent automata, each busily working away in parallel, providing data when and where needed. This dream is an enduring one and has appeared in many fields under many guises. "If this computer can't supply enough horsepower to run the objects fast enough, then just move some of them to another computer and have them send their messages over the network."

Of course, this dream has by no means arrived, object-oriented programming or not, because concurrency is not that simple. In fact the problems quickly become so complex that nothing useful can be gained without first pinning down the key questions: What is the concurrent system to do? What can it leave undone?

Coroutines

The simplest concurrency mechanisms simulate concurrency within a single memory address space. A single sequential process, which might be a personal computer or a process within a time-shared system like UNIX, provides its own scheduler to manage multiple simulated processes. Each task receives a share of the CPU in turn, and all share global data and communicate without restriction. They are also unprotected from each other. In most cases, no automatic provision exists for wresting control from a process that is using up more than its share of CPU cycles. The coroutines cooperate voluntarily in sharing all computer resources.

This form of multitasking can be added to nearly any language by merely writing a few subroutines. Some are best written in assembly language, since they must save and restore the stack pointer of the underlying process. The programming language and its support structures don't have to be involved in any way. For example, TaskMaster is a platform-independent library that supports lightweight tasks and exception handling, even for operating systems (like UNIX) that only support heavyweight processes. It contains a class, called Task, that conveys an asynchronous thread of control to its instances. Task instances are a higher-level kind of object, a card-level object as discussed in Chapter 3, that operate as coroutines of each other, and not as subroutines. A concurrent application consists of a number of Task subclasses and a main routine that creates as many instances as needed. Each task is linked together and every task can quickly determine which task is next. Multiprocessing begins by sending one of them a wakeup message whereupon it will compute briefly and then send itself a sleep message. The sleep message causes a task to save its own execution state and restore the state of the next one in sequence.

This is done with an assembly language function of two arguments, the first the location in which this task's execution state (stack register) will be saved, and the second the stack that was saved when the next process was last put to sleep. The function simply modifies the hardware stack register and returns normally. By changing the stack register, the return address from the function is also changed such that the function returns via the return address in the just-restored context; right where the saved process left off.

This basic scheme can be enhanced almost arbitrarily with tools for coordinating, controlling, displaying, synchronizing concurrent tasks, queueing tasks and messages, and generating and displaying various kinds of event distributions. Smalltalk-80 and Simula both provide a rich library of these classes which is largely responsible for their reputation as languages that support concurrent simulations. However this has relatively little to do with the programming language or whether it is object-oriented, and particularly, it has absolutely nothing to do with the fact that Smalltalk-80 programmers like to call a dynamically bound function a message. It has much more to do with the libraries available in these languages.

Coroutine-based tasking is simple to implement, highly efficient, relatively portable (except for the small assembly language function), and highly popular for building simulation models inside a single real process. The simplicity derives directly from the fact that all simulated processes share the same global identifier space, so that interprocess communication does not involve the range of uniqueness issues discussed in the previous section.

Distributed Systems

Object-oriented programming has also drawn the attention of those who envision highly concurrent systems implemented via large numbers of relatively small computers, working independently except when they need to share data. What could be more natural for building factory automation systems, for example, than a large number of microcomputers each monitoring and controlling some local aspect of the factory in real time and communicating its results to other computers with different responsibilities? It is appealing to think of these systems as large numbers of objects, each containing both procedure and data, operating concurrently yet communicating by messages. This trend is already strongly in place in factory automation, avionics, telephony switching systems, and robotics. It is cropping up in large-scale scientific computing as researchers turn to concurrency to achieve higher throughput, and the personal computer trend is bringing the very same issues into office automation and even traditional data processing.

In such systems terminology problems can really get out of hand. Imagine a large office automation system distributed over personal workstations, file servers, and conventional shared systems. Shouldn't this system provide an object-oriented user interface? Shouldn't its software be organized into objects as described in this book, using messages for encapsulation and inheritance? Shouldn't the file system be organized around objects as well, which move automatically into memory when needed there? Shouldn't the network be organized around objects in the sense of concurrently active servers communicating via network packets, also called messages?

There may be a common unifying concept beneath these radically different meanings, but it is unclear as to whether this unity can be meaningfully exploited to build pragmatic, useful software systems. Successful system building is a matter of exercising skilled judgment in making multiple, interlocking trade-offs, balancing programming costs, hardware costs, and user satisfaction. No panaceas are available to make this easy, but I certainly hope that this book has provided some useful tools.

Coordination Systems

This book has examined system-building problems from the perspective of those who build them. It has been concerned with ways to organize ordinary computers, operating systems, and programming languages to build larger, more manageable units. The theme has been to point out how system building can be turned from a cottage industry into an engineering discipline by exploiting the same prefabrication techniques that are now widely used in electronic hardware manufacturing.

I'd like to close on a different note by devoting this final section to the point of view that drew me to object-oriented programming in the first place. This involves putting aside the robe of system-building craftsman and donning the one of visionary, putting aside matters of "How to build it?" to consider instead "What should be built?"

Although system builders often speak of office automation systems, such systems hardly even address office productivity at all, let alone automate it. Office automation systems are primarily tools to be used by the individuals in an office to enhance their personal productivity, using the computer as a solitary tool. We've barely begun to tap the potential of computers as coordination tools, or tools for helping individuals cooperate toward a common goal.

What is an office, but a group of cooperating individuals? Some of their activities are solitary, and those we pretty much know how to support on the computer. Other activities are coordination tasks, and these are far more difficult because coordination tasks are by definition concurrent. Everything of importance about the word organization revolves around words like role, responsibility, actions, resources, space, and time that have no meaningful counterpart in the computing lexicon of today, not at any level, be it hardware, programming language, operating system, or ultimately, the so-called office automation system itself.

For example, consider the difference between a paper paycheck (perhaps delivered by the inter-office mail service), and an electronic instance of class PayCheck mailed by electronic mail. No amount of gussying about with electronic whizbangs like encryption algorithms, secure networks, or data logging will ever make that electronic check cashable, short of making some person legally responsible should the system be misused. While most computer scientists will hold that the two checks are merely different representations of the same information, any shop clerk will tell you that they are not; and the clerk would be right and the computer scientist wrong. Distinctions of this nature do matter and the computing industry sometimes seems unaware of how much they affect every interaction between the computer and the real world. With a physical check you can buy lunch, or with a signed agreement on paper you can win points in office politics. A true office automation system has to be able to carry similarly binding agreements for it to succeed at coordinating office activities.

The store clerk has a deep practical understanding for words like role, individual, responsibility, and concurrency, and recognizes that they embody what is truly important about cashing that check. Any equivalence between the electronic and physical representations is an illusion, because the representations are non-equivalent in every way that truly matters. These four words are examples from a long list of terms that are important in real world organizations. These words matter, but they are never mentioned in computer reference manuals, technical journals, conference proceedings, panel discussions, faculty interest lists, or proposals to funding agencies. These terms determine the outcome of tremendous financial transactions, power struggles in board meetings, and the balance of international relations. They also control interactions between chaffinch couples, the aggregation behavior of slime-molds, light dominance in rain forest canopies, and the outcome of street brawls. But the way these concepts are influenced when mediated electronically is seldom if ever discussed. How can we, a group that calls itself a science, think of programming languages, syntax-directed editors, and local-area networks as research areas, but never fund a serious discussion like, "Here's why electronic checks aren't cashable and here's how to fix it"?

One missing element in the electronic check system is responsibility; a specific person to turn to if things go awry. For example, the electronic check becomes legal tender when some agent is made legally obligated to make up losses that occur through the system. If the check never arrives, he can be sued, or if the check is cashed more than once, he can be sued. The electronic system has been changed in no way, but it can now be trusted (except perhaps by the agent). The change is one of the fundamental issues I spoke of, the matter of responsibility. You cannot sue electrons, or computers.

I'm reminded of the tremendous energy and skill that is being poured into artificial intelligence systems. The real world impact of these efforts is strongly affected by the simple question, "Who is responsible here?" For example, Mycin[3] was an early expert system for diagnosing infectious diseases. Eventually this system contained so much information about diseases, their symptoms, and testing procedures that it was more accurate than most physicians. However the real world impact of this remarkable technical achievement has been relatively small, because physicians are not prepared to shoulder responsibility for facts that come to them through a chain with so many tenuous links as are found in any computer system.

Offices are organizations; coordinated teams of individuals each playing one or more roles. Each role is a region in organizational space which contains organizational resources. The individual that plays this role is responsible for these resources in a fundamentally important, legally binding way that is lost as soon as the transfer medium is electronic. Organizations revolve around issues of time and space that are barely recognizable in computing systems. Computing hardware is organized around unilateral action. Operators act unilaterally on operands, functions act unilaterally on data, messages act unilaterally on objects, or network packets are sent unilaterally to transaction handlers. If it matters whether the receiver is ready for (receptive to) an action, this must be arranged by adding something that is outside the basic unilateral action, such as a queue and other synchronization machinery at each transaction handler.

Organizations, by contrast, revolve around the concept of interaction, not unilateral action. Interaction implies that two parties rendezvous in space and time only when both are receptive to the interaction, whereupon both undergo a change in state, coincidently. To pay the tab at a restaurant, the cashier and the customer rendezvous at the checkout counter when both are receptive, whereupon the transaction commences for both, coincidently. At some point the customer owns the money and the cashier doesn't. An instant later, the cashier owns the money and the customer doesn't. The state of both parties has been changed coincidently by the interaction. Introducing a buffer, for example, by paying the waiter instead of the cashier, doesn't change the primitiveness of interaction. It simply decomposes the transaction into a pair of interactions, one between the customer and the waiter and a subsequent interaction between the waiter and the cashier, each one controlled by legally binding responsibilities.

[3]E.H. Shortliffe, *Computer-Based Medical Consultations*, American Elsevier, New York, 1976.

Imagine this scenario modeled in an object-oriented simulation language. The cashier and the customer could be modeled as concurrent objects, perhaps using the Task class mentioned earlier to provide them an asynchronous thread of control. Each would have private data, and a set of procedures for regulating access to that data. So far so good. But how should the algorithm for the money exchange transaction be expressed? Accurately modeling this simple transaction depends on a number of factors that depend on concurrency and the cooperation of both parties. The unilateral tell-an-object-what-to-do kind of communication described in this book is not at all a good model for what goes on here. The restaurant example assumes continual awareness on the part of both parties. The customer cannot leave until the cashier notices and cooperates, and the customer is simultaneously prevented from leaving because he fears the cashier will notice. Yet the cashier is forced to respond briskly, because of a complex system of moves and countermoves available to both parties that control the possible outcome.

Computers have proved their worth as tools for automating solitary office tasks. But that next step to true office automation is a big one. It requires concepts, tools, and methodologies capable of describing coordination events far more complicated than the customer-cashier example. Is object-oriented programming the answer? Absolutely not. It merely helps develop large, complicated, but basically conventional systems.

I'm not even sure that there is an answer. I do believe that computer science should invest more time than has been spent to date in finding it.[4]

---

[4] I would like to acknowledge the contribution of Dr. Anatol Holt of the ITT Advanced Technology Center. Tolly is a computer scientist. His work has centered on exploring the questions raised in this last section.

| Appendix A

Specification Sheets

In this appendix, the word Software-IC will be reserved to mean a class as represented in a binary file. When the distinction between compile-time, link-time, and run-time is immaterial to the discussion, class will be used exclusively.

This appendix provides specification sheets for the Software-ICs shown in Figure A.1, organized alphabetically by class name.

About These Specifications

In principle, specification sheets should describe a Software-IC in sufficient detail that an experienced Objective-C programmer can use it without access to its sources. However this amount of detail would not be appropriate in this book and is not provided. These eight Software-ICs are a subset of the eighteen Software-ICs that are routinely delivered with each Objective-C compiler license, and the full documentation for all eighteen is nearly the size of this book. This subset was chosen to provide a representative sample of a typical Software-IC library, large enough to demonstrate how such libraries can be built and documented, yet small enough to be manageable.

The Software-ICs described here are the same as those in the commercial library. However, fewer classes are described here, and not to nearly the same level of detail. Details that would be more appropriate in a reference manual have been ruthlessly pruned. Names of functions and selectors have been modified for greater readability, and in some cases the algorithms themselves were changed to hide irrelevant coding details or to make the code more understandable.

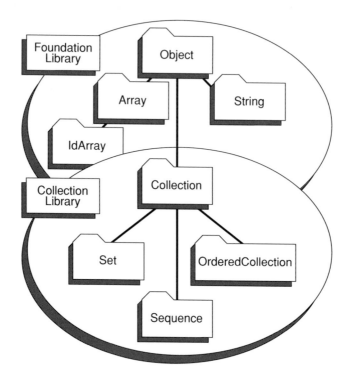

Figure A.1. The specification sheets for these classes are presented in this appendix in alphabetical order. In a few cases, the code itself is different because of the changes made since the standard library was released.

Although this should be rare, this library will occasionally differ from the commercial one. For example, in the commercial library, OrderedCollection and Collection are named OrdCltn and Cltn to avoid name length restrictions with some older C compilers and linkers. In a few cases, the code itself is different, due to optimizations in the commercial library that would only confuse the concepts in this book.

Technical Specification Section

Each specification sheet provides a table of technical specifications, a functionality description, and descriptions of each method. In general, methods that exist primarily to support other functionality have been removed for brevity, consistent with the goal of describing only the interface between this library and its user, not internal interfaces inside the library.

The technical specifications section in each sheet provides the following information:

ClassName. This is the name of the class implemented in this Software-IC.

Superclasses. This lists each of this class's superclasses, in sequence.

Other classes referenced. This lists the classes, not including superclasses, that are referenced via explicit external references from this class and each of its superclasses. This represents any additional classes that this one needs to function properly. The classes in this list represent hidden dependencies that must be added to the application's class table explicitly.

Used by. This lists those classes that reference this one indirectly, i.e., other than by inheriting it. Only the classes shown in Figure A.1 are considered.

Inherited by. This lists the subclasses of this class. Only the classes shown in Figure A.1 are considered.

Source bulk. This provides the source bulk of this class's class description file as computed by the UNIX word count (wc) utility (# lines, # words, # characters).

Binary bulk. This provides the binary bulk of the compiled class as computed by the UNIX size utility.

Maturity index. This presents supplier's judgment as to the likelihood of this class changing in such a way that consumer's code will be impacted, using index values of infantile, adolescent, adult, mature, senile, etc. Classes are infantile as long as they have been used in only a single application. Those that have been used in several applications written by other than the class's author are mature. The classes described here are all relatively mature.

Declaration. This provides the class's declaration, including instance variable declarations.

Factory methods. This provides the declaration for each factory method. Methods of purely internal interest will in some cases be listed here, but without subsequent discussion.

Instance methods. This provides the declaration for each factory method. Methods of purely internal interest will in some cases be listed here, but without subsequent discussion.

Global Declarations

The specification sheets often use the following typedef names in preference to C type names. These are defined in a standard header file, objc.h.

typedef char *STR; The STR type is used for pointers to a null-terminated array of characters; i.e., a C string.

typedef char *SEL; The SEL type is used for Objective-C selector codes. Objective-C currently implements selector codes as pointers to a unique copy of a character array containing the selector's characters.

typedef char BOOL; The BOOL type is used for booleans that hold YES or NO values (see below).

typedef id (*IMP)( ); The IMP type is used for pointers to C functions that implement methods.

typedef struct __iobuf *IOD; The IOD type is used as descriptors for stdio streams.

typedef struct __SHARED *SHR; The SHR type is used as a pointer to structures that describe the shared part of any object.

This file also defines several preprocessor symbols and macros. These are used as abbreviations throughout:

#define IV(obj) (((STR)(obj)) + (obj)->isa->clsSizInstance). The IV() macro replies a pointer (of type STR) to the first indexed instance variable of any array instance.

#define YES (BOOL)1. This defines the value of YES, the Boolean TRUE.

#define NO (BOOL)0. This defines the value of NO, the Boolean FALSE.

#define Nil (SHR)0. This defines the value of Nil, which is used as the id of the Nil class.

#define nil (id)0. This defines the value of nil, which is used as the id of the one and only instance of the Nil class.

The classes are supported by a substrate of functions that are described next. These functions are not called directly but through pointer variables so that applications with unusual requirements can replace parts of the substrate at run-time by storing new values into these variables.

id (*__alloc)(aClass, nBytes) SHR aClass; int nBytes; The function identified by this variable is called to allocate memory for the named variables of a new instance of aClass, with an extra nBytes at the end for indexed instance variables. The space is initialized with zeros (nils), and the first word (the isa link) is initialized to aClass. The function returns the address of this space as the id of the new instance of aClass.

id (*__dealloc)(anObject) id anObject; The function identified by this variable is called to deallocate anObject's private memory for reuse. The function replies nil. It is illegal to reference this object subsequently. To help trap such illegal references, the object's isa link is zeroed before its space is released, and the messager reports messages to such objects as messages to released objects. There is no guarantee that this will catch all such errors because the object's space may be turned to other uses at any time after the object is deallocated.

id (*__realloc)(anObject, nBytes) id anObject; int nBytes; The function identified by this variable changes the amount of space at the end of anObject's named instance variables to nBytes, repositioning anObject in memory if necessary. The function returns the new address of anObject.

id (*__copy)(anObject, nBytes) id anObject; int nBytes; The function identified by this variable replies the id of a new object produced by copying anObject's named instance variables plus nBytes of its indexed instance variables.

id (*__error)(anObject, aFormatString, anArgument) id anObject; STR aFormatString; The function identified by this variable is called to handle serious error conditions. The aFormat String argument provides the text of an error message ala printf. The function prints the error message, calls prnStack() to print the activation record stack to describe the pending function and message returns, and calls the function bye() to abort the run. This behavior is commonly overridden by either providing a custom version of bye() or by installing one's own function in __error.

BOOL (*__storeOn)(aFileName, anObject) STR aFileName; id anObject; The function identified by this variable is called to passivate anObject to the file named aFileName as discussed in Chapter 7.

BOOL (*__fileOut)(anIOD, anObject) IOD anIOD; id anObject; The function identified by this variable is called to passivate anObject to the stdio file description anIOD. This allows objects to be passivated directly to UNIX devices like pipes or network sockets.

id (*__readFrom)(aFileName) STR aFileName; The function identified by this variable is called to activate an object given a passivated record of the object's private data content. The file, aFileName, is assumed to contain a passivated object. The function recreates (activates) the object in memory, replying its id to the caller. Various error conditions are possible; if no object can be constructed (the file does not exist, parsing errors, etc.) the function prints a diagnostic message and returns nil.

id (*__fileIn)(anIOD) IOD anIOD; The function identified by this variable is called to activate an object by reading the stdio I/O file descriptor, anIOD, which is assumed to represent a passivated object. The function recreates (activates) the object in memory by parsing the bytes, returning the id of the new object to the caller. Various error conditions are possible. If no object can be constructed, the function prints a diagnostic and returns nil.

id (*__cvtToId)(aClassName) STR aClassName; The function identified by this variable is called to locate the factory object by that name, by searching for the string in a table of known classes. This is used during activation to determine the shared part of each incoming object (the isa link information is encoded as a classname, to avoid having to store methods of passivated objects).

SEL (*_cvtToSel)(); The function identified by this variable is called to convert a C string to the a selector code, by searching for the string in a table of selector codes. Selector codes are currently implemented as pointers to a unique copy of a string representing the selector's bytes.

Array
Abstract Array Superclass

ClassName	Array
Superclass	Object
Other classes referenced	⟨none⟩
Used by	⟨none⟩
Inherited by	IdArray IntArray
Maturity index	relatively mature
Source bulk	54 lines, 229 words, 1734 chars
Binary bulk	text 676, data 260, bss 0, total 936, hex 3a8
Declaration	@interfacetoArray:Object { unsigned capacity; }

Factory methods	
(int)ndxVarSize	new:(int)nElements
Instance methods	with:nArgs
(BOOL)isCopyOf:anObject	(int)hash
(BOOL) isEqual:anObject	(unsigned)size
(STR)describe	boundsViolation:(unsigned)anOffset
(unsigned)capacity	capacity:(unsigned)nSlots
	copy
	sort

Array is the abstract superclass of a number of subclasses that support indexed instance variables of various types; IntArray holds integers, IdArry holds object identifiers, etc.

Indexed instance variables are like named instance variables, but they are accessed by integer offsets instead of names. Their location is computed relative to the base address located in the elements instance variable. It is the responsibility of the subclass to correctly access the information pointed to by the elements pointer and to return the information with the correct type. For example, IdArrays define the at: and at:put: methods to return ids, while the IntArray types them to return integers.

A programmer who is preoccupied with efficiency may use the IV(obj) macro defined in objc.h to directly access the indexed instance variables. The IV() macro is defined to return a value of type STR that points to the first indexed instance variable of obj. In order to be useful, the value returned by IV() must be cast to the correct type. This is typically done on a per class basis by defining a macro named FIRST that points to the first element by correctly casting the result of IV(). For example, the definition of the FIRST macro used when accessing IdArrays is:

```
#define FIRST ( (id *) IV(self) )
```

The most basic way of creating array instances is to send a new: message to the appropriate factory with an argument that indicates the number of indexed variables and therefore the capacity of that instance. Once created, it is not straightforward to increase an Array's capacity. This usually relocates the array in memory, thus changing its id. Arrays are best used as low-level building blocks, a substrate for higher level classes that can hide the identifier problem from their consumer. For examples of how this is done, see Collection.

Each array subclass provides its own set of methods for accessing instance variables. IdArray provides at: and at:put: methods for reading and writing indexed variables of type id, and IntArray provides intAt: and intAt:put: methods that read and write integers.

Declaration

unsigned capacity   This variable specifies the number of indexed instance variables held by this instance. Notice that since this variable is of type unsigned, this limits the maximum capacity of IdArrays and the classes that use them (Collections) to 2^{32} on typical machines.

void *elements   This variable specifies a pointer to the indexed instance variables contained in the instance.

Instance Creation

+ new:(unsigned)nElements   This factory method replies a new instance with nElements indexed instance variables. The implementation determines the number of bytes per instance variable by sending ndxVarSize to self and allocates space by calling the substrate function (*_alloc)().

+ with:(unsigned)nArgs, argumentList   This factory method creates a new instance with nArgs indexed variables and initializes them from the method's (variable length) argument list. The implementation is a subclass responsibility since the C types of the argument list varies with the subclass. This method is useful for creating initialized arrays, like this:

```
id a = [AnyArraySubclassFactory with:3, entry1, entry2, entry3];
```

Memory Management

- (unsigned)size   This method replies the size of the array. For IdArrays, the size is the number of non-nil array members. For arrays of other C types size is equivalent to capacity.

- (unsigned)capacity   This method replies the number of indexed variables held by the receiver. This meaning is assumed by the activation/passivation logic and should be changed only with great care.

- capacity:(unsigned)nSlots   This method changes the receiver's capacity to nSlots. It replies the receiver's new identifier. This new identifier is in general different from the old one because the receiver may be repositioned in memory, invalidating the old identifier. The implementation uses the substrate function (*_realloc)().

Error Handling

- boundsViolation:(int)anOffset   This method is used by subclasses to report array bounds errors. It is implemented as

```
- boundsViolation:(int)anOffset {
    return [self error: capacity > 0
        ? "bounds violation: %d outside range [0..%d]"
        : "zero capacity array", anOffset, capacity-1];
}
```

Collection
Abstract Collection Class

Class Name	Collection
Superclass	Object
Other classes referenced	IdArray Sequence
Used by	⟨none⟩
Inherited by	OrderedCollection Set
Maturity index	relatively mature
Source bulk	96 lines, 468 words, 3499 chars
Binary bulk	text 1888, data 340, bss 0, total 2228, hex 8b4
Declaration	@interfacetoCollection:Object { id contents unsigned capacity; }

Factory methods
  new:(int)anInt
  with:(int)nArgs; id Arg1;
Instance methods

(BOOL)contains:anObject
(BOOL)isCopyOf:anObject

(BOOL)isEmpty

(int)offsetMatching:anObject
(int)offsetMatchingSTR:(STR)aStr
(int)offsetOf:anObject
(int)size
add:newObject
addContentsOf:aCollection
addContentsTo:aCollection

asIdArray
asOrdCltn
asSet

eachElement
eachElementPerform:(SEL)aSelector
  with:anArgument
eachElementPerform:(SEL)aSelector
  with:arg1 with:arg2
eachElementPerform:(SEL)aSelector
expand
find:anObject
findMatching:anObject
findSTR:(STR)aStr
free
freeContents
remove:oldObject
removeContentsFrom:aCltn
removeContentsOf:aCollection

Collection is the abstract superclass of a number of classes that are modeled loosely after Smalltalk-80's collection classes.[1]

This class defines the basic message protocols for managing arbitrary numbers of other objects as a unit. This includes instance creation, adding and removing elements, converting between collections of different types, testing membership, and memory allocation.

Different subclasses are generally implemented in radically different ways. However, the methods discussed here assume that the subclasses use the instance variable, contents, to identify an IdArray that holds identifiers for

---

[1]See Goldberg and Robson, *Smalltalk-80: The Language and Its Implementation*, Addison-Wesley, 1983.

the members of the collection. This assumption is valid for most common collections including OrderedCollections and Sets, but it is not true for all collections, such as collections based on list or tree data structures. Sub-classes are responsible for overriding methods whose assumptions regarding the contents variable are not valid.

Enumeration is a property of all collections, the ability to sequence through the collection members one by one. Enumeration is implemented by a parallel hierarchy of classes, Sequences, which encapsulates the details of how to enumerate over the different kinds of collections so that these details do not spread to the consumer's code. The following enumeration protocol is guaranteed for any kind of collection

```
aSequence = [anyCollectionInstance eachElement];
while (nextMember = [aSequence next]) {
    ... process nextMember
}
[aSequence free];
```

Collection classes that use data structures other than the default one (i.e., an IdArray) override eachElement to create a Sequence subclass that performs enumeration for that data structure.

The descriptions that follow all presume the default case of data structures based on IdArrays.

Instance Variables

id contents   This variable identifies the data structure in which the members of the collection are managed. The methods implemented in this class presume that this data structure is an instance of IdArray.

unsigned capacity   This variable identifies the amount of space allocated for the array based on the number of elements the array can hold. This variable is updated whenever the collection is expanded or contracted and is used by Collection's methods to determine the bounds of the IdArray that contains the actual object ids.

Instance Creation

+ new   This factory method replies a new instance of the receiver's class. The contents variable is initialized with a default size IdArray.

+ new:(int)anInt   This factory method replies a new empty instance of the receiver's class whose capacity variable has been initialized to the value returned by [IdArray new:anInt].

+ with:(int)nArgs; id Arg1;   This method replies a new instance of the receiver whose contents are initialized from the nArgs subsequent arguments.

The method is implemented as

```
+ with:(int)nArgs; id Arg1; { register id *p = &Arg1;
    self = [self new:nArgs];
    while (nArgs--) [self add:*p++];
    return self;
}
```

This method is used like this:

```
flagColors = [ OrderedCollection with:3, red, white, blue ];
```

Adding Members

The collection class defines an abstract protocol for adding elements to any kind of collection. These implementations are normally overridden in subclasses.

- add:newObject   This method adds newObject to the collection. The implementation is a subclass responsibility.

```
- add:newObject { return [self subclassResponsibility]; }
```

- addContentsTo:aCollection   This method adds the contents of the receiver to aCollection and replies aCollection. The implementation is

```
[contents addContentsTo:aCollection]; return aCollection;
```

- addContentsOf:aCollection   This method adds the contents of aCollection to the receiver and replies the receiver. The implementation is

```
[aCollection addContentsTo:self]; return self;
```

Removing

The Collection class defines an abstract protocol for removing elements from any kind of collection. The implementations are usually overridden in subclasses.

- remove:oldObject   This method removes oldObject from the receiver and replies oldObject if the removal succeeds, nil if the remove failed (for example, because object was not found). The implementation is a subclass responsibility.

```
- remove:oldObject { return [self subclassResponsibility]; }
```

- removeContentsOf:aCollection   This method removes any members from the receiver that are also members of aCollection and replies the receiver.

```
- removeContentsOf:aCollection
    { [contents removeContentsOf:aCollection]; return self; }
```

Enumeration

- eachElement   This method replies a new instance of Sequence suitable for enumerating over the members of the receiver. The caller owns the sequence instance and is responsible for releasing it when finished. For efficiency reasons, many collection classes assume that the collection will not be changed while enumeration is occurring. Implementors of collection subclasses should override eachElement if the default implementation provided here and in class Sequence does not match the way the receiver is implemented.

```
return [Sequence array:contents];
```

This default implementation (unless overridden) sacrifices safety to provide speed. All methods assume that the contents variable references a private data structure. Yet this method passes a reference to this structure to a Sequence. If the data structure changes while the Sequence is open (for example, by increasing the capacity of an IdArray), the data structure might be relocated in memory and the Sequence will not be notified. A safer implementation would be to pass the sequence a copy of the array, but this might decrease performance to the point that the way enumeration is implemented across diverse collections could not be kept hidden from performance-conscious programmers.

- eachElementPerform:(SEL)aSelector

- eachElementPerform:(SEL)aSelector with:argument1

- eachElementPerform:(SEL)aSelector with:argument1 with:argument2   These three methods broadcast the message aSelector to each member of the receiver. The three methods support messages of zero, **one, or** two arguments: They are implemented as

```
- eachElementPerform:(SEL)aSelector
    { if (contents) _msg(contents, _cmd, aSelector); return self; }
```

Converting between Collection Types

The following methods convert collections of one type to another, by creating an instance of the new type and then adding each member of the receiver to the new collection. For example, [anOrderedCollection asSet] serves to eliminate duplicate members from an ordered collection.

- asSet   This method replies a set to which the receiver's members have been added. The method is implemented as

```
return [self addContentsTo:[Set new:([self size]*4)/3]];
```

- asOrdCltn   This method replies an OrderedCollection to which the receiver's members have been added. The method is implemented as

```
return [self addContentsTo:[OrderedCollection new:[self size]]];
```

Testing

- (unsigned)size   This method replies the number of elements in the receiver. The following default implementation is often overridden.

```
return [contents size];
```

- (BOOL)isEmpty   This method replies whether the receiver contains any members. The implementation is

```
return [self size] == 0;
```

- (BOOL)contains:anObject   This method replies whether the collection contains anObject.

```
return [self find:anObject] != nil;
```

Searching

- find:anObject   This method replies whether the collection contains a member whose id is the same as anObject; nil otherwise.

```
return [contents find:anObject];
```

- findMatching:anObject   This method replies a member such that [aMember isEqual:anObject]; nil otherwise.

```
return [contents findMatching:anObject];
```

- findSTR:(STR)aStr   This method replies a member such that [aMember isEqualSTR:aStr]; nil otherwise.

```
return [contents findSTR:aStr];
```

- (int)offsetOf:anObject

- (int)offsetMatching:anObject

- (int)offsetMatchingSTR:(STR)aString   These methods parallel the find methods, but they return the offset of the matching element. They reply a negative number (-1) to indicate failure.

Memory Management

- free   This method deallocates the receiver and the object identified in the contents variable. Collection members are not freed (see IdArray).

```
- free { [contents free]; return [super free]; }
```

IdArray
Array of Object Reference

ClassName	IdArray
Superclass	Object, Array
Other classes referenced	⟨none⟩
Used by	Collection Set OrderedCollection
Inherited by	⟨none⟩
Maturity index	relatively mature
Source bulk	173 lines, 975 words, 6107 chars
Binary bulk	text 2768, data 336, bss 0, total 3104, hex c20
Declaration	@interfacetoIdArray:Object
Factory methods	
(int)ndxVarSize	with:(unsigned)nArgs; id Arg1;
Instance methods	
(BOOL)contains:anObject	eachElement
(BOOL)isEqual:anObject	eachElementPerform:(SEL)aSelector
	with:anArg with:anotherArg
(STR)describe	eachElementPerform:(SEL)aSelector
	with:anArg
(int)hash	eachElementPerform:(SEL)aSelector
(int)offsetMatching:anObject	exchange:(int)aOffset
(int)offsetOf:anObject	and:(int)anotherOffset
(int)offsetSTR:(STR)aStr	find:anObject
(int)size	findMatching:anObject
add:anObject	findSTR:(STR)aStr
addContentsTo:aCollection	freeContents
asIdArray	packContents
at:(int)anOffset	remove:anObject
insert:anObject	removeAt:(int)anOffset
at:(int)anOffset put:anObject	removeContentsFrom:aTbl
at:(int)anOffset	sort
addContentsOf:aCollection	
packContents	

IdArray is a subclass of Array whose indexed instance variables hold references to other objects. IdArrays are system-level building blocks that manage arbitrary numbers of object identifiers. They are primarily used to build other classes, such as Collections, and are rarely used directly by user-level code.

Instance Creation
+ **with:(unsigned)nArgs; id Arg1;**   This factory method creates a new instance with capacity to hold nArgs references, initializing it by adding (add:) the remaining members of the argument list. The method is used like this:

```
bigCities = [IdArray with:3, [String str:"NewYork"],
    [String str:"Los Angeles"], [String str:"Chicago"]];
```

Accessing (as an Array)

These methods allow the receiver's indexed instance variables to be read or modified according to an integer offset between zero and capacity -1.

- **at:(unsigned)anOffset**   This method replies the contents of the indexed variable at anOffset.

- **at:(unsigned)anOffset put:anObject**   This method replaces the contents of the indexed variable at anOffset with anObject and replies the prior contents of this slot.

Adding

In a few limited respects, primarily adding and removing elements, IdArrays emulate collections with a fixed maximum capacity.

- **add:anObject**   This method adds anObject to the first empty slot in the receiver (i.e., the first slot that contains nil). It replies self if successful, or [self boundsViolation:capacity] if no empty slot exists.

- **addContentsTo:aCollection**   This method executes [aCollection add: aMember] for each nonnil member. It replies aCollection.

- **addContentsOf:aCollection**   This method adds the contents of aCollection to the contents of the receiver. This method doesn't check the capacity of the receiver's IdArray before it starts, and therefore might generate an error if it runs out of room to complete the addition.

Removing

- **removeAt:(unsigned)anOffset**   This method packs the elements behind anOffset into the slot at anOffset and replies the prior contents of slot anOffset.

- **remove:anObject**   This method searches for a member whose id equals anObject (aMember == anObject) and replies anObject if the search succeeded, otherwise nil. Nil is stored into the now-empty slot.

- **removeContentsFrom:aCollection**   This method executes [aCollection remove:aMember] for each non-nil member.

- **packContents**   This method is used to remove the nil slots in the IdArray while preserving the original order of the elements. Collections use this method to eliminate 'holes' left from using the remove: method.

Comparing and Sorting

IdArrays obey the requirements established by the Set class and function properly as set members.

- (BOOL)isEqual:anObject   This replies whether the receiver is equal to anObject. An IdArray is equal to anothertoObject if they are both instances of the same class, have the same capacity, and the members of both reply true to isEqual:.

- (unsigned)hash   This replies a hash code based on the class of the receiver, its capacity, and the hash value computed by each member.

```
register unsigned n = capacity;
register unsigned code = (int)isa ^ n;
id *p = (id*)IV(self);
while(n--) code ^ = [*p++ hash];
return code;
```

Testing

-(unsigned)size   This method reports the number of non-nil elements in the array, determined by counting them.

-(BOOL)contains:anObject   This method replies YES if receiver contains anObject, implemented as

```
return [self find:anObject] != nil;
```

Searching

These methods report the results of various membership tests applied to each member. The methods reply nil if no match succeeds.

find:anObject   This method replies the id of any member for which member == an Object.

findMatching:anObject   This method replies the id of any member for which [member isEqual:anObject].

findSTR:(STR)aString   This method replies the id of any member for which [member isEqualSTR:aString].

Offset Determination

These methods report their findings as offsets into the array. Negative findings are reported by returning an illegal offset; −1.

- (unsigned)offsetOf:anObject   This replies the offset of the member for which [member = = anObject].

- (unsigned)offsetMatching:anObject   This replies the offset of the member for which [member isEqual:anObject].

- (unsigned)offsetSTR:(STR)aStr   This replies the offset of the member for which [member isEqualSTR:aStr].

Enumerating

- eachElement   This method replies a Sequence that can be used to enumerate the members. The caller owns the sequence and is responsible for releasing it when through. This method is implemented as

```
- eachElement { return [Sequence array:self]; }
```

- eachElementPerform:(SEL)aSelector

- eachElementPerform:(SEL)aSelector with:argument1

- eachElementPerform:(SEL)aSelector with:argument1 with:argument2
These three methods broadcast the message aSelector to each member of the receiver. The three methods support messages of zero, one, or two arguments.

Deallocating

IdArrays inherit the free method of the Object class. Notice that freeing an IdArray does not automatically free its members, but only the receiver itself.

- freeContents   This method frees each member of the receiver by sending [member free] and storing nil into its slot in the receiver. The IdArray is not freed.

Indexed Variable Typing

These methods report the size and type of its indexed variables to meet requirements established in the activation/passivation logic.[2]

+ (int)ndxVarSize   This method replies sizeof(id).

- (STR)describe   This method replies the string $"@"$, a coded value signifying type 'id'.

---

[2]The details of the activation/passivation logic and its interaction with these classes are not described.

Object
Abstract Class of all Object

ClassName	Object
Superclasses	⟨none⟩
Other classes referenced	⟨none⟩
Used by	⟨none⟩
Inherited by	Array IdArray String Collection OrderedCollection Set
Maturity index	relatively mature
Source bulk	124 lines, 591 words, 4188 chars
Binary bulk	text 1496, data 572, bss 0, total 2068, hex 814
Declaration	@interfacetoObject { struct__SHARED *isa; short attr, objID; }

Factory methods
    (STR)ndxVarType   new
    (int)ndxVarSize   poseAs:(SHR)aFactoryId
    free   readFrom:(STR)aFileName
    initialize
Instance methods
    (BOOL)isCopyOf:anObject   deepCopy
    (BOOL)isEqual:anObject   doesNotRecognize:(STR)aMessage
    (BOOL)isKindOf:(SHR)aClass   error:(STR)aCStr; va__dcl
    (BOOL)isMemberOf:(SHR)aClass free
    (BOOL)isSame:anObject   idOfSTR:(STR)aClassName
    (BOOL)notEqual:anObject   notImplemented
    (BOOL)notSame:anObject   perform:(STR)aSelector
    (BOOL)respondsTo:(STR)aSelector with:anObject
    (BOOL)storeOn:(STR)aFileName perform:(STR)aSelector
                                    with:firstObject with:secondObject
    (STR)describe   perform:(STR)aSelector
    (STR)name   print
    (STR)str   printOn:(IOD)anIOD
    (int)capacity   self
    (int)compare:anObject   shallowCopy
    (int)hash   shouldNotImplement
    (int)size   show
    asGraph:(BOOL)unique   subclassResponsibility
    awake   superClass
    class
    copy

This class is the most generic class in the system. It is the root of the inheritance hierarchy and a superclass of all other classes in this appendix. It establishes how the object concept is managed in computer memory, and defines a repertoire of behaviors that will be inherited by all other classes. Its factory methods are inherited by all other factory objects to provide the basic protocol for instantiating objects of any class. Object is an abstract superclass, in that instances are rarely created as such. Its variables and methods are used by inheriting them into specialized subclasses.

Implementation Note

This class is based on a large collection of supporting functions that are maintained and documented as detachable units. This allows the substrate to be changed without changing the source for the class itself. These substrate functions are accessed through global function pointers called locator variables to allow substrate functions to be changed either at link-time or at run-time. For example, bulky functionality like the activation/passivation machinery could be removed in a space-critical application that doesn't need this functionality by defining dummy allocation/deallocation machinery and overriding the locator variable values at link-time. Conversely, the behavior of the error handler can be changed at run-time by storing the address of a custom error handler into its locator variable.

Only the intended meaning for each method can be described here. The actual meaning, and thus the method's real implementation, is determined by the locator variable. Summary documentation for these functions is provided at the beginning of this appendix.

Instance Creation and Deletion

The most basic way to create an instance of any class is by sending new to that class's factory object. The factory object returns an id that can be used to access the instance until the instance is sent a free message. After this time, it is illegal to access the object further. Its memory has been deallocated and possibly turned to other uses.

+ new   This factory method allocates a new instance of the receiver and replies the id of this new instance. The implementation allocates the amount of memory stated in the receiver's clsSizeInstance variable, sets the first word in that block to the receiver, and fills the remainder of the space with nil (0).

```
+ new { return (*_alloc)(self, 0); }³
```

This method is commonly overridden in subclasses for which nil instance variables are not acceptable. The recommended way of doing this is by using the special receiver, super, as follows:

```
@implementation SomeObjectSubclass ...
+new {
    id newInstance = [super new];   // allocate an instance
    [newInstance initialize];       // initialize as needed
    return newInstance;             // reply the instance
    }
```

---

³The properties of this function were discussed in Chapter 5 under the pseudonym allocNil-Block.

- free   This method deallocates the receiver and replies nil. It is illegal to access the receiver again. To aid in checking for this, the method zeroes the receiver's isa link before releasing its memory. The messager checks for and reports messages to an object whose isa == nil as messages to freed objects.

```
+ free { return nil; } // Factories are not on the heap!
- free { return (*_dealloc)(self); }
```

Computed Selectors

A computed selector is a selector code held in a C character pointer. The compiler provides a special syntax for initializing such variables, and the library provides dynamic functions (cvtToSel()) that convert C strings to selector codes.

- perform:(SEL)aSelector

```
return _msg(self, aSelector);
```

- perform:(SEL)aSelector with:anObject

```
return _msg(self, aSelector, anObject);
```

- perform:(SEL)aSelector with:firstObject with:secondObject

```
return _msg(self, aSelector, firstObject, secondObject);
```

Error Handling

The object class defines a set of standard responses to error conditions. The most basic way to report an error is

```
return [self error:"cannot handle this"];
```

The default implementation of (_error)() prints a message describing the problem and terminates the program by calling the function bye(), and so the return statement will never be executed. This default behavior is modifiable, by, for example, providing your own function bye() or by overriding error: in a subclass. The other methods in this group are implemented in terms of error:.

- error:(STR)aFormatString; id Arg1;   This method defines the standard way that error conditions will be handled. Override this method to recover from the condition and return control to the caller. The same effect can be obtained for all classes by overriding the exit function bye() or even exit(). The default implementation calls the standard error handler through the locator variable (_error)(). This function prints the error message provided by its arguments, prints the stack of messages that led to the problem, and exits. The arguments to this method are as for the stdio printf function.

- **subclassResponsibility**   Abstract superclasses define protocols that must be reimplemented by all subclass builders by implementing the method that must be overridden as return [self subclassResponsibility]. A standard error message will result if the subclass builder forgets to override the message.

```
- subclassResponsibility
    {return [self error:"Subclass should override this message."]; }
```

- **doesNotRecognize:(STR)aMessage**   The messager reports failure to discover aMessage in the receiver's dispatch table by sending it the message doesNotRecognize: instead. The implementation is

```
- doesNotRecognize:(STR)aMessage
    { return [self error:"%s does not recognize %s", [self name], aMessage]; }
```

Indexed Instance Variable Types

Generic operations (deepcopy, activation, passivation) learn about the C types comprising an instance's indexed variables through the following message protocol. This implementation is appropriate only to those classes that lack indexed instance variables and must be overridden in every class that defines indexed variables. These methods are best understood by referring to Array classes that override them, such as IntArray and IdArray.

- **(unsigned)capacity**   This message must reply the number of indexed instance variables held by the receiver, returning zero except for those classes that support indexed variables. The requirements for this method are established by the activation/passivation machinery. The default implementation is

```
- (unsigned)capacity { return 0; }
```

+ **(int)ndxVarSize**   This message must reply the width of an indexed instance variable in bytes. The default implementation is

```
+ (int)ndxVarSize { return 0; }
```

+ **(STR)describe**   This message must reply a string describing the C type(s) comprising the indexed instance variable. The default implementation is

```
+ (STR)describe { return ""; }
```

Activation/Passivation

Passivation produces a file containing a symbolic representation of the receiver plus all objects referenced by that receiver. Activation converts such a representation into a fully functional memory-resident copy of the original object.

- storeOn:(STR)aFileName   This method causes the receiver to convert itself
to a symbolic representation stored on file aFileName. The implementation
is

```
- (BOOL)storeOn:(STR)aFileName {
    extern id (*_storeOn)();
    return (*_storeOn)(aFileName, self);
}
```

+ readFrom:(STR)aFileName   This method reads a symbolic representation
stored on file aFileName to produce a functioning object in memory, replying
the identifier of the newly created object. The implementation is

```
+ readFrom:(STR)aFileName {
    extern id (*_readFrom)();
    return (*_readFrom)(aFileName);
}
```

- show   This method creates a symbolic representation of the receiver on
the user's terminal. This method is used during debugging as a convenient
way to use the passivation logic to produce a printable representation of any
object and its descendents. By default, the printing is done by the same logic
that is used for the storeOn: method.

```
- show { extern id (*_show)(); return (*_show)(self, 0); }
```

Utility Methods
This is a collection of methods for providing convenient access to information held in every object's shared part.

- class   This method replies the contents of the receiver's isa variable. This
result is variously called the class of the receiver, the id of the receiver's factory object, and the address of the receiver's shared part. These terms are
synonymous in Objective-C.

```
- class { return (id)isa; }
```

- (char*)name   This method replies the classname of the receiver as a character string.

```
- (STR)name { return isa->clsName; }
```

- (char*)str   This method replies a pointer to a character string that describes this instance. It is identical to str unless overridden in a subclass.
String overrides str to describe the characters held by the receiver.

```
- (STR)str { return isa->clsName; }
```

- (unsigned)size   For instances like Arrays and Collections, which can hold any number of other instances, size reports the number of objects they hold. In all other cases, size returns 0.

```
- (unsigned)size { return 0; }
```

- (BOOL)isKindOf:(SHR)aClass   This method reports whether the receiver is an instance of aClass or any of its subclasses. This method is used to do class-dependent checks on arguments passed into methods from outside. For example, Points implement the isEqual: method as

```
- (BOOL)isEqual:anObject {
    return [anObject isKindOf:Point]
       ? x == [anObject x] && y == [anObject y]
       :NO; }
```

- (BOOL)isMemberOf:(SHR)aClass   This method reports whether the receiver is an instance of aClass.

- (BOOL)respondsTo:(SEL)aSelector   This method reports whether the receiver recognizes a specific message.

Comparing

Collections (particularly Set) assume that all members can rank themselves with other members via three basic comparison methods—compare:, isEqual:, and hash. These methods must be consistent with each other and therefore should all be reimplemented in synchrony. No meaningful default implementation for these methods can be provided at the Object level. However, the method name and meaning is defined here, along with a default implementation that generates a standard error if the default is not overridden.

- (unsigned)hash   This method replies an integer whose value is the same for all objects which compare equal according to isEqual:. Collisions, or nonidentical objects that return identical hash values, are inevitable and this is handled by the classes that use hashing. This method is used by classes like Set to spread different objects across a hashing arena, yet send identical objects to a consistent location. The search is refined from there by comparing each object in the collision pool via isEqual:. This method is implemented as

```
return [self subclassResponsibility];
```

- (BOOL)isEqual:anObject   This method replies YES if the receiver is equal to the argument.

```
return [self subclassResponsibility];
```

- (int)compare:anotherObject   This method replies an integer which is less than, equal to, or greater than zero according to whether the receiver is less than, equal to, or greater than anotherObject. This method is implemented as

```
return [self subclassResponsibility];
```

The following methods are commonly inherited as they stand:

- (BOOL)isSame:anObject   This method reports whether the receiver is identical to anObject (i.e., whether they are the same object).

```
return self == anObject,
```

- (BOOL)notEqual:anObject

```
return ![self isEqual:anObject];
```

- (BOOL)notSame:anObject

```
return ![self isSame:anObject];
```

Copying

Copying produces a new object whose private part duplicates the receiver's. A deepCopy does this for all objects that can be reached from the receiver as well.

- copy   This method works the same as shallowCopy.

- shallowCopy   This method replies the id of a duplicate copy of the receiver's private part. Objects referred to inside the receiver are not duplicated, but are now referenced from both the receiver and its copy.

- deepCopy   This method traces all objects reachable from the receiver, building a new copy of the entire graph. The new object and its descendent objects are guaranteed to occupy storage distinct from the receiver and its descendents.

OrderedCollection
Ordered Collection Class

ClassName	OrderedCollection
Superclasses	Collection Object
Other classes referenced	IdArraytoSequence Object
Used by	⟨none⟩
Inherited by	⟨none⟩
Maturity index	relatively mature
Source bulk	44 lines, 173 words, 1385 chars
Binary bulk	text 624, data 196, bss 0, total 820, hex 334
Declaration	@interfacetoOrderedCollection:Collection { unsigned firstEmptySlot; }
Factory methods	⟨none⟩
Instance methods	
(BOOL)isCopyOf:anObject	at:(unsigned)anInteger
(unsigned)lastIndex	boundsError:(unsigned)anInteger
(unsigned)size	firstElement
add:anObject	lastElement
at:(unsigned)anInteger put:anObject	remove:oldObject
	expand

The OrderedCollection class is a kind of Collection that maintains the order in which members are acquired (added). The version described here allows elements to be added and removed from one end only.

OrderedCollections manage their members in an IdArray, referenced from the contents variable inherited from Collection. This array normally has excess capacity, with the first unused slot identified by firstEmptySlot. Elements are added by checking that unused capacity remains (expanding the IdArray when more space is needed) and storing the id of the new member in the first unused slot. OrderedCollections silently reject attempts to add nil members.

Instance Variables
unsigned firstEmptySlot;   This variable holds the offset of the receiver's first unused slot.

Accessing
Bounds are always checked; violations are reported via

```
return [self boundsError:anInteger];
```

- **at:(unsigned)anInteger**   This method replies the value in slot anInteger.

- **firstElement**   This method replies the first element in the collection

```
return [self at:0].
```

- **lastElement**   This method replies the last element in the collection

```
return [self at:firstEmptySlot-1].
```

Testing
- (unsigned)size   This method replies the number of members of the receiver

```
return firstEmptySlot.
```

- (unsigned)lastIndex   This method replies the offset of the last nonempty slot;

```
return firstEmptySlot -1;
```

Adding
- add:anObject   This method appends anObject to the end of the collection, automatically acquiring additional space as needed. The method is implemented as

```
- add:anObject {
      if (anObject == nil) return self;
      if (contents == nil || firstEmptySlot >= capacity)
            [self expand];
      FIRST [firstEmptySlot++] = anObject;
      return self;
}
```

Removing
- remove:oldObject   This method removes the first member whose id matches oldObject and replies oldObject, or else nil if oldObject was not found. The remaining members are packed to fill the gap. This changes the offset of all objects behind it in the array.

Error Handling
- boundsError:(unsigned)anInteger   This method overrides the boundsError: method inherited from Collection.

```
return [self error:"cannot access element %u (firstEmpty=%u capacity=%u)",
    anInteger, firstEmptySlot, capacity ];
```

Sequence
Enumeration over Collections and IdArrays

ClassName	Sequence
Superclasses	Collection Object
Other classes referenced	IdArray Sequence
Used by	Collection
Inherited by	⟨none⟩
Maturity index	relatively mature
Source bulk	62 lines, 344 words, 2119 chars
Binary bulk	text 652, data 176, bss 0, total 828, hex 33c
Declaration	@interfacetoSequence:Collection
	{ unsigned offset; }
Factory methods	array:anIdArray
Instance methods	
(BOOL)isCopyOf:anObject	next
(int)size	previous
first	rewind
free	toFirst
last	toLast

Sequences implement a uniform protocol for enumerating (sequencing over) the members of all classes that collect objects into groups.

Sequence is the root of a hierarchy of classes that roughly parallels the Collection classes. This root class handles those collections in which enumeration can be implemented as an index and a reference to an IdArray. Subclasses must be developed to handle other data structures like linked lists, trees, etc. Each collection is responsible for providing enumeration methods (such as eachElement) to deliver a properly initialized sequence that is suitable for enumerating the members of that receiver.

To make sequencing as efficient as possible, the heavily used collections like Set and OrderedCollection do not allocate a unique copy of their private IdArray when creating a sequence. Instead they provide a reference to their private copy. This violates important assumptions they make elsewhere about the privacy of this store. This makes it unwise to operate on the collection in such a way that its IdArray might be repositioned in memory while a sequence is operating over it. Specifically, do not add elements to a collection while a sequence is active.

Instance Variables
unsigned offset   This defines the sequences state with respect to the collection. This offset is modified by [sequence next].

Allocation/Deallocation
+ **array:anIdArray**   This factory method creates a new sequence initialized to sequence over the members of anIdArray. To reduce memory allocation overhead, memory for the new sequence is obtained from a shallow cache (depth 1).

```
+ array:anIdArray { extern id IdArray;
    if (anIdArray == 0) return nil;
    if ((id)anIdArray->isa != IdArray) returnto[self error:"IdArray needed"];
    if (cache && (cache->isa == Nil)) cache->isa = (struct _SHARED *)self;
    else cache = (*_alloc)(self, 0);
    cache->offset = 0; cache->contents = anIdArray; return cache;
    }
```

- free   This method releases the sequence. To reduce memory deallocation overhead, the most recently freed is cached and reused in the next instantiation.

```
- free { contents = nil; offset = 0;
    if (cache == self) cache->isa = n; else [super free]; return nil; }
```

Sequencing

- next   This method replies the next nonnil object in the sequence or nil if there are no more objects in the sequence.

- previous   This method replies the prior nonnil member in the sequence, or nil if there are no more members.

- toLast   This method positions the sequence to just past the last member.

- toFirst   This method positions the sequence to the first member.

- first   This method is implemented as

```
- first { [self toFirst]; return [self next]; }
```

- last   This method is implemented as

```
- last { [self toLast]; return [self previous]; }
```

- (unsigned)size   This method reports the number of elements in the entire sequence (i.e., the number remaining in the sequence).

Set
The Class of Sets

ClassName	Set
Superclasses	Collection Object
Other classes referenced	IdArray Sequence
Used by	⟨none⟩
Inherited by	⟨none⟩
Maturity index	relatively mature
Source bulk	127 lines, 747 words, 4730 chars
Binary bulk	text 1672, data 204, bss 0, total 1876, hex 754
Declaration	@interfacetoSet:Collection { unsigned tally; }
Factory methods	⟨none⟩
Instance methods	
(BOOL)contains:anObject	filter:newObject
(id*)findElementOrNil:anElement	find:anObject
(int)occurrencesOf:anObject	findSTR:(STR)aStr
(unsigned)size	intersection:aSet
add:newObject	remove:oldObject
difference:aSet	replace:anObject
expand	union:aSet

Sets are collections that reject duplicate entries. Duplication is determined by the entries, not by the set. Sets are often used as symbol tables, and they are implemented for high efficiency in this type of application. Duplicate entries are detected as they are added (add:). Sets expect that every entry will implement a pair of comparison methods which must behave in a coordinated fashion.

1. [newElement isEqual:oldElement] is expected to report whether newElement is equal to oldElement, according to whatever equality definition is appropriate for that kind of element.

2. [newElement hash] is expected to return an unsigned integer which is equal for all objects for which isEqual: is true. Sets are prepared to deal appropriately with collisions on this integer.

For example, consider a class of points where aPoint is equal to someObject if and only if someObject is also a point and its coordinates are the same as the aPoint's. The Point class would implement this definition as

```
- (unsigned)hash { return ((unsigned)isa) ^ xLoc ^ yLoc; }
- (BOOL)isEqual:anObject {
    return [anObject isKindOf:Point] && xLoc == anObject->xLoc &&
      yLoc == anObject->yLoc; }
```

Strings would have a different equality test, for example, comparing bytes one by one.

Hashing trades space to gain speed. To keep efficiency high, sets automatically expand by doubling their capacity when their tally exceeds 75% of their capacity.

To enumerate the members of a set, see Sequences. Sets enumerate their elements in random (hashed) order.

Instance Variables

unsigned tally   This variable maintains a count of the number of elements in the set.

Adding

- add:newObject   This method adds newObject as a set member, unless an oldMember exists such that [oldMember is Equal:newObject). The method replies nil if successful, newObject if not.

- filter:newObject   This method adds newObject as a set member, unless an oldMember exists such that [oldMember isEqual:newObject]. If no equivalent member is found then newObject is added and newObject is replied. Otherwise, the method executes [newObject free] and replies oldMember.

- addContentsTo:aCollection   This method executes [aCollection add: member] for each member of the receiver and replies aCollection.

Combining

- union:aCollection   This method replies a new instance of the receiver's class which contains the contents of receiver and aCollection; the sum of the two collections. The method's implementation is

```
return [[[isa new] addContentsOf:self] addContentsOf:aCollection];
```

- intersection:aCollection   This method replies a new instance of the receiver's class containing the intersection of the two collections; i.e., those elements that are in both receiver and aCollection. The method's implementation is

```
id sum = [self union:aCollection], tmp;
[sum removeContentsOf:tmp = [self difference:aCollection]]; [tmp free];
[sum removeContentsOf:tmp = [aCollection difference:self]]; [tmp free];
return sum;
```

- difference:aCollection   This method replies a new instance of the receiver's class which contains the difference of the two collections, those elements that were in the receiver but not in aCollection. The method's implementation is

```
return [[[isa new] addContentsOf:self] removeContentsOf:aCollection];
```

Testing

- (unsigned)size   This method replies the number of set members.

- find:anObject   This method replies oldMember such that [oldMember isEqual:anObject]. This method replies nil if not successful.

- (BOOL)contains:anObject   This method replies YES if any oldMember exists such that [anObject isEqual:oldMember].

Removing

- remove:anObject   This method removes oldMember such that [oldMember isEqual:anObject] and replies oldMember.

Private

- expand   This method increases the capacity of this Set.

- (id*)findElementOrNil:anElement   This method replies a pointer to either an empty internal storage slot or to the id of aMember for which [aMember isEqual:anElement]. The search begins at a slot determined by [anElement hash], and continues circularly through the buffer to deal with hash collisions. The method replies address of the first slot such that *slot = = nil or [*slot isEqual:anElement].

String
String of Characters

ClassName	String
Superclasses	Object
Other classes referenced	⟨none⟩
Used by	⟨none⟩
Inherited by	⟨none⟩
Maturity index	relatively mature
Source bulk	111 lines, 545 words, 3705 chars
Binary bulk	text 1380, data 252, bss 0, total 1632, hex 660
Declaration	@interfacetoString:Object { unsigned length, size; char*string; }

Factory methods
  sprintf:(STR)fmt; VA__TYPE
    va__alist;
  str:(STR)aStr
Instance methods

(BOOL)isCopyOf:anObject	(double)asFloat (int)asInt
(BOOL)isEqual:anObject	(int)compare:anObject
(BOOL)isEqualSTR:(STR)aSt	(int)compareSTR:(STR)aStr
(STR)describe	(unsigned)hash
(STR)str	(long)aslong
(char)charAt:(unsigned)anOffset put:(char)aChar	concat:anObject
(char)charAt:(unsigned)anOffset	concatSTR:(STR)aCString
	sort
(STR)strcat:(STR)aBuf	str:(STR)aStr

String is a subclass of Object. Its instance variable string holds a character array terminated by the null character, '\0'. Strings provide low-level string-management similar to those of ordinary C strings. They differ from C strings in that:

1. Strings are objects, so they can function in conjunction with other classes that assume objects. For example, Strings can be stored as container members (see Set, OrderedCollection), but C strings cannot.

2. String can be modified by subclassing, while C strings cannot. For example, consider a String subclass called Symbol. Its instances can be stored in Sets to produce a ready-made symbol table.

3. Strings maintain their length and size so they can be dynamically changed without requiring the user to update their reference. Normal C strings, when reallocated, might change their position in memory, requiring the user to update all references to the string.

Support Functions

There are several string manipulation functions defined in the String implementation file that permit safe and efficient manipulation of C null-terminated strings. They are safer than the standard C library string manipulation functions, since they allow NULL parameters. Also, they improve efficiency by avoiding length calculations whenever possible. The functions provided are:

```
static unsigned slen(char * a);
static char * scopy(char * a, char * b);
static char * sncopy(char * a, char * b, unsigned n);
static char * scat(char * a, char * b);
static char * sncat(char * a, unsigned n, char * b, unsigned m);
static int scmp(char * a, char * b);
static void slower(char * a);
static void supper(char * a);
```

Declarations

unsigned length   This instance variable specifies the length of the null terminated string contained by this instance.

unsigned size   This instance variable specifies the current size of the buffer used to store the C string.

char *string   This instance variable points to the storage buffer used to hold the actual string.

Instance Creation

+ str:(STR)aStr   This factory method replies a new instance initialized with the characters in the C string aStr.

+ sprintf:(STR)aFormatString, STR firstArg;   This factory method replies a new instance initialized the same way that the stdio sprintf() function works. The following methods produce equivalent results:

```
firstString = [String str:"10 pounds in a 5 pound sack"];
secondString = [String sprintf:"%d pounds' in a %d pound sack", 10, 5];
```

Type Conversion

The following methods use the C functions atoi, atol, and atof to perform the indicated conversions on the receiver's character contents, where contents means IV(theReceiver).

- (STR)str   This method replies a C pointer to the first character in the array. It is implemented as

```
return string;
```

and is used like this:

```
printf("This string contains %s\n", [aString str]);
```

- (int)asInt   This method reports the integer value represented by the receiver's characters. It is implemented as

```
return atoi(string);
```

- (long)asLong   This method replies the long value represented by the receiver's characters. It is implemented as

```
return atol(string);
```

- (double)asFloat   This method replies the floating value represented by the receiver's characters. It is implemented as

```
return atof(string);
```

Accessing (As an Array of Characters)
These methods allow individual characters to be read or written according to offset, where legal offsets range from 0 to capacity − 1. Bounds checking is performed, with errors reported by

```
return [self boundsViolation:theErroneousOffset];
```

- (char)charAt:(unsigned)anOffset   This method replies the character at offset anOffset.

- (char)charAt:(unsigned)anOffset put:(char)aChar   This method stores aChar into offset anOffset and replies the prior contents of that slot.

Concatenation
These methods allow the user to add to the current contents of the receiver's string.

- (STR)strcat:(STR)aBuf   This method concatenates the receiver's C string to aBuf. It can be used to make a copy of the receiver's C string in a local memory area without having to directly access the instance variable that points to the receiver's string. No length checking is possible to ensure that aBuf is large enough.

- concat:aStr   This method concatenates aStr, which is an instance of String or one of its subclasses to the end of the receiver's string.

- concat:(STR)aCString   This method concatenates aCString, which is an ordinary C string, to the end of the receiver. This method returns self.

Comparison and Hashing

These methods are defined to meet requirements established in class Set. Most are based on the internal function, scmp, which compares two strings and replies negative, zero, or positive according to whether the first string is less than, equal to, or greater than a second string.

- (int)compareSTR:(STR)aCString   This method compares the contents of self with the C string, aCString. It is implemented as

```
return scmp(self->string, aCString);
```

- (int)compare:anObject   This method compares the contents of the receiver and anObject. It is implemented as

```
return scmp(self->string, [anObject str]);
```

Notice that unless anObject is a String, [anObject str] evaluates to the name of its class.

- (BOOL)isEqual:anObject   This method replies whether the receiver is equal to anObject

```
return scmp(self->string, [anObject str]) == 0;
```

- (BOOL)isEqualSTR:(STR)aStr   This method replies whether the contents of self are equal to the C string, aCString.

```
return scmp(self->string, aStr) == 0;
```

- (unsigned)hash   This method replies an integer hash code involving each of the receiver's characters that was generated using the __strhash() function. The semantics of isEqual: and hash are closely coupled as discussed in the specification for class Set.

```
- (unsigned)hash { return _strhash(IV(self)); }
```

Appendix B

Hand-coded Dependency Graph Application

$\mathbf{T}$his code was produced by starting with the object-oriented dependency graph application in Chapter 6, and making the following transformations:

1. An include file was created to declare each of the data types as structures instead of objects.
2. Each occurrence of the type id was replaced with one of the data types declared in the include file.
3. Each message expression was rewritten using conventional C coding constructs. In many cases message expressions were replaced with function calls. In others, statements were expanded inline.
4. C functions often had to be created to handle operations that had previously been inherited from generic classes. For example, the methods of lower level classes, like String and Object, were handled by implementing them inline in some cases, and in others by calling a function.

The effect of these transformations was to increase the interdependency between modules such that each class that impinges on another now states that dependence explicitly in the source, rather than by leaving it to the messaging routine to resolve at run-time.

Except for how binding is accomplished, the algorithms, parameter settings, and overall layout should be identical across the two implementations, so that performance comparisons can be meaningful.

Declarations File: Gr.h

The file, gr.h, declares each of the data types used in the application. The
C preprocessor includes this file inside each separately compiled module,
so that all data types have global scope. The file appears in each of the program files at the locations marked by #include "gr.h" statements.

```
#include "objc.h"
#define DIM 1

/* Node declarations */
#define SET struct _SET
typedef struct _NODE {
    SET *references;    /* set of referenced nodes */
    BOOL isMarked;      /* node is marked */
    BOOL isDefined;     /* node is defined */
    char name[DIM];     /* name of this node */
}NODE;
#undef SET

/* Set declarations */
typedef struct _SET {
    int tally;          /* number entries in set */
    int capacity;       /* capacity of contents */
    NODE **contents;    /* contents of set */
} SET;

/* Graph declarations */
typedef struct _GRAPH {
    SET *nodes;         /* set of nodes */
} GRAPH;

/* Set operators */
SET *   setNew();
NODE**  setFindNode();
NODE*   setFind();
int     setSize();
BOOL    setContains();
NODE*   setAdd();
NODE*   setFilter();
SET *   setExpand();

/* Graph operators */
GRAPH*  gphNew();
NODE*   gphDefine();
NODE*   gphAdd();

/* Node operators */
NODE*   nodNew();
NODE*   nodAdd();
NODE*   nodMark();
NODE*   nodDefine();
BOOL    nodIsMarked();
BOOL    nodIsDefined();
```

```
NODE*  nodPrint();
int    nodHash();
int    nodIsEqual();
```

C typedef statements are used extensively to define new typenames. For example,

```
typedef struct { ... } NODE
```

defines the symbol NODE to be a synonym for the structure declared in the same statement. This allows a node to be referred to as a NODE, not as a struct __NODE, and a pointer to such structures as a NODE*. The remainder of the file declares the type returned by various C functions. To help keep these straight, a naming convention was used. The first three letters of each function name indicate the class to which it belongs.

The purpose of this file is to make every data type public across every source file. Such a file was not needed in Chapter 8 because classes had no need to know such detailed information about their neighbors. The presence of a file with such global effects is the antithesis of encapsulation. However, it is undeniable that hundreds of useful programs have been written quite successfully with this antiquated technique.

Node Class: Node.c

Transforming the Node class as outlined above produces the following hand-coded version, node.c:

```
/* Node in singly linked graph of named nodes */
#include "gr.h"

/* Create a new node named nodeName */
NODE *nodNew(nodeName)
    STR nodeName;
{
    NODE *self = (NODE *)zeroAlloc(sizeof(NODE) + strlen(nodeName));
    strcpy(self->name, nodeName);
    return self;
}
/* This node references anotherNode. */
NODE *nodAdd(self, anotherNode)
    NODE *self, *anotherNode;
{
    if (self->references == 0) self->references = setNew(10);
    setAdd(self->references, anotherNode);
    return self;
}
/* Mark myself and my dependents as reachable. */
NODE *nodMark(self)
    NODE *self;
```

```
{
    if (self->isMarked == YES) return 0;
    self->isMarked = YES;
    if (self->references) {
        register int n; register NODE **p;
        n = self->references->capacity;
        p = self->references->contents;
        for (; n--; p++) if (*p) nodMark(*p);
    }
    return self;
}
/* Mark myself as "defined" */
NODE *nodDefine(self)
    NODE *self;
{
    self->isDefined = YES; return self;
}
/* Reply whether this node is reachable or not */
BOOL nodIsMarked(self)
    NODE *self;
{
    return self->isMarked;
}
/* Reply whether this node is defined or not */
BOOL nodIsDefined(self)
    NODE *self;
{
    NODE *self;
    return self->isDefined;
}
/* Print this node */
NODE *nodPrint(self)
    NODE *self;
{
    printf("%s ", self->name);
    return self;
}
/* Compute hash function on this node */
#       define iabs(anInt) (anInt & 0x7fffffff)
#define EOS     '\0'
#define TST() if (*s == EOS) break;
#define SHFT(N) (*s++ << ((N)*8))

int nodHash(self)
        NODE *self;
{
        register unsigned int hash = 0; register char *s = self->name;

        for (; ; ) {
                TST();
                hash ^= *s++;
                TST();
                hash ^= SHFT(1);
                TST();
```

```
                hash ^= SHFT(2);
                TST();
                hash ^= SHFT(3);
        }
        return iabs(hash);
}
/* Test equality of two nodes */
int nodIsEqual(self, anotherNode)
    NODE *self, *anotherNode;
{
    return strcmp(self->name, anotherNode->name) == 0;
}
```

The implementation is similar in broad outline to the dynamically bound version but substantially different in particulars. For one thing, code that had been inherited before now appears explicitly. The instance creation function, zeroAlloc(), is now called directly alongside a string copy function call, strcpy(), that initializes the node name. This had been accomplished before with a [String str:aNodeName] message. This version also duplicated the functionality of the hash and isEqual messages, in the nodHash() and nodIsEqual() functions. This code is nontrivial, and so the duplication increases not only code bulk, but also complexity.

Graph Class: Graph.c

Similar transformations, applied to the Graph class, produces the hand-coded implementation shown here:

```
#include "gr.h"
/* Allocate a new graph */
GRAPH *gphNew(siz) {
    GRAPH *self = (GRAPH *)zeroAlloc(sizeof(GRAPH));
    self->nodes = setNew(siz); return self;
}
/* Define a new node */
NODE *gphDefine(self, s) GRAPH *self; STR s;
{
    return nodDefine(gphAdd(self, s));
}
/* Add a new node to self */
NODE *gphAdd(self, s) GRAPH *self; STR s;
{
    return setFilter(self->nodes, nodNew(s));
}
```

Set Class: Set.c

The code that follows was totally missing in the object-oriented implementation, because its functionality was acquired directly from the library and reused without change.

```c
/* Set: C version */
#include "gr.h"
#define expansionPredicate(tally, capacity) (tally >= ((3 * capacity) >> 2))

    NODE **findElementOrNil();
    SET *setErr();

/* Allocate and zero memory */
char *zeroAlloc(n)
    register int n;
{
    register char *p, *q = (char*)malloc(n);
    for (p = q; n--; p++) *p = 0;
    return q;
}
/* Instance creation */
SET *setNew(siz)
{
    SET *newSet = (SET *)zeroAlloc(sizeof(SET));
    newSet->contents = (NODE**)zeroAlloc(siz*sizeof(NODE*));
    newSet->tally = 0; newSet->capacity = siz;
    return newSet;
}
/* Reply aNode if in set, else nil. */
NODE *setFind(self, aNode)
    SET *self; NODE *aNode;
{
    return *findElementOrNil(self, aNode);
}
/* Replies the number of elements in set. */
int setSize(self)
    SET *self;
{
    return self->tally;
}


/* Reply if aNode is in self. */
BOOL setContains(self, aNode)
    SET *self; NODE *aNode;
{
    return *findElementOrNil(self, aNode) != 0;
}


/* Adds newNode, replying 0 if actually added; newNode if not */
NODE *setAdd(self, newNode)
    SET *self; NODE *newNode;
{
    if (newNode) { NODE **p;
        if (expansionPredicate(self->tally, self->capacity)) setExpand(self);
        p = findElementOrNil(self, newNode);
        if (*p == 0) { *p = newNode; self->tally++; return 0; }
    }
    return newNode;
}
```

```
/* Add newNode and reply it if add succeeds. Else free it and reply
 * the prior object blocking its slot in the set.
 */
NODE *setFilter(self, newNode)
   SET *self; NODE *newNode;
{
   if (newNode) { NODE **p;
       if (expansionPredicate(self->tally, self->capacity)) setExpand(self);
       p = findElementOrNil(self, newNode);
       if (*p == 0) { self->tally++; return *p = newNode; }
       else { free(newNode); return *p; }
   } else return (NODE*)setErr(self, "cannot filter");
}
/* increase my capacity. Rehashes all contents. */
SET *setExpand(self)
     register SET *self;
{
     register int n; register short oldCapacity = self->capacity;
     register NODE **oldContents = self->contents;
     register NODE **now, **end, **begin;
     NODE **origContents;
     self->capacity *= 2;
     self->contents = (NODE**)zeroAlloc(self->capacity*sizeof(NODE*));
     n = self->capacity; begin = self->contents; end = begin + n;
     origContents = oldContents;
     for ( ;oldCapacity--;oldContents++) {
          if (*oldContents) {
               now = begin + nodHash(*oldContents) % n;
               while ( *now ) if (now >= end) now = begin; else now++;
               *now = *oldContents;
               }
          }
     free (origContents); return self;
}

/* Reply address of slot that contains node in contents; If not there
 * reply the address of first empty slot after hash pt (circular search)
 */
static
NODE **findElementOrNil(self, node)
   SET *self; NODE *node;
{
   register int n; register NODE **end, **now; NODE **begin;
   for (;;) { /* until an empty slot exists */
       n = self->capacity; begin = self->contents;
       now = begin + nodHash(node) % n; end = begin + n;
       for (; n--; now++) { if (now >= end) now = begin;
            if (*now == 0 || nodIsEqual(*now, node)) return now;
       }
       setExpand(self);
   }
}
#include "stdio.h"
static SET *setErr(self, fmt, args)
   SET *self; STR fmt, args;
{
```

```
    _doprnt(fmt, &args, stderr);
    exit(1);
}
```

This version was produced by applying the same techniques used for graph
and node to the Objective-C implementation described in Chapter 8. Whereas
the object-oriented set used dynamic binding to adapt itself to the needs of
this application, this implementation lacks that ability. It declares its nonre-
usability explicitly and repeatedly; in the data type declarations for NODE
and in the function calls nodIsEqual() and nodHash().

Driver Routine: cDriver.c

The main difference in the driver routine is it uses a fast hand-coded loop
to sequence through the sets for printing, while the object-oriented version
used message expressions.

```
#include "stdio.h"
#include "gr.h"
    GRAPH *graph = 0;
    NODE *definition = 0;
    char yytext[BUFSIZ];
    extern STR root;
cDriver() { int n; NODE **p;
    graph = gphNew(10); yyparse();

    /* Mark all nodes reachable from root */
    nodMark(gphAdd(graph, root));

    /* Print reachable nodes */
    printf("Reachable from %s:\n", root);
    n = graph->nodes->capacity;
    p = graph->nodes->contents;
    for (; n--; p++) if (*p && (*p)->isMarked) nodPrint(*p);
    printf("\n");

    /* Print unreachable nodes */
    printf("Not reachable from %s:\n", root);
    n = graph->nodes->capacity;
    p = graph->nodes->contents;
    for (; n--; p++) if (*p && !(*p)->isMarked) nodPrint(*p);
    printf("\n");

    /* Print undefined nodes */
    printf("Undefined nodes:\n");
    n = graph->nodes->capacity;
    p = graph->nodes->contents;
    for (; n--; p++) if (*p && !(*p)->isDefined) nodPrint(*p);
    printf("\n");
}
#define DefAction(s) definition = gphDefine(graph, s);
#define RefAction(s) nodAdd(definition, gphAdd(graph, s))
#include "Syntax.m"
```

Notice that the parsing logic (Syntax.m) is shared by both the object-oriented and the hand-coded versions.

Parsing Logic: Syntax.m

In both implementations, the logic that actually builds the graph is hidden inside the parsing function, yyparse(). The #include "Syntax.m" statements include this function in the respective driver routines. The drivers tell the parsing logic how to build the graph by defining a pair of macros, DefAction() and RefAction(). These implement the action of defining or referencing a newly read token, according to whether the token appears first on a line.

```c
#define WRD 1
#define EOL 2
/* Handcoded parser */
yyparse() { register int c;
    for(;;) { /* for each line in the file ... */
        switch(c = yylex()) {
        case WRD: DefAction(yytext);   /* define a node */
            for(;;) { /* for each reference in the line ... */
                switch(c = yylex()) {
                case WRD: RefAction(yytext); /* reference a node */
                    continue;
                case EOL: break;
                default: yyerror("syntax error 2"); continue;
                } break;
            } break;
        case 0: return 0;
        case EOL: continue;
        default: yyerror("syntax error 1");
        }
    }
}
#include "ctype.h"
/* Lexer */
yylex() { register int c;
    while ((c = getc(stdin)) != EOF) {
        if (c == '\n') return EOL;
        else if (isspace(c)) {
            do { c = getc(stdin); } while (isspace(c));
            ungetc(c, stdin); continue;
        } else { register char *p = yytext;
            do { *p++ = c; c = getc(stdin); } while (!isspace(c));
            ungetc(c, stdin); *p = 0; return WRD;
        }
    }
    return 0;
}
```

Index